FREE

Also by Amanda Knox:

Waiting to Be Heard

FREE

My Search for Meaning

Amanda Knox

H
HEADLINE

Copyright © Amanda Knox 2025

The right of Amanda Knox to be identified as the Author of the Work has been asserted by her in accordance with the Copyright, Designs and Patents Act 1988.

First published in the US by Grand Central Publishing, Hachette Book Group, Inc.

First published in the UK by Headline Non-Fiction
An imprint of Headline Publishing Group

1

Apart from any use permitted under UK copyright law, this publication may only be reproduced, stored, or transmitted, in any form, or by any means, with prior permission in writing of the publishers or, in the case of reprographic production, in accordance with the terms of licences issued by the Copyright Licensing Agency.

Cover design by Caitlin Sacks
Cover copyright © 2025 by Hachette Book Group, Inc.

Cataloguing in Publication Data is available from the British Library

Hardback ISBN 978 1 0354 2815 1
Trade Paperback ISBN 978 1 0354 2814 4

Offset in 11.85/17.5pt Adobe Caslon Pro by Jouve (UK), Milton Keynes

Printed and bound in Great Britain by Clays Ltd, Elcograf S.p.A.

FSC
www.fsc.org
MIX
Paper | Supporting responsible forestry
FSC® C104740

Headline's policy is to use papers that are natural, renewable and recyclable products and made from wood grown in well-managed forests and other controlled sources. The logging and manufacturing processes are expected to conform to the environmental regulations of the country of origin.

Headline Publishing Group Limited
An Hachette UK Company
Carmelite House
50 Victoria Embankment
London EC4Y 0DZ

The authorized representative in the EEA is Hachette Ireland, 8 Castlecourt Centre, Dublin 15, D15 XTP3, Ireland (email: info@hbgi.ie)

www.headline.co.uk
www.hachette.co.uk

Contents

Prologue .... *xi*

How to Play a Paper Piano

Claustrophobia 3
Possessed 13
Ikigai 19
Tutto Fa Brodo 26
Desire 31
Amicus Fidelis Protectio Fortis 39
Tunnels 45
Tapestries 52

Libertà

Just Enough and Not at All 59
Self-Help 68
Public Property 74
Defensive Maneuvers 79
Just Ignore It 86

The Bunker 92
Ex-Conned 102

Not Alone

We Know 113
Sisterhood of Ill Repute 121
Just Amanda 129
Punching Down 137
Joy 143

Inferno

The Only Way Out Is Through 153
In Bocca al Lupo 163
Coraggio 171

Purgatorio

Dear Giuliano 181
A New Life 188
Una Vita in Gioco 194
Rudy Goes Free 201
An Uncertain Miracle 205
Life Isn't Fair 217

Paradiso

Preemptive Closure 225
Homecoming 232

Faccia a Faccia 240
A Dream Deferred 254

Blessings

The Other Side of the Coin 263
The Art of Freedom 270
A Benediction 276

Acknowledgments *279*

To Eureka and Echo, who embody my freedom, and to Chris, for always believing in me.

Prologue

The only path I've spent more hours walking than the loop around the prison yard was the path through my neighborhood to Oma's house. My mom was single and raising two daughters, but we lived within walking distance of her mom, and just about every day after school, we'd strap the leashes on the dogs and walk as a pack over to Oma's for dinner. Goulash, potatoes, and pickled red cabbage, zwetschgenknödel for dessert. On one of those walks, coming back from Oma's house on a brisk fall evening, Mom said to me, "Amanda, I think you're going to live an extraordinary life."

My mom was in the habit of saying prophetic things offhand. Maybe that's true of all moms, simply because they never know what random thing they say will land just right, planting itself in your mind forever. But I don't think she could have imagined how out of the ordinary my life would be, or how painful. If she could have seen the future, her daughter thrown into a foreign prison, accused and convicted of a murder she didn't commit, if she could have seen the death threats, the tabloid slander, the trauma rippling through our whole family for decades to come, would she have wished me a simple, *ordinary* life?

In the fall of 2007, a twenty-one-year-old British student named Meredith Kercher was studying abroad in Perugia, Italy. She shared a cottage with three roommates—two Italian law interns and an American girl. Two months into her stay, a burglar named Rudy Guede broke into her cottage when no one was home. When Meredith returned, Guede raped and killed her, then fled the country.

We know this beyond any doubt because Guede left his fingerprints and footprints in her blood; he left his DNA in and on her body. The MO of the break-in matched his previous burglaries. He was known to carry a knife. He later admitted to being at the scene. But before the forensic evidence came back identifying Guede, the authorities, desperate to find the killer, with the eyes of the global media upon them, questioned the American roommate for fifty-three hours over five days, in a foreign language, without a lawyer, eventually coercing her in the dead of night into signing statements that implicated herself and others. They arrested her and accused her of Meredith's murder, all before a single piece of forensic evidence was analyzed.

I am that American roommate, and I should have been nothing more than a footnote in this tragic story. Instead, Guede was charged with the lesser crimes of conspiracy and rape in a separate fast-track trial. Rudy was officially convicted of rape and of "committing murder with others." In Italy, they do not distinguish between "participating in murder" and murder. Which is to say that he was never accused of wielding the weapon that killed Meredith, but he was convicted of murder. He was sentenced to thirty years, reduced to sixteen on appeal. And then I became the main event, along with a young Italian man named Raffaele Sollecito, with whom I'd been romantically involved for just a week.

The investigation and trial took two years, and the prosecution presented a baseless theory of a sex game gone wrong, a drug-fueled orgy that devolved into murder. In that story I was portrayed as a cunning manipulator, a sadist in sheep's clothing who convinced my one-week fling, Raffaele, and Guede, a man whose name I didn't even know, to rape my roommate and then hold her down so I could plunge in the knife.

There was precisely zero evidence to support this story, and mountains of evidence to refute it, but the media couldn't get enough. They amplified every imagined detail, cementing the image of that character, the man-eater "Foxy Knoxy," in the minds of millions around the world. When the trial finally reached a verdict, I assumed this absurd case would collapse like the house of cards it was, but instead, the judge pronounced, "Colpevole." *Guilty.* The jury convicted Foxy Knoxy and sentenced her to twenty-six years in prison. But the guards couldn't handcuff that invented person. They couldn't escort that fiction into a cell. That was me, the naïve twenty-two-year-old exchange student; I was the one dragged back to that windowless prison van and driven once again to those high cement walls topped with barbed wire.

After four years in prison, I was acquitted on appeal in 2011 when independent experts concluded that the minuscule trace of DNA supposedly linking me to the crime was the result of lab contamination. I returned to my home in Seattle, bewildered and traumatized. But I was finally free, right? Not exactly. I was trapped in my childhood bedroom, hiding from the news cameras across the street, and psychologically stuck in a story that had taken on a life of its own. I was the girl accused of murder. *Did she or didn't she?* Everyone I met already thought they knew who I was, what I had or hadn't done, and what I deserved. I was threatened with abduction, torture, and death. Strangers sent me lingerie and love letters.

I didn't feel free.

Then, two years later, prosecutors appealed my acquittal, arguing the verdict was "lacking in logic," and it was overturned. I was retried in absentia, reconvicted of the same crime, and resentenced, this time to 28.5 years. Once again, I was a convicted killer, now facing extradition. Once again, the media cashed in, presenting me as a figure to be judged and condemned. Once again, I appealed.

The final ruling in my nearly eight-year legal ordeal was delivered on March 27, 2015, by the Court of Cassation, Italy's highest court. They definitively acquitted me and my codefendant, Raffaele Sollecito, of the murder of Meredith Kercher, "per non aver commesso il fatto"—*for not having committed the act*. It was an unprecedented decision from the court, which usually remanded cases back to an appeals court for retrial. Instead, they exonerated us on the grounds of factual innocence, citing stunning errors in the prosecution's case and culpable omissions, essentially wagging their finger at the state for ignoring exonerating evidence. It was a clear vindication after a series of Kafkaesque trials. This final ruling is now the legal truth in Italy regarding what happened to Meredith Kercher, but it is not the *truth*.

Meredith's actual killer, Rudy Guede, was never held fully accountable for his actions; after serving just thirteen years, he was released from prison in 2020. In 2023 he was rearrested for assaulting another young woman. His trial was still pending as this book went to print. The final ruling from the Court of Cassation, while exonerating Raffaele and me, maintains several falsehoods: that I was present at the house the night of the murder, and that the murder was committed by multiple assailants. It also upheld my conviction for slander against Patrick Lumumba, a pub owner I worked for in Perugia whom I was coerced into naming as the murderer during the interrogation that led to my arrest. Even though I had been denied the assistance of an interpreter or an attorney, I was blamed for the outcome of that interrogation and sentenced to three years' time served.

If that all sounds confusing, it's because it is. And I am not the only one who was deeply unsatisfied with this result. It labeled me a convicted liar, and pointed to fictitious accomplices for a crime Guede

Prologue

clearly committed alone, both lessening his guilt and denying the Kercher family a sense of closure.

Then, in 2019, the European Court of Human Rights vindicated me further, ruling that my rights were violated during my interrogation. I used this ruling to sue Italy to overturn my slander conviction, and in October of 2023, the Court of Cassation did just that and sent the case back to the appellate level for retrial. I became a defendant yet again. And on June 5, 2024, I returned to the Court of Appeals in Florence to defend myself. In a decision that shocked me as well as the press, the court upheld my conviction, sentencing me yet again to three years' time served. Italy's highest court, the Court of Cassation, upheld that verdict on January 23, 2025. I am now exploring the possibility of appealing this unjust conviction in the European Court of Human Rights once again. Believe it or not, eighteen years after my arrest, the legal drama is still not over. But *none* of that is what this book is about.

I wrote my memoir, *Waiting to Be Heard*, a year after I was released from prison, at the age of twenty-five, while I was still on trial. There were already thousands of news articles, dozens of books, and even a TV movie about what people thought had happened to me in Italy. A chorus of strangers had been authoring my experience for years, and I thought by adding my lone voice to that chorus, I might finally be able to move on. I was done being a tabloid staple, eager to return to my life as an anonymous college student.

If I'm consistently good at anything, it's being naïve.

Waiting to Be Heard was my attempt to dispel the big lie—created by my prosecutor and furthered by the media—about who I was and what I had to do with Meredith's murder. If you want the play-by-play of the investigation and the trials, I urge you to read it. But I've realized, as the years have passed and that haunted feeling has remained, that *Waiting to Be Heard* still wasn't really *my* story. It was the story of what

Rudy Guede had done to Meredith, and of what the Italian justice system had done to me. It was the story of what happened *to* me, and it left little room for anything I actually did.

The problem was, back then, I hadn't done much. Or at least, that's what it felt like. I had survived prison—that's no small thing. And in the first part of this book, I'm going to take you into prison in a way I never have before. I'm also going to take you into the world of "freedom," where I stumbled a lot trying to reintegrate, knowing Foxy Knoxy, the false version of me in the public imagination, was walking into every room before I entered. I'm going to show you how my loneliness and isolation began to dissipate when I connected with other wrongly convicted and publicly shamed people. Their stories gave me a glimpse of real freedom. But even so, I didn't feel like the protagonist of my *own* story. My life was still the product of other people's mistakes. No matter what I did, the world treated me like a killer or dismissed me as tabloid trash. I was lost. I was stuck in a tragic narrative that afforded me only two possible roles: villain or victim. And I feared that nothing I would ever do could define me more than the worst thing that ever happened *to* me.

I just wanted my old life back, but that life no longer existed. My face was in newspapers and magazines and on billboards in Times Square, but my world was so, so small. I had to try something else, be something else. That something else is what this book is about.

What I've only recently realized is that freedom is not a state of being. It's a practice. And for the last few years, I've been making meaning out of my misfortune. I've been creating my own freedom. If *Waiting to Be Heard* answered the question "What?!," this book answers the question "So what?" It is a road map of my personal evolution as I directly confront the existential problems I've faced ever since I was first arrested and charged for a terrible crime I didn't commit: Could I ever be anything more than "the girl accused of murder"? Would I ever be truly "free"?

Prologue

Trying to answer those questions led me to study stoicism, Zen Buddhism, and research on resilience and post-traumatic growth. I hope to share the wisdom I've gained from those disciplines and from my own reflections. It's been said that pain is inevitable but that suffering is a choice. This book is a guide to making that choice—and then making that choice matter. It is the story of what I've accomplished despite overwhelming obstacles.

And what I've accomplished I owe in some sense to my antagonists, the people who locked me in a cell for years. And I have to thank life for testing me. But above all, I owe it to my mom, who, late one summer in my childhood, offered another offhand prophetic remark.

The blackberries were exploding in the alleyways between the small suburban houses on our block. I was maybe eight years old. I had been building forts deep in the blackberry bushes, riding my bike with the neighbor kids. After playing a breathless game of tag in our backyard, I went inside and asked Mom if I could make everyone peanut butter sandwiches. While helping me spread the peanut butter, she said, "Of all the things I hope for you, Amanda—that you're successful, and smart—I hope most that you'll be kind."

She couldn't have known that I would take her wish so deeply to heart that it would lead me to risk my safety and my freedom by returning to Perugia, an olive branch in hand, to meet face-to-face with my prosecutor, Dr. Giuliano Mignini.

That story is *my* story. It is a story that truly speaks to who I am in a way that all the things that have happened to me never could. My circumstances may be extraordinary, but the challenges I've faced are universal. We all want to persevere through hardship, and you don't have to be in a prison cell to feel trapped in your own life. You can feel hemmed in by the stories others tell about you, even if they aren't headlines splashed across international publications. I hope that my successes and my failures can be illuminating for your own journey toward equanimity, resilience, and wellbeing.

I thought about beginning this book with a quote. Perhaps this line often attributed to C. S. Lewis...

> Hardship often prepares an ordinary person for an extraordinary destiny.

Or this from Viktor Frankl...

> When we are no longer able to change a situation, we are challenged to change ourselves.

But I don't need anyone else to speak for me. I can write my own damn quote.

> To be free is to be powerful, and if your power is kindness, you are always free. No one can stop you from being kind.
>
> —Amanda Knox

How to Play a Paper Piano

Surviving Prison

Claustrophobia

FOR AS LONG AS I can remember, I've disliked small, enclosed spaces. When playing hide-and-seek, I hid behind things rather than in them, or better yet, in places with a vantage point—high up in tree branches, on top of the swing set. I've never willingly crawled into a snug spot, especially if it offered only one way out. Ever since I lost consciousness under water when I was six, I've had a fear of drowning—of some hostile element closing in on me from all sides. Growing up, I lived in a small, one-story house. I shared a room with my sister, Deanna. But I didn't spend all that much time inside. Mostly, I was out in our backyard or biking around the neighborhood. We lived close to a greenbelt, and every day Mom would take us and the dogs for walks into the patch of woods where Deanna and I would run and leap, sticks for swords, playing at being Xena the warrior princess.

I was an outdoor kid, rain or shine. I took to camping like I was born in the woods. I even did some pretty vigorous backpacking during middle school: a five-day trip out on the Olympic peninsula, packing everything in and everything out, hiking at least five miles a day and pitching my own tent. At twelve, I was helping to build trails in state parks. All that felt normal in the Pacific Northwest. I knew that my home was bigger than my backyard. It didn't occur to me *not* to roam, to fully immerse myself in the most compelling natural resources we had—the mountains and the forests.

In high school, I was out on the soccer pitch every single day. I especially loved those early mornings, frost on the grass, sun cresting the horizon, the adults cold, bundled, and grumbling, drinking coffee in the stands while I stretched and sprinted around the big, open field wearing just shorts and a t-shirt. It was as invigorating as a Russian ice bath. That wide-open space was synonymous with movement for me.

In college, I got into rock climbing and went on weekend trips to go bouldering. My then-boyfriend, DJ, and I did a lot of camping, even in the middle of winter. There is something magical about how quiet the world gets when it's blanketed in snow. Deep in the woods, I loved listening to the dripping of water, the rustling of small animals, the crunch of snow under my feet as we walked through dense forest to emerge onto a precipice with a view stretching to distant peaks. Camping was so essential to me that I couldn't imagine going to Italy without bringing my camping gear. And it took up a lot of space! I had visions of camping on the banks of Lago Trasimeno, just outside of Perugia.

By the time I arrived in Italy, I knew all this about myself. Expansiveness was a deep part of me, and it informed every aspect of my personality. I choose to face the anxiety of the unknown over the despair of the known every time. I am not the kind of person who will stay in an unhappy relationship or an unsatisfying job because I'm afraid of change. I'll chop off twenty inches of hair that took me three years to grow just to see what I look like with a pixie cut.

So you can imagine how I reacted to being trapped in a small concrete box for four years. Or, for that matter, for hours overnight in an interrogation room.

The thing is, I didn't know it was an interrogation room. I didn't know I was being interrogated. It wasn't like what you see on TV: an empty room but for a table and two chairs, a one-sided mirror across the wall, a cop slamming down a folder full of crime scene photos, *You have the right to remain silent. Anything you say can and will be used against you*... It was just a small, cramped office; there were two desks, file cabinets, framed certificates and photos on the walls. It was a room I, and Meredith's other roommates and friends, had already spent countless hours in over the last few days, answering questions as collaborators with the investigation.

"The pubblico ministero is here to see you," Officer Rita Ficarra said matter-of-factly, seemingly oblivious to the fact that I was curled up in the fetal position. My head was still ringing from the buzzing of my cell phone—my mom's attempts to contact me that Ficarra did not allow me to respond to—and the feel of Ficarra's hand slapping me as she shouted, "Remember! Remember!" The interrogation had gone on and on into the early hours of the morning, as a rotating cast of officers twice my age had badgered me with the same questions in a language I barely understood, refusing my answers again and again, until I started doubting my own sanity, and I began to believe them when they said that I was so traumatized by something I'd witnessed that I'd blacked it out. Threatened with thirty years in prison, I leapt out the only window they offered me, unsure how high up I was or where I might land. It didn't feel like a choice. I had to escape that cage of circular questioning. I signed the statements they typed up implicating myself and others—my boyfriend, Raffaele Sollecito, and my boss, Patrick Lumumba. "You need to talk to the pubblico ministero about what you remember," Ficarra said.

"Pubblico ministero"... it was a deceptively easy term to translate—"public minister"—but what did *that* mean? I thought back to a call I'd received from a representative at the UW, my hometown university, a day or so after the news of Meredith's murder broke. She'd expressed her condolences and said something about local government officials being there to assist me—with what, I wasn't sure. Perhaps this was what she had meant. I guessed the pubblico ministero was someone like the mayor, come to my rescue. Would he let me out of this tiny room?

Ficarra started clearing her seat and desk. While she shuffled papers around, I tried again: "I'm really confused right now. I don't feel like this is remembering..."

She didn't even look up. "Pazienza. Your memories will come back."

Then the pubblico ministero, my rescuer, appeared in the doorway. He struck me as an old-man version of my stepdad, on the heavier side, with a round face that sat like a scoop of ice cream on his suit collar. He had a brusque, businesslike demeanor; he didn't so much greet me as acknowledge my presence as he sat down behind Ficarra's desk. But he was calm, and after being screamed at all night, I actually felt hopeful that, together, we'd be able to straighten everything out.

His name, he reminded me, was Dr. Giuliano Mignini. Apparently, we had already met outside my house on one of the days previous. But I didn't remember him, had no recollection of ever seeing his face, which only made me doubt myself further. He wanted to hear what I had to say, he said.

Relieved, I launched into desperate rambling. My mom was on her way to Perugia and trying to contact me. I was trying to help, really, but I was scared and confused after a nightmare of a night. He glanced at the statement I'd signed earlier. "You're scared of this... Mr. Lumumba?"

"I don't know? I'm just...scared...and confused."

His brow furrowed, and he began walking me through the vague and confused scenario represented in the document and asked for further details. Every time I tried to explain that I didn't know if those fuzzy and disconnected images were memories or things I'd imagined, he pushed back. "What do you mean *you don't know?* You must have heard *something*. Why are you hitting your head? Why are you crying?" I could muster only meek, self-deprecating complaints about being hit and yelled at. I felt his impatience, his incredulity, and my heart sank. Even he, the mayor, or whoever he was, couldn't, or wouldn't, believe me. Talking to him was like knocking on a stone wall, hoping it would open. Defeated, I gave up a second time. I agreed to his suggestions. I signed his paperwork. I would do what they said until I could see my mom again. It would only be a few hours until she arrived in Perugia. We would get a hotel room, and we would get some rest, and then *she* would help me straighten everything out.

I dissociated. It was like playing hide-and-seek with myself; I was safe drifting above and at a distance, merely observing as they took me into another room and told me to strip naked. A male doctor minutely examined my neck, my hands, my genitals and pointed out details for a photographer, reassuring me that they were only looking for signs of sexual violence. They snapped metal cuffs around my wrists, reassuring me that it was merely a formality, and ushered me down the stairs and out into the parking lot.

"Where are we going?" I asked finally.

"You are being taken to a holding place for your own protection," a male police officer said. "It will only be for a few days."

It was early morning in Casa Circondariale Capanne. I was escorted by a man and a woman wearing military uniforms. The man was like a half-melted candle; his back was hunched, the skin on his face drooped, and he flickered warm to cold, eager to indifferent. The woman reminded me of a vampire—pale, with perfectly styled hair dyed blood red. Downstairs, after my handcuffs had been removed, the man introduced himself as Vice Commandante Argirò, and as if to affirm his own importance, he insisted that I was to ask for the vice commandante, and only the vice commandante, should I need to talk. ("Vice Commandante"—*Vice Commander*—but what did *that* mean?) The woman simply introduced herself as Agente.

Our footsteps echoed over the cement floors of a long hallway lined on either side with doors unlike any I had ever seen: they were solid sheets of metal with no handles, just a hole where the handle should be, and a small viewing window closed with a shutter. It was quiet; I assumed that the rooms behind these doors were empty. When we reached the last door at the end of the hallway, Agente turned a large metal key in the lock, and used the key as a handle to open it, revealing another door, this one made of steel bars—again, no handle. Agente used the same key to open this door as well.

Inside, there was a steel bed frame painted pumpkin orange, a green foam mattress, and a coarse wool blanket. Vice Commandante Argirò led me inside and pointed to a boxy object mounted six feet up on the wall wrapped in a black garbage bag and duct tape. "Don't touch!" he barked, "and don't speak to anyone." This last part confused me; there was no one else here. And it was like he was admonishing me, like he, too, was mad at me.

As I searched his and Agente's faces for some indication of my status—was I a guest, under their protection, or a pest, under their boot?—Vice Commandante Argirò marched out of the room, and Agente closed and locked both doors behind them.

The quiet and the cold closed in on me. I thought about my mom, how she probably thought I was dead. I started to panic, hyperventilating. *This was all a big mistake. This was all my fault. And what was this room? Why were there bars?* But then I reminded myself what they had promised: *They were keeping me here for my own protection. It would only be for a few days.* I cried myself to sleep.

Free

It was not "a few days." It was 1,428 days, and if it were up to the police and prosecution, including one Dr. Giuliano Mignini, I never would have left.

The next morning, still cold, still numb, lying on my bunk, my gaze averted from the locked door, I heard knocking. It was soft but firm, unobtrusive and unmistakable, as if to say, "I'm here! I hope that's all right..." From the very beginning he was different. *He knocked.*

I turned and rose from the bed obediently. The outer metal door opened on a man with a squarish, stubbly face, his brown eyes almost hidden behind self-transitioning rectangular glasses. He wore a fleece pullover with a zippered collar, a casual blazer, slacks, and sneakers. Compared to the crisp lines and perfectly plucked eyebrows of so many of the cops and prison officials, his relaxed style felt almost...Pacific Northwest.

Even so, I approached warily. I think he interpreted this as shyness, but I wasn't shy, and I never have been. It wasn't shyness that kept my head bowed and my body recoiled, that had me communicating in muted gestures and muttered words.

I realized who—or what—he was by the small silver cross pinned to the collar of his blazer.

"Hello," he said, his voice like honey mixed with sand. "Do you understand Italian?"

I understood that sentence at least. I nodded.

"I'm Don Saulo," he said. "I'm a priest. I'm here to help. Would you like to talk?"

I shook my head apologetically. "I'm not religious."

This is what I'd told the nun who had come by earlier that morning in her starched gray habit. She'd told me that I was no better than an animal without God.

But the priest merely chuckled, which surprised me. "How about I ask the agente to bring you down to my office in a little bit? We can talk about whatever you want."

I thought about the invitations to talk I'd been offered by the police, by the pubblico ministero, by Vice Commandante Argirò, and how none of them ever felt like a choice. "Okay," I said.

He nodded goodbye and gently pushed the outer door partially closed, not to shut me in, but out of politeness.

A while later, Agente opened the barred door and gestured for me to step outside. She followed close behind as I walked down the deserted hallway, now bright from light streaming through the window at the far end. I could feel the eyes of invisible women peering out from their own partially closed doors.

Through a barred gate, down the stairs, through another barred gate, into another hallway. Don Saulo's office was narrow, with a low couch on the left and a tall cabinet on the right. Past these, the old priest sat at his desk facing the door, the sunlight haloing him from the window at the far end of the room. He looked up as I entered, thanked Agente, who closed the door behind me, and gestured for me to sit in the chair across from him. I obeyed.

I don't remember how he broke the ice. By asking me how I was doing? All I know is that I found myself gushing desperation. "There's been a mistake. I didn't do it. I shouldn't be here. No one believes me. No one believes me!"

He reached across the table and patted my hand, saying something along the lines of "You're here for a reason." He meant it in the "God is looking out for you" kind of way, but I couldn't help hearing it as "Well, you must have done *something*," and I silently castigated myself for my stupidity.

I tried to explain: "I'm innocent, but they yelled at me, and I got confused. Now the police are mad at me. They won't listen. They don't believe me.... Do *you* believe me?" I was rambling, unraveling. It's not that I needed *him* of all people to believe me; I just needed *someone* to believe me.

He covered my hand with his own, protectively, and chose his next words carefully. "I believe you are...sincere," he said. Again, he meant to be kind. He didn't know me, he didn't know what happened; what else could he say? But still, I couldn't help hearing it as "I believe you *want* to be innocent." I was crushed. Slowly, dejectedly, I withdrew my hand and held it in my lap.

I had nothing to say; no—there was nothing I could say. His kindness rolled off me like rain off a stone statue in a deserted piazza.

It took me a while to realize that the room I was kept in was in fact a cell, *my cell*, that the outer metal door was called a "blindo," and to learn that "Agente" meant "guard." Eventually, I would come to consider the red-haired woman who locked me in that first night and all the other guards as one many-faced Agente. Even their interchangeability was a kind of box that no message or plea could penetrate. Even the priest was separated from me by the infinite distance of divinity. It seemed there was no one in this place I could reach. I was trapped not only by the walls of my cell and by the barrier of language, but by the indifference of those who kept me here.

Someone—the police? the warden?—ordered that I be kept in isolation for the duration of the investigation, so for my first eight months of prison I had no access to common areas. I was not, however, in solitary confinement. For the first several weeks, I shared a cell with one other woman. Scabs covered her body from her incessant and compulsive scratching. I don't know how long she'd been locked up. When Agente moved me in with her, she reassured me that she was a veteran of sorts.

I could only imagine what traumas she'd endured. Whatever they were, they left her irritable and erratic. Navigating her mood swings meant staying small and quiet—yet another way I felt trapped.

In my life before prison, I'd had the invisible luxury of spending time in places that radiated freedom—the woods, the wide-open soccer pitch, the family trips each summer to Lake Roosevelt in Eastern Washington. I gravitated to those places. It didn't feel like a choice. Now, walled off from that open world, freedom felt like an impossibility.

I took every chance I could to leave my cell, pacing circles in the small courtyard adjacent to the chapel reserved for me alone. I did jumping jacks, I jogged, I skipped. Even when it was pouring rain, I circled that courtyard like a dog at a fence line, feeling the blood pump through my body, calming me.

And I sang. I sang the Beatles, Dido, the Eagles. I sang Christmas songs, "The Star-Spangled Banner." I sang every song I knew by heart. It was enough to feel the vibrations in my body and to hear my voice echo down the hallways and out beyond the prison walls, a small sliver of me riding the wind.

As the days passed, I learned that how free I felt in any given moment was as much about my physical reality as my point of view—literally. If my view was the locked door, I started hyperventilating. If my view was the old stone tower on the hillside a few kilometers from the prison, or the tiny bunnies frolicking in the grass below, that changed everything. That choice was always available to me. And when I chose not to stare at the many things boxing me in, I became free to discover possibilities within that concrete box that I never could have anticipated. I began to sketch the contours of a small circumscribed life, a life I never would have chosen for myself, but a life worth living.

Possessed

I'VE LOVED BOOKS FOR AS long as I can remember. I have my schoolteacher mom to thank for that. Some of my earliest memories are of sitting in her lap, flipping page after page. I was also the kid dressed in my homemade wizard cloak, waiting in line at midnight to purchase the next installment of the Harry Potter series. When I wasn't running around outside, I was cuddled up with a dog and a book. I got deep into manga in middle school—*Magic Knight Rayearth*, *Sailor Moon*, *Ranma Nibun-no-Ichi*—which inspired me to spend three weeks in Japan at age fourteen. In college, I fell in love with Shakespeare. I loved immersing myself not just in the intricate plots and unforgettable characters but in the words. I'd get chills when a scene or a sentence unfolded *just so* through unique combinations of linguistic flourish and restraint, with turns of phrase that were events in and of themselves. By the time I was preparing for my study abroad in Perugia, I was enamored of the Italian language, which sounded so singsong to my ear, all those vowels at the ends of all the words. I figured I'd have countless hours to peruse Italian bookstores, searching for "authentic" copies of *Invisible Cities*, *The Decameron*, and *Pinocchio*.

A few days after I was arrested, I asked for a dictionary. I had tried to order deodorant and a hairbrush from the commissary list, and accidentally ended up with a beard comb and hair remover cream. I had attempted asking Agente about access to a washing machine to do my laundry and was pointed to the bidet in the bathroom. Agente took pity on me and gave me magazines other inmates were throwing out. Translating them, looking up words one by one in the dictionary, was a slog. A few weeks into my stay, I painfully and begrudgingly overcame my sense of denial and acknowledged to myself that I really wasn't going home "in a few days" as the police had promised. As consolation, I held out hope that I might eventually be returned to the custody of my family on some kind of house arrest. In the meantime, I finally asked for a book. Agente brought me down to the library, a glorified closet next to the warden's office, and allowed me to pick out a single volume. The closet was mostly filled with Italian romance novels. There were a few Italian classics that I knew nothing about: *L'Amore Molesto* by Elena Ferrante, *Il Gattopardo* by Giuseppe di Lampedusa, *I Promessi Sposi* by Alessandro Manzoni. But then I had what felt like the only stroke of good fortune I'd had in a long time: I saw a copy of *Harry Potter and the Goblet of Fire* in Italian.

I struggled through that book with unbridled joy. Having read it at least four times in English, I knew what was happening even when I couldn't parse a sentence. And that was often. Especially at the beginning, I got stuck a dozen times on every page. Every time I did, I would write that sentence down in a notebook and deconstruct it with the Italian-English dictionary until I figured it out. *Harry Potter* was crucial in helping me learn Italian.

I was eventually allowed up to three books in my cell, but there wasn't much to choose from in that impoverished library. My family occasionally brought me books, but they often didn't know what to get me—they were reading things like the Twilight series, which was not my style. But in those early days, Giuseppe Leporace, an Italian professor at the University of Washington, arranged for me to keep earning credit through independent study. He sent me packets of Italian poetry, parables, and short stories like those in *Il Novellino*, to analyze and translate into English.

As I was still in isolation, I wasn't allowed to do things like visit the school room, where an elementary school teacher volunteered once a week to help teach inmates how to read and write. I thought she might be able to help me translate one of the poems Professor Leporace had sent me. I asked Agente if the teacher could come visit my cell when she had a moment. She arrived in a huff. I told her about the poem I was translating, and she scoffed and said I was wasting her time. After refusing to help me, she left. Her look said it all: *Who do you think you are? Poetry? You're never getting out of here.*

Aside from my three books, I wasn't allowed much in my cell. Two pairs of shoes, five pairs of socks, two pens, one metal plate... In prison, everything you have is numbered. There was not much logic to the rules around possessions. Though we were allowed to have a camp stove that produced an open flame, we couldn't have nutmeg—presumably because a woman on the cellblock had tried to snort it. We could clean with bleach, but we were forced to wear socks on our hands when it got cold, because we weren't allowed to wear gloves.

Aside from my books, my most precious belongings in my cell were the photographs of my family and friends. After months and months in isolation, with only brief, limited contact with anyone outside of Capanne, that world and everyone who occupied it started to feel like half-forgotten dreams. To remind myself of my mother's realness—her relentless optimism, her *Seahawks* shirts covered in dog hair, her voice—I would prop a picture of her against the wall as I wrote her a letter. I did that with each family member, trying to really visualize them as I wrote. I was allowed to keep ten photographs with me at a time. I have a big family, which meant choosing which ten people I wanted to be able to imagine clearly that week. Then I would have to write a "domandina"—a *request form*—to the warden asking to swap out one batch of photos for another, trading this cousin for that one, letting one friend into my immediate world while another lost definition in the fuzzy strokes of memory as they were sealed back into the storage locker where the prison kept all those things I was not allowed to have in my cell.

That storage locker eventually filled up with books thanks to two Italian men: Rocco Girlanda, a local politician, and his colleague, Corrado Daclon. Representatives of the Italy USA Foundation, they worked to establish ties of friendship between the United States and Italy. They asked me if I needed anything, and I said one word: Libri. From that day on, my literary world expanded dramatically. Rocco and Corrado brought me as many books as I could devour by my favorite Italian authors: Umberto Eco, Alberto Moravia, Italo Svevo, Leonardo Sciascia.

I was still allowed just three books in my cell at a time, and had to beg Agente once a week to go into storage and swap them out for others. I don't know exactly how many books I read in prison. My best guess is I read around two hundred books during my entire stay at Capanne.

I'll mention just one: *Man's Search for Meaning* by Viktor Frankl. This book was both a model and an inspiration for me. Simply put, it's a stark account of Frankl's life in a concentration camp, and a meditation on how others can learn from his experience. Frankl went on to develop and popularize logotherapy and existential analysis, which concerned itself with helping people realize meaning in their lives. It was not just his practical advice (look for ways to make each individual moment valuable; discover a unique vocation that only you can accomplish) but his raw nerve to exist in the face of hopeless struggle that resonated, and continues to resonate, with me.

The edition I had in prison was black with gold lettering, and it was the closest thing I had to a "How to Survive Prison" manual. Obviously, I was not being tortured to the extent that prisoners in concentration camps were, and I was not subject to starvation and slave labor, but there were parallels to Frankl's experiences and those of my fellow prisoners. I, too, was shocked upon admission, and struggled with feelings of apathy as I slowly became accustomed to my new reality. I depersonalized, feeling as if I were watching myself from outside and above my own body. I witnessed how bitterness poisoned the personalities of many of the women around me—prisoner and agente alike—but also how some "decent" agenti and prisoners resisted the pull of moral deformity, quietly finding a sense of purpose, either through work or in caring for others, embodying a sense of dignity despite their circumstances.

That sense of dignity, especially, was a gift from Frankl's book, and from the world of books in general. Books were my escape from the clatter and the overwhelming sadness of Capanne. They were my tutors in the language I would need to navigate the prison world safely and to defend myself in court. They were my therapists and my gurus, and my friends when my flesh-and-blood peers were across the planet. And even as they came to represent such noble things to me, the indignity of prison was visited upon them as well. If you were to peruse my library now, you could identify many of the books I read in prison by their missing spines. We weren't allowed hardcover books, and so when my family or supporters sent me one, the cardboard cover and spine had to be ripped off, leaving a wiggly bundle of pages swimming inside its dust jacket. Still, they remained beautiful in their disfigurement.

But as precious as my books and photographs were, the longer my stay at Capanne stretched on, it was the immaterial things that I began to truly treasure. Even my body, like all the other possessions I had in that environment, wasn't really under my control. Full-body pat-downs were a multi-daily occurrence, and I had to strip naked before and after each visitation. My body was trapped in a box; it moved from one box to another at the whim of others. Do you own a thing if you don't get to choose how and when to make use of it?

What I could control was my mind—my thoughts and memories, my sense of myself. I protected these fiercely, even as the world was swirling with falsehoods about who I was, what I thought, what I cared about, and what I deserved. But none of that could change what I knew to be true, and none of that truth could be taken away from me.

Material things can reveal your inner world—you can tell a lot about a person by what objects they surround themselves with—but material things don't create that inner world, or sustain it, even if it seems like they do. The *Does it bring you joy?* test, popularized by Marie Kondo, may be a good strategy for evaluating whether to keep or donate the things that fill up your life, but analyzing possessions in isolation—*Does this pair of shoes bring me joy?*—doesn't answer the aggregate question: *How much stuff should you have, even if it all individually brings you joy?* For me, it's certainly more than three books and ten photographs, but being forced to live that spartan lifestyle shifted my baseline and helped me to realize that while there are certain physical necessities for survival—food, water, and shelter—any sustainable form of joy or peace must come from within. It can't be grounded in what you can hold, what you can buy, or what you can treasure. No thing has that power. Life is inevitably going to deliver upsets and left turns and catastrophes. Your things will be ruined, lost, or given away. But it's possible to detach your joy from things entirely, while still finding pleasure in that photograph of your mother or that spineless copy of Dante's *Divine Comedy*. It's not the paradox it seems. I learned to value what I had precisely because it could all be taken away in an instant. When I was stripped of nearly everything, the one thing I still had was myself, and I was enough.

Ikigai

SHE FIRST CAME TO ME a good year into my imprisonment, once I had been moved into gen-pop, my trial was underway, and it was dawning on me how much trouble I was really in. She sat on the bunk next to me, cross-legged. She was eleven years old, maybe twelve. Her hair was long and tangled, her face freckled. She wore an oversize red-and-black flannel shirt that draped her skinny, athletic body. She had a curious energy about her, and she looked at me as if to say, *What the heck are you doing here?*

I still didn't have a satisfying answer to that question. I had long since given up on the possibility of house arrest, and I was frightened by how the prosecution's case was developing. Dr. Giuliano Mignini and his colleagues had dreamed up a scenario that didn't make sense unless you were forced to grant the premise: Amanda *must* be guilty. Which meant that it wasn't enough that I was simply not guilty; I had to somehow *prove* my innocence. And I didn't know how.

I turned away from the little girl as I heard a hiss from the corridor, another inmate shooting a dagger of a word at me: "Infame!" *Snitch*. I was in the middle of a particularly rough week. I was still the new, gawky kid on the block. Eight months in isolation meant that I hadn't yet figured out the social dynamics of prison. And as the lone

American, whose case was being covered on every Italian news channel, I was constantly under scrutiny from agente and prisoner alike. It made for a lonely, paranoid existence, even when people were mostly ignoring me.

But now, the whole cell block was giving me the evil eye. A few women had even spat at me, while others aggressively shouldered me in the yard. I didn't know why until Agente shook a tabloid in my face—it had somehow leaked that I'd told my mom I'd been harassed by one of my previous cellmates, a woman who watched me shower. My mom hadn't told anyone, which meant the prison officials themselves had taped our conversation and leaked it to the press.

I turned back to the girl sitting across from me. "This is what's going to happen to you," I said. "They're going to lock you in prison for a crime you didn't commit. The guards and the prisoners will harass you, and when you complain about it to your mom, they'll spit at you and call you a snitch. You're going to be sad. And you're going to be alone. And none of it will make any sense."

She didn't seem scared by any of this news. More surprised, incredulous. Her expression seemed to say, *Wait, what? Tell me more.*

She began visiting me often, always when I was alone in my cell. Never in the yard, never with others nearby. She came from her world of soccer, gymnastics, *Pokémon*, and *Harry Potter*. The air of freedom around her spoke of easy friendships and family dinners and climbing trees. Although she sat across from me, she couldn't see my cell and asked me to describe things to her. I told her about the view of the cypress trees from my window, about the gristle they served us twice a day, the barred door I could barely stand to look at.

She didn't say much. Mostly I talked to her about what I was up against, what was coming next, reassuring her that she would get through it. Not just the daily trauma of this or that conflict—a guard refusing to give me the food my family brought on visitation day, a cellmate accusing me of stealing her tobacco (I don't smoke)—but the bigness of it all, feeling trapped and unsafe day after day after day. "You'll survive this," I said.

How?

"I don't know how, but you will. I promise."

Okay... I guess so. Always that cautious optimism.

As excited as I'd been to enter gen-pop, sharing a cell with four other women came with its own downsides, as did navigating the yard each day. Mostly because I was the odd one out. Being the only American and "famous" was *not* a good thing. When the TV screens weren't tuned to game shows and soap operas, my face was plastered across them, accompanied by salacious speculation about drug-addled sex-fiend Foxy Knoxy. I would have given anything to blink that media coverage out of existence. But the other women, many of whom had been ignored or forgotten by society to begin with, and who felt even more neglected and forgotten in prison, were jealous of the attention, however negative it was. This made me a target.

It didn't help that I also was one of the few prisoners who routinely had visitors and received mail each day. In fact, so much mail came—not just correspondence with my family and friends, but marriage proposals and death threats from total strangers—that the agenti complained to me about how long it took them to open and inspect it all. Sometimes my family brought me food or clothing. I quickly learned to share or sometimes give it all away to my cellmates. Not only did they need it more than I did, but it gave them one less reason to resent me.

While violence was not a daily occurrence in the women's block of Capanne prison, it wasn't unheard of. I'd seen women punch each other in the face. One of my own cellmates ripped my journal from my hands and tore it to shreds because she thought I was writing about her. In the yard one day, while I was walking with a cellmate, or concellina—an Italian word I coined that Don Saulo found quite clever—another woman ran up behind us. I'd seen her rubbing her palms together, as if in maniacal anticipation of something. It was worse than that. She'd taken the glue out of a glue stick and was mashing it into her palms. She jumped on the woman next to me and began ripping her hair out in a frenzy. I froze, and then my legs gave out beneath me. Another cellmate pulled me out of the fray.

When that little girl came to me later that day, I didn't have words for her; I was too upset by the violence I'd witnessed. Instead, she reminded me that I was tough: *You broke your foot playing soccer and kept playing!* But she didn't know me the way I knew her. She knew who I was, not who I was becoming. I was the big sister, the one giving her the guidance and reassurance I so desperately needed in the present moment. And she didn't know, couldn't know, that sometimes when I told her she'd survive, it felt like I was lying.

As big as I made myself for her, when she wasn't there, I became small, turtling into myself as much as I could. My initial survival strategy was to stick earplugs in and keep my face in a book. Most of my fellow prisoners suffered from some combination of trauma, mental illness, and drug addiction. They struggled with impulse control and emotional triggers. Crowded together in tight quarters, we came to view one another, quite rationally, as potential threats and competition for scarce resources. Being forced to adapt to a world that rewarded violence and punished vulnerability dwarfed any positive effect from the occasional rehabilitation programs offered, like theoretical beekeeping. Seriously, beekeeping without the bees?

But as my Italian improved, and the others learned that I was not a threat, I began to recognize the prison marketplace of time and energy. Alessia, who worked in the commissary, was like the black-market

FedEx. She'd pass notes and CDs and cigarettes between cells. We were allowed to cook, but we had shit ingredients to work with, which is why it paid to be friends with Wilma, who worked in the kitchen and had access to coveted garlic cloves, and who, if you were lucky, would clip you a sprig from the rosemary bush.

And what about you? How do you help? my younger self asked me. The women around me had many needs. They needed dental work. I was one of the few prisoners who had all my teeth. They needed to be loved. I was one of the few who routinely had visitors. They needed legal help. I was one of the few with a lawyer actively working on my behalf. I couldn't bring their family to them, or treat their illnesses, or give them legal advice, but I realized I could facilitate all of those things, because I could read and write. So many of the women around me were illiterate and uneducated. I taught one cellmate how to read the analog clock. I was shocked when I discovered, while trying to explain how far away my home was, that she also didn't know the earth was a sphere.

Most evenings, I visited the Nigerian women who nicknamed me "America." They'd have the table set up by the time I arrived. They'd greet me with a juice box (always pear, my favorite). Then, one by one, I'd translate their court documents and letters from their boyfriends, and write out their innuendo-filled responses, translating the pidgin English they'd picked up from the King James Bible into proper Italian.

Even Agente called me in when my services were needed. It didn't matter what language. Once I was brought in to help a Chinese woman explain a medical problem to the doctor. So I grabbed a Chinese-English dictionary that my family had brought me (I'm a language nerd) and muddled my way through it, translating from Chinese to English to Italian.

"This is how you will find your place," I explained to my younger self, "by looking at what you have to offer and at what the women around you need. You will become the unofficial prison translator and scribe."

And that will keep me safe?

"As safe as you can be," I said. "But it will also feel good."

This was the truth. The social capital I earned through my literacy helped me more safely navigate the pitfalls of prison life. And helping these women gave me a sense of purpose. I wasn't just languishing. I was contributing something to the small, deprived society of the cellblock. My prison hustle taught me that there is no inherent conflict between selfishness and selflessness. There is always some sliver of a Venn diagram where what serves you and what serves others overlaps. The Japanese even have a name for this: ikigai. It's the intersection of your talent, your passion, what the world needs, and what you can get paid for. I've always had a passion for languages, and I'd gone to Perugia to study Italian, thinking one day I'd work as a translator. Translating court documents and love letters in prison wasn't exactly what I'd imagined, but it checked all four boxes. I was able to do something I loved, I was good at it, it was desperately needed in my community, and it got me paid, at least in the currency of prison: juice boxes, safety, and respect.

"Ikigai" literally means "reason for being." We all have one, and judging by my experience, it's possible to find it even in the direst of circumstances. In the West, we tend to focus on just two of those four circles—your talent and what you can get paid for—and often just the latter. Your passion? *That's just a hobby.* What's good for the world? *This is a business, not a charity!* But that latter one is especially important, because generosity is rewarding in a way that monetary compensation isn't. It gave me the feeling of vitality and purpose.

Kindness is a form of self-interest. This is something that my younger self knew instinctually. It not only feels good, but it comes back to you in unexpected ways. I had stopped celebrating my birthday in prison—why bother?—but when I turned twenty-three, my friend Laura, who worked in the kitchen, insisted on baking me a chocolate cake. The illicit treat got wrapped in a garbage bag and passed through many hands before Alessia came by and squeezed it through the bars of my cell with a wink. It was smashed and gooey and delicious.

I never saw my younger self again after I got out of prison. I felt giddy when I saw pictures of her in the photo albums at my mom's house—smiling at me from the amber of the past—but I never experienced her with that same presence she had in my cell, so real I could smell the dirt underneath her fingernails, the sweat on her flannel from endless games of tag, the peanut butter still on her breath.

Perhaps what I really needed in those moments was for some future me, the thirty-five-year-old me, to travel back in time and tell the confused, terrified twenty-year-old sitting in front of her that I'd get through the nightmare. But without that future reassurance, all I could do was pay it backward in time to twelve-year-old me. Doing that took the crushing weight of my existential crisis off my shoulders and placed it in front of me so I could examine it, even learn from it. And looking squarely at what I faced, at what I could control and what I couldn't, somehow gave me the will to make that promise to my younger self, even when it felt like a lie: *You will survive this. You will!*

I know now it wasn't a lie. I did survive it. I did get through it. I learned from it. And I have her visitations to thank for that. She is the one who helped me see that when I couldn't get what *I* needed, I could still give what someone else needed.

"Why did you come here?" I asked her, the very first time she appeared. She looked at me curiously, as if the answer were so obvious that the very fact of the question surprised her.

Because you needed me.

Tutto Fa Brodo

I LIKE TO EAT. AS a kid, my family called me a bottomless pit. I would stuff myself with as many waffles as I could, order the biggest hamburger on the menu, and unashamedly lick every last bit of sauce off a plate. I had a surprisingly large appetite because I was uncommonly active. I was playing three sports at one time and constantly running around, a twelve-year-old with a high-octane metabolism.

But consuming food is not the same thing as making it. At my dad's house, food mostly came from a box or the freezer. We ate a lot of Hamburger Helper and Costco hot dogs. At my mom's house, cooking was simple: steam some rice, sauté some chicken, season it all with lemon pepper. I remember Mom becoming so excited when she discovered a recipe for orzo salad with peppers and olives and tomatoes. But I ate most often at Oma's house. Oma was always cooking something, and it was usually German food. Once in a while, she tried making spaghetti, but it turned out horribly—mushy noodles, sauce from a can. Germans aren't exactly known for their pasta. There was always too much food at Oma's, so I'd take leftovers to school, and while other kids were eating their ham and cheese sandwiches, I was slurping up lentil stew with ham hock. My classmates thought my food looked gross, but I reveled in eating it in front of them, making a display of how delicious it was. They were missing out on all the savory and pickly goodness of German food.

Though I helped Oma make rouladen at Christmas—beef stuffed with pickles and onions and topped with gravy—I didn't cook all that much as a kid, or even as a young adult. In my first years of college, I lived off takeout Thai food and cheap sushi. I remembered how good authentic Italian food was from a family trip to Rome when I was fourteen, and as I packed for my semester abroad, salivating over the thought of handmade pizza, I had no idea how much my relationship with food was about to change.

When I arrived in Italy, I did so with an open mouth. I filled it with the ripest tomatoes and the freshest mozzarella. The simple ingredients were so exquisite I didn't even need to cook. I loved Italy for a lot of reasons, but this was near the top. The Italians are serious about food—about cooking it, about eating it, and about building their social world around it. In the span of five short weeks, my culinary world was transformed. And then it was transformed again...

People often say to me, half in jest, "Hey, at least the prison food must have been better in Italy!" Or if I'm going out to dinner with someone and they choose an Italian restaurant, it's "Sorry, you're probably sick of it!" But the thing is, I didn't eat real Italian food for those four years. I ate prison food. Prison food is prison food, and Capanne was no exception.

Each morning we'd receive a hot beverage for breakfast. I usually took the instant coffee, which tasted strangely (but not badly) like toast. For lunch and dinner, you'd hand your metal dish through a slot in the barred door and they'd slop on a starch, a veggie, and some meat. The starch was typically pasta drizzled with olive oil. I rarely ate it. I love vegetables, but what I got in prison was bland and boiled to death. Boiled carrots. Boiled spinach. Boiled potatoes. Starch upon starch.

The protein was usually more cartilage than meat, and I could rarely tell what animal it had come from. I never touched it.

My whole life, I'd eaten with gusto and I'd moved with vigor, and that was now gone. Without room to run around, and without anything nourishing or delicious, I became a bit emaciated. My body was a reflection of my mind.

Occasionally, all we'd get were the leftovers from the men's side of the prison. It was the same food, just cold by the time it arrived. Once, they simply ran out of food, and we got nothing but bread. But we were allowed to buy food from the commissary. Often, when the meals were too disgusting to eat, I'd subsist on a pouch of precooked lentils. We could also do some rudimentary cooking of our own. We could buy basics, like oil and spices.

One day, they served us boiled potatoes for lunch, and my cellmates decided we ought to pool our servings together to make gnocchi. I looked at them blankly. *You don't know how to make gnocchi?* I only knew how to microwave a Hot Pocket, but I was eager to learn. Making gnocchi wasn't that difficult; it just took a little time. We mashed the potatoes up and kneaded them together with egg and a little flour to make the dough, then pressed them in our palms with a thumb. A quick boil, a little olive oil and salt—*mwah!* They were delicious.

This is how I learned to cook. My cellmates and I took the crummy ingredients the prison provided and used whatever was at our disposal to conjure up something tasty. We could buy flour and yeast, which meant we could make pizza dough. But how do you roll it out? With a broomstick, of course. A pot on top of the camp stove was our makeshift pizza oven. I learned to love ingredients I never would have thought to buy back in Seattle. Raw fennel became one of my favorites—I rejoiced when that was the day's veggie instead of boiled greens. I learned to make a salad out of the raw fennel with olives and oranges I purchased from the commissary.

But these delicious moments were the exception, not the rule. I longed for actual food, especially sushi. I fantasized about it. But even more than the food, I fantasized about the family meals I was missing, everyone gathered around for company as much as sustenance. I knew that back home, Oma was lighting a candle at the table to represent me whenever the family sat down for dinner.

On good days, I felt a bit like that candle: wavering, fragile, but bright. Prison taught me that I could kindle that warmth even in a cell, that a little effort, a little ingenuity, and some humble ingredients could make a worthy meal, and to always be thankful for it.

There's a saying in Italian: "tutto fa brodo"—*everything makes broth*. Broth is made by boiling down the leftovers and scraps of food—vegetable peels, chicken bones, fish skins. The stuff you'd otherwise throw away becomes the foundation of everything you make. Everything has a purpose; everything is important.

Capanne was chock-full of throwaways. Alessia, the eighteen-year-old thief, who fondly recalled pickpocketing tourists and stealing Vespas just for the sake of an afternoon joy ride. Francesca, the thirty-year-old lunatic who drank spoiled milk and muttered under her breath about being God incarnate. Giulia, the stay-at-home mother who stashed cocaine for the mafia and spent her days endlessly crocheting. Cera, the twenty-eight-year-old model convicted of murdering her boyfriend, who chain-smoked and read voraciously. Sergio, the drug-dealing trans man who shamelessly flirted with every pretty girl on the cellblock.

What kind of broth did we make?

So often, I felt estranged from the environment around me. I didn't smoke, I didn't gossip, I didn't watch soap operas, I didn't get into fights. More often than not, I wanted to be left alone. I couldn't be where I truly belonged, and all too often, I couldn't relate to the experiences of everyone around me, nor they to mine.

But then Giulia showed me how to make gnocchi. Alessia taught me how to belly dance. Cera let me borrow her Fabri Fibra CD and helped me translate poetry. Sergio made me laugh. Francesca...well, Francesca was mostly harmless and doing the best she could. For better or worse, I was exposed to the humanity of the women trapped alongside me in Capanne, women who had committed crimes both petty and grave, women who continued to struggle with mental illness, impulse control, and emotional instability.

They were not my friends, exactly. I guess they were my peers, in that we were all boiling in the same pot together. We all knew what it was like to be cast off, thrown away. We all knew what it was like to live deprived of opportunity and purpose. And every day, as we rubbed shoulders watching our lives slipping away, we each found new opportunities and purposes in one another, in something as small as shaking boiling milk in an empty two-liter water bottle until it turned into foam. Like so many of the makeshift delights of prison, making a cappuccino during siesta was only worth the effort if the whole cell was gathered around the percolator.

Our circumstances isolated us from one another like the dividers on a cafeteria tray, as we slid our plates through the slot in the bars to receive our personal allotment of slop. And we could have coveted those scraps of food like wary animals. But breaking bread together was an act of resistance; it was freedom. It allowed us to conjure a new family, at least for the duration of a meal.

Desire

WHEN LENNY FIRST ARRIVED AT Capanne, she was sulky and withdrawn. She paced the yard alone with her head bowed and her shoulders hunched. This was not unusual for a transfer. Each prison is its own delicate ecosystem, so to be uprooted and replanted, without warning, was a jarring, even frightening experience. I sized her up—petite, slight belly, messy hair. By the way she closed in on herself, I guessed that she'd only lash out if cornered. She wasn't a threat to me.

Lenny watched me jog around the yard every day and eventually worked up the nerve to say hello. I was cautiously friendly; as the "famous one," I didn't trust when others took a special interest in me. But I also didn't object to her accompanying me as I walked around the perimeter, the cement walls so high I could only see the sky above us. She immediately informed me that she was a lesbian and asked if I had a problem with that. "Of course not," I said. I told her how I had helped found the gay–straight alliance at my Catholic high school. Lenny informed me that in Italy people were still very closed-minded and judgmental. I sympathized. When I was fourteen, I was ridiculed when a rumor went around that I was gay. That's part of why I became an ally in the first place.

Over the next few weeks, I let Lenny borrow my CD player and

CDs; she liked Norah Jones and Dido. I taught her how to play chess. When she got a janitorial job, she loitered outside my cell for a sip of espresso and a chat whenever she was on break. Lenny didn't really have anyone else, and I knew she looked forward to our time together. I received multiple letters a day, and I was visited every week, usually by one of my parents. All my touchstones were out there, in the free world. But Lenny's sole source of connection was quickly becoming me. I had been in long enough at this point to know where that might lead. And I wondered and worried whether she was drawn to me, or to Foxy Knoxy...

It was a soccer nickname originally. I played top of the diamond, the first line of defense. My job was to pounce on the ball, and I was good at it. I knew the nickname was cheeky; that's why it stuck. We were a team of thirteen-year-old girls, after all. We called my friend Trish "Trash" and Martinez was "Martini." What I didn't know was that my stupid nickname would become a curse.

The tabloids jumped on "Foxy Knoxy" when they discovered my abandoned MySpace page. "Foxy Knoxy" was translated into Italian as "Volpe Cattiva"—*wicked fox*—and it bolstered the image of me as sexually deviant.

In the courtroom, my prosecutor, Dr. Giuliano Mignini, fabricated the details of this character. "To vent her resentment," he explained in his closing arguments, "it is probable that Amanda violently pushed Meredith against the wall, bruising her neck. Meanwhile, Raffaele grabbed Meredith's hair from behind, immobilizing her as Amanda's fingers pressed forcefully beneath Meredith's chin... Raffaele had to defend his position as the boyfriend, while Rudy did everything he could to win Amanda's affection. Meredith was, unfortunately, the victim caught in the middle. She fell... They undressed her. The assault had now turned into a sex game. They stripped off her jeans, and Meredith probably ended up on her knees. Amanda pulled out the knife and stood in front of her friend, watching Raffaele and Rudy grope and abuse her... It's easy to imagine that Amanda, furious with Meredith for criticizing her casual promiscuity, called her a prude, insulted her, and perhaps said, 'You're such a goody two-shoes... Now we'll show you... Now we'll force you to have sex!'"

This narrative was catnip to the global media, who spread and further developed that image of me as a sex-crazed girl-gone-wild, as a femme fatale.

Stuck inside Capanne, I tried to be invisible. I was quiet and withdrawn. I wore baggy sweatsuits. Eventually, I cut off all my hair. I sometimes thought back to when I had been propositioned, at age nineteen, by the guy who worked the counter at Scarecrow Video, to pose for a "tasteful, softcore" amateur porn film. "No sex! Just showering!" He offered me two thousand dollars. I was holding down a full class load and two part-time jobs to save for my upcoming study abroad. I cringed to think what the tabloids, and Dr. Giuliano Mignini, would have made of *that* had I gone through with it.

But my efforts to be invisible didn't help. In the early days, I'd spent a couple weeks enduring mandatory evening visits with Vice Commandante Argirò. Alone with him in a private office, he hovered over me and made comments about my figure, my face, my pretty "blond" hair. He interrogated me about my underwear, my sex life, and propositioned me for sex. Months later, on the fourth of July, just days before my twenty-first birthday, a male agente cornered me in a bathroom, grabbed me around the waist, and tried to kiss me.

Meanwhile, Raffaele was writing me letters from his cell, reassuring me that we would get through this together. He even dropped the L-bomb, but I wasn't sure if Italians used the word "love" more casually. We had only known each other for a week before both our worlds were turned upside-down. I was touched, but maintaining any sort of romantic relationship was the last thing on my mind. I recoiled and dreaded being the object of anyone's desire, even the soft and sincere yearning in Raffaele's letters. I made it very clear to him that however intimate our relationship had been in those days before we were arrested, it was a thing of the past. Romance was not what I needed to get through this ordeal.

But to many of my fellow inmates, romance was a lifeline. Women who enter prison are more likely to have suffered poverty, mental illness, and abuse, and what familial ties they have are often strained and weakened by incarceration. So they build a family on the inside.

Most of the inmates belonged to established social groups within the prison, drawn largely down racial and ethnic lines: Italian, Nigerian, Romani. (I only learned this more polite term after I was released. The Romani I met referred to each other as "zingare," *gypsies*.) Prisoners formed cliques, families, partnerships. It was very common for the Nigerians to refer to one another as "Mama" and "Daughter." They often called one another the names of their sons. *Mama Daniel. Mama Lucas.* The Romani called one another the Romani word for "cousin." As the lone American, I didn't belong to any of these groups. That gave me something of an anthropologist's view of the social world around me. And I noticed that it was common for the women to form intimate relationships that, while not necessarily sexual, had all the qualities of a romance.

Inmates got crushes on each other. The boundaries of friendship slipped. They passed love letters through the bars, gave each other presents: drawings of flowers, little crocheted satchels to carry a CD player. One half of a notoriously tumultuous couple sulked and glared whenever her partner acted too friendly with other inmates. There were tear-drenched breakups, and sometimes fist fights between new partners and exes. But for as many couples who acted like star-crossed teenagers, there were just as many who were as unshakably self-contained as if they had been married for twenty years.

So when Lenny wanted to hold my hand and started to say things like, "I can do things for you that no man can," I knew what was happening. When I informed her that I wasn't interested, she merely took that to mean that I was playing hard to get. One day, she swooped in and kissed me. I didn't feel in danger, but it was unwelcome, and I told her that since she couldn't respect my boundaries, we couldn't be friends anymore. It was tense after that. On a break from work, Lenny loitered outside my cell, pouting and arguing that I was overreacting. I was relieved when she was finally released, though she often wrote to me, sending CDs, which she inscribed on the inside jacket, "Love always, Lenny." I never replied.

A part of me felt bad for being so cold toward her. She wasn't just trying to turn me "gay for the stay"—a term that reveals a deep ignorance of what prison relationships are like. There are all sorts of reasons why people form romantic relationships. Sex isn't always the first thing, the main thing, or even a necessary thing. We all have a need for companionship, for intimacy, a need to give and receive care; we need someone to be vulnerable around, someone to share our fears, concerns, hopes, and dreams with, someone to touch. These needs are even more paramount in an environment that is designed to humiliate, isolate, and punish. That's what makes prison such an awful place: it is designed to deny people their strongest, best instinct, necessary for their sanity and survival—the desire to connect.

I didn't find intimacy in prison through connection with my fellow inmates, either emotional or sexual, but I did slowly start to explore my own sexuality. It was a big deal for me, and difficult. I had to fight through so much shame to even start thinking about it.

There was the general shame floating in the ether of my childhood, that puritan strain in American culture that led my mom to plug her ears when I asked her about sex as a teenager. There was the low-key misogyny that permeated my early college years, the double standard that made sexually active men *players* and sexually active women *sluts*. And of course, as I was on trial for murder, I was mercilessly slut-shamed. That first month in Perugia had been a spark for me, a kindling curiosity about the world of sex and romance. It was *Italy*, after all. I'd read my mom's copy of *Under the Tuscan Sun*. Though I wouldn't have said it was the *reason* I was going to Italy in the first place, a part of me looked forward to that chance encounter of a lifetime, the kind you see in movies. I caught myself fantasizing about riding on the back of a Vespa, hugging the waist of my handsome sweetheart, like at the end of *Amélie*. It didn't go exactly according to plan, though. I hooked up with two young men, one whom I met on a train to Florence who gave me oral herpes, and another who introduced me to the Bellini but was rough with me in bed. I eventually met the young, handsome sweetheart I'd dreamed about, Raffaele, but that, too, didn't exactly go according to plan.

Looking back, I'm still a bit astonished that my experience of rediscovering my sexuality occurred during the period of my life when my privacy was the most violated, when I was being more shamed and vilified than most people will ever be in their entire lives. But perhaps it makes sense, because sexual intimacy is essentially vulnerability, and I had never been so vulnerable.

Intimacy is also inevitable. Like language, we require it to develop into healthy adults, and like food or water, we become desperate without it, willing to risk everything for a morsel. I think of the gay people in Iran who are murdered, or the women who for centuries were diagnosed with "female hysteria," forced into insane asylums, and given hysterectomies for daring to exhibit sexual desire.

How entitled we are to quash and control other people's consensual expressions of sexuality. How vicious and foolish we are to judge and shame one another. And how cruel we are, especially toward women, to those exploring and nurturing their own sense of intimacy.

I was aware, too, that I was developing as a sexual woman in the midst of an unimaginable maelstrom of misogyny. Plenty of other writers have diagnosed the extreme sexism at play in my trials, but looking back on it, I'm still flabbergasted at just how bad it was. There wasn't a single word uttered about Rudy Guede's sexual depravity for violently raping Meredith. Instead, it was my supposed sexual deviancy that became the focus of eight years of trials and countless tabloid stories.

Going through it, I only vaguely understood that there was some sort of double standard when it came to sex. I hadn't read about how common it was—in the context of a sex crime—for male violence to be treated not as deviant but rather as normal and inevitable, so much so that a female victim is often blamed for dressing too provocatively, as if the man's uncontrollable lust was just a known factor every woman should be expected to work around lest she be raped.

I had but a foggy grasp of the scope and history of this misogyny, and how my situation had many precedents. But I saw quite clearly how my own sexuality was being used against me, how it had been twisted to vilify me, how I was hated not just as a supposed killer but as a sexually active woman.

At trial, Dr. Giuliano Mignini had treated the vibrator found in my toiletry bag like a smoking gun, putting one of Meredith's friends on the stand to question her about it. "And when Meredith told you about this and you saw it...was Meredith angry with Amanda about this?" Mignini suggested.

The vibrator was about five inches long, bright pink, and shaped vaguely like a bunny. It had been a gag gift from my best friend back in Seattle. I had only used it once or twice, unsuccessfully.

"Not really," Meredith's friend testified. "It just seemed a little strange to her more than anything else."

The tabloid headline the next morning: DEAD GIRL FEARED KNOXY'S SEX TOY.

My sexual spark had been crushed like a cigarette beneath a polished Italian leather boot. I had every reason to want to repress and even hate my sexuality, to blame it for what had happened to me. But somehow, I intuitively understood that there was nothing wrong with it. Perhaps because the public perception of my sexuality was so exaggerated and distorted, I saw how completely unreasonable the hatred was. Whoever, or whatever, was hated was not me; it was a gross, pornographic fantasy created by my prosecutor and the media. Ironically, the discrepancy between that fantasy and who I actually was reinforced for me that my sexuality was normal and healthy. It was those who conjured this twisted fantasy who were disturbed. That realization allowed me to eventually breathe those embers of my sexuality back to life.

I waited until my cellmates were asleep. I moved with absolute silence, careful to not even rustle a blanket. I was clumsy at first and didn't get anywhere near orgasm before the agente patrols. They came by every fifteen minutes or so to open the small cell windows and peer inside. But like many things in life, constraints can be useful. The agente rotation forced me to figure out my body and find the right mental space efficiently. In those fleeting moments of pleasure, my body felt like my own again, but more important, I felt defiant. I was reclaiming something natural, healthy, and delightful, something my prosecutor had used as proof of my corrupt moral character. He was wrong, the tabloids were wrong, and if I let all that alienate me from my own body, that would be just one more thing in the long list of what they'd stolen from me.

Amicus Fidelis Protectio Fortis

THERE IS NO GOD. DEEP down I knew this the day Mom's boyfriend, a devout Catholic, chased me through the house, fury in his eyes. I must have been five, and I'd gotten into a spat with his son, who was three or four. I hid in the closet, but the boyfriend soon found me and bent me across his knee to spank me. By the sound of my first scream, Mom ran in to save me—she didn't believe in corporal punishment. I can still see the small, golden cross hanging from his neck, swaying gently with each slap, but that's a detail I might have invented.

There were things about the boyfriend I liked. He volunteered in a clown troupe, and I got to dress up in a clown costume and join him in the parades. He let us drink Tang and play Elton John's "Crocodile Rock" at full blast to have a dance party. I didn't like that he dragged us to church every Sunday. Then, one day, he was gone, and it was just me, my sister, and Mom again. Years later, Mom told me that a large reason she had broken up with him was that he was pressuring her to put Deanna and me into catechism classes, wanting our family to live a more religious life.

My mom was a public elementary school teacher, and though my education began there, by the time I approached high school, I started looking at private schools, even though we couldn't afford it. I collected

Pokémon cards and loved anime and manga, and the only place I could study Japanese was at Seattle Prep, a Jesuit high school across town. Mom, who understood the value of a quality education, supported me, and somehow found financial aid to make it possible. What I didn't anticipate was that I'd be required to take religion class and attend mass during school.

In religion class, we learned about a variety of theologies, but spent the lion's share of our time close-reading Christian texts. We had to write personal essays about how religion played a role in our lives. Most of my classmates had grown up going to church, attending Catholic elementary and middle schools, and this was just the water they swam in. But I often felt like I couldn't breathe. All around me was the assumption that God exists, that he is benevolent, that he has a plan for you, me, and everyone. I didn't know why this seemed so wrong, and wouldn't figure that out until prison, but I felt it nonetheless. This was the first time I was forced to put a name to what I believed, and so I started identifying as agnostic to get people to stop asking me about God. In religion class, my rebellious side came out, and I wrote essays about paganism. I didn't so much believe in Wicca as I found it fascinating and fun. Years later, I would meet Damien Echols of the West Memphis Three—we were released from prison mere days apart. He had a similar interest in Wicca, which was used to vilify him as a devil worshiper, and which led to his wrongful conviction and death sentence. Thank goodness my prosecutors never found those essays I wrote for religion class! To the credit of my teacher, he praised my writing, gave me good grades, and told me that at the root of every good Christian is a good pagan.

My relationship with religion became much more fraught the moment I was arrested. As the seat of Roman Catholicism, religion pervades almost all aspects of life in Italy, including the justice system. That became painfully clear to me the first day I was brought into a courtroom for pretrial hearings, eight months into my imprisonment. There was a large crucifix on the wall, the limp body of Christ looking over the judge's shoulder. As my trial started, I began to understand how much that Catholic worldview would determine my fate.

I was a pretty normal twenty-year-old American girl. If anything, I was a little sheltered. I'd had sex with seven people in my entire life, but that was misrepresented in court and in the press as the number of people I'd slept with in my few weeks in Perugia.

Meredith was also a normal girl in her early twenties. She'd had a few boyfriends. She was casually hooking up with an Italian boy in Perugia, just as I was. She had no shame about asking me for a condom when she and Giacomo were becoming intimate. We were entirely unremarkable for college girls, both of us closer to the naïve end of the spectrum than "girls gone wild." And yet, while my sexuality was magnified and distorted into deviancy, Meredith's was erased. I became the slut, and she became the virgin.

This was no accident. These are the two most prominent female roles in the Bible: the two Marys, the Madonna and the whore, the virgin and the prostitute. Those archetypes had traction with the jury, the judge, and the world. They were roles in a fantasy about good and evil. It was a lot easier to paint me as pure evil, as the ultimate sinner, by painting Meredith as pure good, the ultimate saint. And it was a disservice to both of us.

Watching this unfold, some members of my family recommended that I start wearing a cross to court. They were realizing, just as I was, that appearances seemed to matter more than the truth, and that my fate might depend on something as simple as whether or not I fit the image of a good Catholic girl. But I refused to lie. I didn't believe in God, and I wouldn't misrepresent that I did. I was still convinced, naïvely, that the truth was sufficient to clear up this whole mess, that

I could just show them who I was. That didn't go well. When my stepmom bought me a Beatles shirt that read, "All you need is love," I decided to wear it to court on Valentine's Day. I thought it was like wearing a Christmas sweater on Christmas. Of course, it was somehow seen as further proof that I was a bizarre, twisted psychopath. No matter what I did, the prosecution and the media found a way to see it as evidence of my guilt. If I saw my family across the courtroom—one of the few times I was allowed to see them—and I smiled to let them know I was surviving despite it all...I was portrayed as an attention whore, "smiling for the cameras." If I didn't smile, I was portrayed as cold and calculating. It wasn't just the prison cell that made me feel trapped, but this sense that no matter what I did, my life spun further and further out of control, and my chances of ever being free again slipped further and further away.

So you can imagine how I reacted to the idea that this was all part of God's plan. That's essentially what Don Saulo told me that first day we spoke: *You're here for a reason.* I couldn't hear him then. But he could hear me, literally. He heard me singing from my cell, or from the small outdoor courtyard where I could stretch my legs while I was still in isolation.

He'd been stopping at my cell door each morning for weeks, as he made his rounds, checking in on all the women in the cellblock. And each time he came by, he repeated his offer for me to visit his office to chat. I turned him down day after day. After that first visit, I knew the priest couldn't help me. But then one day, he asked if I played any instruments. "I used to play guitar," I told him, "before I was stuck in here."

"I have a guitar!" he said. "You could play it during mass. You could even come to my office to practice."

I didn't love the idea of mass, but it was a chance to leave my cell and to play the guitar—one small link to the life I was living before this nightmare. And so began our musical relationship. Once or twice a week, I was allowed to spend an hour in Don Saulo's office practicing hymns on the guitar, and then during mass on Saturdays, I'd play and sing those religious tunes.

The chapel was the nicest room in the whole prison. The plexiglass and bars of one wall revealed a small garden that let in natural light. In front of the simple wooden pews, there was a wood-paneled alcove with a podium where Don Saulo would give his homilies and where I would play hymns beneath paintings of Jesus and the Virgin Mary. The other inmates would sing along, happy to be there. The atmosphere was even festive at times. It was a warm, inviting, and contemplative oasis compared to the rest of the prison, and those weekly masses warmed me to Don Saulo.

He also had a small electronic keyboard in his office, on which he taught me to play the piano. I didn't just play hymns, though. As the months went by, Don Saulo let me come to his office to play whatever I wanted. He'd listen and do paperwork while I'd play Beatles songs. When he learned about my love of languages, he started teaching me Latin phrases: "Credo ut intelligam" (*I believe so that I may understand*), "Amicus fidelis protectio fortis" (*A faithful friend is a sturdy shelter*). I asked him to listen to a song on my CD player and help me with the piano fingering. Back in my cell, I taped some sheets of paper together and I drew out a piano keyboard from memory. I put my headphones on and practiced playing on my paper piano. To my cellmate, I was like Poe's raven—she couldn't hear the music, only my incessant *tap tap tapping*. I learned to tap more quietly, my paper piano getting me through the week until the next time I was allowed to visit Don Saulo's office.

Don Saulo was such a curious mix of soft and hard, tough and tender. I remember him crying at the end of *Kung Fu Panda*, a film he had brought in for us to watch during one of the rare movie screenings in the education room. But he was also incredibly rigid. His honesty was always unflinching, even as it was compassionate. And as the date of my verdict approached, I needed that energy. I found myself lingering in his office as much as I could. I found myself looking forward to mass. I still didn't need the ministrations of a priest, but I needed comfort. Without my even realizing it, Don Saulo had become my best friend.

I had been so allergic to religion, so at the mercy of religious thinking in my trial, that I'd developed a blind spot. Don Saulo had made himself comfortable in that blind spot, for nearly two years, until I learned to see him. At the close of my trial, awaiting the verdict, he held my hand in his office, just as he had that first day I met him. And as he did so, I probed that wound he'd left, the sting of what he had said in our first conversation, that he did not know whether I was innocent, but that he believed I was sincere. The sting was gone. That sentence no longer felt like a dismissal. I saw it now for what it was: an act of hard-edged compassion. He had respected me enough to offer me the truth.

Tunnels

THE DAY AFTER I WAS convicted of murder, I had the first epiphany of my life. I didn't know what an epiphany should feel like, but it was cold, like a breeze blowing in and brushing the back of your neck, making your hairs stand up. Suddenly, I knew something deep down that I hadn't known before, and I spent the next several months peering into that epiphany, trying to consider all its implications, like watching the ripples spreading out from a drop in a pool of water.

I silently swept a corridor of the cellblock during my work shift, the word "colpevole," *guilty*, echoing in my head. I overheard one agente say to another, "Poor thing. She doesn't understand what just happened." They thought, since I wasn't sobbing hysterically, that I hadn't absorbed the fact that I was going to spend the next twenty-six years trapped in this place.

But I was quiet precisely because I was sitting with my epiphany. And it was this: I was not, as I had assumed for the past two years, waiting to get my life back. I was not a lost student waiting to go home. I was a prisoner, and prison was my home. I'd thought I was in limbo, awkwardly positioned between my life (the life that I should have been living) and someone else's life (the life of a murderer). I wasn't. I never had been. The conviction, the sentence, the prison—*this* was my life.

There was no other life I *should* have been living. There was only my life, *this* life, unfolding before me.

My first two years of prison, I believed my mom when she insisted that there was a light at the end of the tunnel. That the truth would win out, and the judge and the jury would see how absurd this entire debacle was. Now that tunnel was stretching out before me, so long that I could not see even a speck of light.

Mom fought to remain optimistic. The tunnel was just longer than we'd thought, but we'd all get through it, we'd reach the other side. Even though I tried, I just couldn't see it that way. I had assumed that the truth would set me free. I now knew how wrong that was. The truth hadn't vindicated me in my first trial. Why should I expect it would do so in my appeal?

The epiphany itself didn't feel good or bad. It was just true. If there was a feeling, it was the feeling of clarity. My life was sad. I was imprisoned for a crime I didn't commit. I would be locked away for the best years of my life. I would likely never fall in love, have children, or pursue a career. My world would be so small, trapped within concrete walls and surrounded by traumatized people, a fair number of whom were a danger to themselves and others. This life would inevitably take me further and further down a path that would alienate me from everyone I loved, who, despite their best efforts to stay connected to me, were on their own paths moving in very different directions.

But—and this was the critical thing, the thing I hadn't been able to see until that moment—no matter how small, cruel, sad, and unfair this life was, it was *my* life. Mine to make meaning out of, mine to live to the best of my ability. There was no more waiting to live. There was only life—right here, right now.

I was alone with my epiphany. I tried to explain it to my mom, but I couldn't find the right words, and she couldn't hear me anyway. My mom and I were fighting different fights, in a way. She was trying to save me. I was trying to survive. Looking down that dark tunnel, I knew I couldn't hold my breath long enough to get through it. I couldn't keep looking for a light I didn't see; I had to start imagining how to live in the dark. But my mom could not, and would not, accept the very thing I had just come to understand. *This* was my life. She thought I was depressed and giving up. She was going to save me, and she just needed me to survive until she did. But I knew if I was going to survive, it would be precisely because I had finally accepted that I was living *my* life, whether I was eventually found innocent and freed or not.

I allowed myself to imagine alternate realities. What if I had been home that night and Rudy Guede had killed me, too? What if I was acquitted and freed in five years? In ten? What if I served my entire sentence and came home in my late forties, physically and psychologically broken? What if I killed myself?

The prison put me on suicide watch after my conviction. I was moved to a smaller cell with a single cellmate, and Agente had eyes on me at all times. I didn't know if that was standard practice for the weeks after a harsh sentence or a special measure for me given the insane media attention on the case. Or maybe they saw something in my demeanor—the way I couldn't meet people's eyes, how I held my body—something that revealed what I was thinking. Because I *was* thinking it.

We all knew the methods. One inmate in my cellblock had broken a plastic pen into shards and tried to swallow them. I heard about a guy in the men's wing who had used his cooking stove and a plastic bag to asphyxiate himself. You could hang yourself with a bedsheet. I even thought that if I threw myself at the bedframe in just the right way, I could hit my head hard enough to bludgeon myself to death.

I imagined each of these methods in detail. If I swallowed the shards of a plastic pen, how long would it take before the internal bleeding drew attention? Would they be able to save me in surgery? I could get bleach from the cleaning cart if I got myself assigned to sanitation duty, but how much would I need to drink? And could they pump my stomach before it did its job? Hanging seemed more reliable, but also extremely unpleasant—the choking, writhing, and desperation.

I eventually settled on slitting my wrists. I could do it with a shattered plastic pen. I would turn the shower on as hot as I could get it. I would wait until my cellmates were out in the yard, I would lie down—two quick vertical slits—and I would let the water carry my life slowly down the drain.

That seemed peaceful. It wouldn't leave a mess. It had a high chance of success.

So why didn't I do it? I knew how much it would hurt my family, especially my mom. I knew she would have traded places with me in an instant, and that she would never forgive herself if I died in there alone. She was already suffering immensely, and I couldn't bear to magnify her pain. And secondly, as scared as I was of facing decades in prison, something inside me just couldn't make peace with the idea. I didn't deserve to die any more than Meredith did, any more than I deserved to be stuck in this cell. Stubbornness stopped me. It's the same reason I never once thought about changing my name when I got out. There was nothing wrong with my name; it was the world that had tied it up with faulty associations: *killer, slut, psychopath*. If I were to kill myself, those lies would win the day. Because as much as I now doubted that the truth would ever save me, I still valued it. For my own sake, for Meredith's, for the principle of the thing. Most essentially, in those moments when I first began to fantasize about suicide, I made a deep, unconscious choice. A choice to live.

I imagined all those possible futures in vivid detail so that they no longer felt like shadows creeping over me from the realm of unconscious nightmares. Once fully realized in my head, I could let them go, one at a time. I'm explaining that choice now in hindsight, but the truth is, staying alive feels like part of my constitution—another way I'm extremely lucky.

What I do know is that before this moment, before seriously considering what it would mean to end my life, before standing there as a critic in front of my own corpse, giving notes on the reliability of the method, the anticipated pain, the mess, life had been an unconscious, unexamined habit—the thing I did when I wasn't doing anything at all. Now, living felt like an active decision, a choice I made every single morning. To be or not to be. To suffer or to take arms against that sea of troubles by killing myself. I chose to suffer. And that choice gave me a sense of responsibility for the shape of my own life. As much as others were to blame for putting me in that cell, for sending me death threats, for ruining any possibility of a quiet, anonymous life, it was my choice to accept all that or to take the emergency exit. And if it was my choice, then blaming the world made little sense. Realizing that made it easier to accept my life and to find a way to fill it with beauty, and love, and knowledge, to kindle the fragile light of truth in that long, dark tunnel. I began to ask myself: how do I make *this* life worth living?

It was a big question, one I couldn't answer in its grandest sense. But there was a smaller version of that question: how can I make my life worth living *today*? I could answer that question, repeatedly. That was entirely within my power. So I did that. I walked endless laps around the small courtyard—concrete walls, concrete floor, not even a blade of grass creeping through a crack. I did thousands of sit-ups on my bunk, my feet tucked under the metal bar at the end of the bed. I sat at the small table facing the wall and stared at photos of my family as I wrote them letters. I put in my earplugs to mute the cacophony of the prison—the clanking doors, the shouting, the Italian soap operas—and read one book after another.

These small accomplishments were enough to make a day worth living. I didn't know if they were enough to make a life worth living, but I remained open and curious to the possibility.

The light, I realized, wasn't at the end of the tunnel, it was inside of me. And it allowed me to see that the tunnel was never a good metaphor for my situation. It suggests a straight, unchanging path with a light at the far end to aim for as you endure the current darkness. It suggests that things are going to stay the same until you get to the other side.

But life is not like that. Nothing in life stays the same. Everything is unpredictable. Neither joy nor pain is stable and unchanging. I take no credit for this realization. It's ancient wisdom rediscovered time and again. The ninth-century Chinese poet Han Shan wrote:

> *Once you realize this floating life is the perfect mirage of change, it's breathtaking—this wild joy at wandering boundless and free.*

Recognizing the impermanence of our situations is both a relief from the feeling of being trapped in your own life and a reminder to treasure the precious moments we are afforded. *This too shall pass*—that formulation of this same idea comes to us from the medieval Persian poets.

Even as one day blurred into the next in an existentially exhausting way, I realized that the tunnel I thought I was in was not everlasting. Though the outward circumstances of my situation didn't change much—two hours of yard time in the morning, soggy pasta for dinner, one ten-minute phone call on Fridays—my inward experience of these circumstances inevitably changed. The "tunnel" was always shifting, changing shape. There was no darkness now and light later. There was no future moment when all things would be all right for all time. That was a false aspiration that prevented me from finding the condition of being all right, right now.

Which isn't to say that it wasn't hard, devastating even, to scale back my hopes and dreams. Letting go of that pure, blinding light at the end of the tunnel meant relinquishing my hold on the answer to everything going wrong with my life. The light I was able to kindle for myself in the midst of that crisis was a pale flicker in comparison. But I was able to cope, and even thrive in a way, in the midst of that crisis because I realized that that far-off light wasn't real. Like everything in the future, it was merely a product of my imagination. The present was all that existed, as imperfect as it might be.

And while my emotional default remained firmly stuck on sad—I woke up sad, spent the entire day sad, and went to sleep sad—it wasn't a desperate, grasping sadness. It was a sadness brimming with energy beneath the surface, because I was alive with the freeing feeling of seeing reality clearly, however sad that reality was. I was slowly and deliberately walking a tightrope across a bottomless foggy abyss, with no clue where I was going and nothing to hold on to but my instinctual sense of balance.

In many ways, though I'm now free and legally vindicated, I'm still walking that tightrope. The abyss is always there. And anyone who's stared into it, as I have, knows the strange comfort of carrying it with you.

Tapestries

DON SAULO NEVER STOPPED OFFERING me his priestly advice, but as our conversations evolved, they became more and more philosophical, especially after my conviction. We debated gay marriage, adoption, the role of women in religious doctrine, vegetarianism, life after death. We disagreed, amicably, about many things. Don Saulo welcomed my skepticism.

"God is weaving a glorious tapestry," he once told me. "And your life and my life and all the joy and suffering in the world, it is all a part of this tapestry. But here on Earth, we can only see the underside, the frayed ends and knots. We must have faith that the tapestry is beautiful, and that we will see it as God sees it when we join him in heaven."

That still didn't feel right to me. I couldn't accept that this life, my friend murdered, me being torn from my family, sentenced to decades in prison, that all that was a part of God's plan. I matched Don Saulo's brutal honesty with my own: "I think God is just a comforting story we tell ourselves to feel better because sometimes life is cruel and unfair." It seemed to me that there was no higher reason for any of this, no celestial tapestry, nothing grander than the tragic actions of mortal men—Meredith's killer, Rudy Guede, and my prosecutor. There was a reason I was stuck in this prison. It wasn't God's plan. It was Dr. Giuliano Mignini.

Don Saulo's faith, as ever, was unshaken. "Reality can only exist as an expression of love," he told me, "because someone loved it into being. Maybe you don't believe it, but it doesn't hurt to pray. Just in case someone loves you... pray to him."

It wasn't the first time he'd said this. I tried my best to see the logic within Don Saulo's religious worldview. But even then, I didn't get it. If you believe in God, and that God has a plan for you, then why pray? Why do what I saw many other prisoners do—cry out to God for relief, for freedom, for money, for cigarettes?! Why bother, when God never answers? Why bother, when your undesired lot was part of his tapestry in the first place?

I cared about this question not because I was tempted by religious faith, but because I respected Don Saulo, and I cared about meaning and purpose. Senseless tragedy had descended upon my life from nowhere, for no reason. What I deserved, what I wanted, what was true even, had nothing to do with it. What was prayer or hope next to that? Wasn't I powerless?

Don Saulo listened with his warm, sad smile. Then he said, "God doesn't give you the life you want. He gives you the life you need." That probably would have resonated with many of the women around me, who certainly believed in God, and who said things like, "If I weren't in prison right now, I'd be dead." God had put them here to save them from a far worse fate. It was a story about their circumstances that lessened their suffering. I saw that, but it didn't work for me.

I balked at Don Saulo. "Why on Earth would I need this?"

Don Saulo always had a way of gently turning things around on me. "If you pray for strength," he said, "God doesn't give you strength. He gives you the opportunity to be strong."

Those words, finally, hit me with the weight of truth. Everything I held dear, everything I thought belonged to me—my home, my freedom, my future—I thought it had been taken away from me, but Don Saulo showed me that in the midst of unjust torment, I could still be smart, kind, generous, curious, creative, funny, sane.

Seen in that way, prayer is an evocation of choice. The choice to not let misfortune get the better of you. To hang on to what matters to you. To intend upon certain values and principles that ultimately define who you are. Next to that intention, painful circumstance is just white noise.

Perhaps not in the way he intended, Don Saulo converted me into a believer in the tapestry. There may be no God, and no divine plan for our lives, but I could weave my own tapestry. I could make my life as beautiful as I wanted. I could love my reality into being.

I still didn't believe in an omnipotent creator, but I began to understand that nihilism wasn't what I was left with. Yes, nothing inherently mattered, and there was no ultimate reason for anything that happened to me or anyone else. But that vacuum of meaning was nevertheless an opportunity unlike anything I'd ever encountered before. I saw that my misfortune could be both senseless and valuable. I was not stuck in a tunnel, with nothing to do but wait for the light. I was in the midst of an extraordinary opportunity for personal growth. I couldn't lie to myself that God was looking out for me, or that freedom was just around the corner. But this story Don Saulo told me about my misfortune being an opportunity was true, whether I took advantage of that opportunity or not.

I slowly embraced this new story, stepping into it like an unfamiliar costume, adjusting and hemming it until it fit me snugly. It helped me survive prison, and it shaped my sense of who I was: someone who was resilient, who would grow and learn in response to hardship.

On October 3, 2011, nearly four years after my arrest, I was awaiting

Free

my appeal verdict and I spent most of that day in Don Saulo's office, playing music and talking with the Catholic priest who had become my best friend in Capanne prison. Though my mom was crossing her fingers hard enough to break them, I had given up hope of a sane outcome, an outcome derived from truth, and I was learning to be at peace with the idea that I would likely spend the next few decades of my life here. I couldn't risk being crushed again, the way I had been with that first guilty verdict. But Don Saulo did not seem worried. He told me I had aged forty years in just four. And then his face took on that look of brutal honesty, the same look he'd given me years prior when we first met. He said, "I believe you are innocent. I know you are going home."

He broke the rules and brought out a tape recorder. He wanted to record me singing and playing the piano because he knew—*he knew*—that he might never hear my voice again. I didn't have that kind of faith, but I played for him. I played and sang the song "Maybe Not," by Cat Power.

> We can all be free
> Maybe not with words
> Maybe not with a look
> But with your mind

Don Saulo was right. When I was brought back to court, the verdict came in—"Assolta!" *Acquitted!* They raced me back to the prison, which had erupted in cheers of "Libertà! Libertà!" as all the inmates, even those in the men's wing, banged their pots and metal dishes against the bars. I didn't have a chance to see Don Saulo as I ran down the hallways saying my goodbyes. A few minutes later, I was whisked away from those concrete walls, and from my best friend.

I have known cruel atheists and kind believers, cruel believers and kind atheists, and I have learned that how you act is more important than what you believe. I'm not interested in convincing anyone that God doesn't exist. If your belief in God leads you to practice compassion and forgiveness, as it does for Don Saulo, the world is a better place for it. By the same token, that kind of grace doesn't depend on God or belief in God. Kindness is its own justification.

I remain an atheist, but Don Saulo taught me to value much of the wisdom in the teachings of Jesus. Turning the other cheek, the golden rule, a radical refusal of judgment, an acceptance of all people—high and low, sinners and saints. No one deserves God's grace, and yet, it is there for everyone. That is how I think about compassion. It is not kindness if it is reserved for the just, the good, the *kind*. As I left the prison that day, I couldn't have imagined that I would one day extend an olive branch to my prosecutor, that I would strive to be kind to the man who'd imprisoned me. But even then, a part of me knew that true compassion, true mercy, must be extended to everyone—even, and perhaps especially, to the people who have hurt us.

Only then can we be free.

Libertà

How I Failed to Reclaim My Old Life

Just Enough and Not at All

IN THE DEAD OF NIGHT, I paced the room, unable to sleep. During the day, my ears pricked at every tiny sound, at every potential threat. A window looked out over the yard where others were allowed to stretch their legs, but not me. That window was shuttered, always. I could barely eat. I washed my underwear in the sink. I sat on the bed, which felt unfamiliar, and stared at photographs of my family—they looked so distant, locked away in some other time I could not remember, while I was trapped in this box where I had spent years of my life.

I'm not talking about my prison cell in Perugia, Italy. I'm talking about my childhood bedroom.

The moment I was acquitted in 2011, my family went into emergency evacuation mode. The combined efforts of a local Italian politician and an ex-FBI agent helped us escape Perugia, paparazzi ramming my stepdad's car from behind, until we lost them in the night, reunited with my mom, and reached a safe house in Rome. I was too jittery to sleep, so I just sat in a chair and watched my mom as she slept across the room. The former FBI agent checked in on me sometime before dawn, finding me wide awake. "Is everything okay?" he asked.

"I can't go to sleep," I said. "I'm afraid this is all a dream and that I'll wake up back in my cell."

"It's not a dream," he said.

A kind supporter who worked for British Airways upgraded me to first class for my flight back to Seattle the next morning. It was a shrewd precaution; journalists on the flight tried to get to me, passing messages, sneaking up the stairs of the 747. When everyone had fallen asleep, I turned on the TV. That's when it hit me. Every single news channel—ABC, NBC, CBS, CNN, Fox, BBC—was blasting headlines about me. In prison, I had been the "famous" one whose case was covered on every Italian TV station, and I knew, from letters I received from around the world, that the case was international news. But still, in my little ten-by-twelve-foot cell, I remained mostly insulated from the global media onslaught. I had been fighting for my freedom in the courtroom. The abstract knowledge that the case was making headlines elsewhere didn't prepare me for what it was like to actually flip through the channels. I began to realize that my problems were far from over.

I had emerged from behind bars and barbed wire only to enter a whole new kind of prison, made of camera lenses and flashbulbs, menacing cars and helicopters. The moment I landed at SeaTac airport was captured live on every news channel, people like Anderson Cooper narrating the play-by-play. After four years in Capanne, I was desperate for some quiet and to spend time with my family; I was instead pushed in front of a microphone where a mob of journalists clamored over each other, some using ladders for a better vantage, to film my homecoming. There were also around fifty supporters who had gathered at the airport to welcome me home, and I felt like I owed these kind strangers at least a few words. Overwhelmed, I stammered some unprepared, incoherent thanks, then we tumbled into three identical SUVs, like in a heist movie. Helicopters circled above, poised to pursue. My mom's house was already staked out with news vans and gawkers.

Free

Each SUV peeled off in a different direction, and we were able to lose the paparazzi. But that also meant I didn't get to go home. Instead, we went to my aunt's, and then to a rental house we hoped would remain secret.

My entire extended family was there, ready to celebrate my return. That night was a blur. I couldn't eat a thing, and I kept slipping into Italian without thinking. We stayed there in secret for a few days until some reporters tailed my dad from his house, and our hideaway was discovered. So we went back to my mom's. The house was completely surrounded. News crews camped out across the street with cameras, telephoto lenses, microphones, and vans topped with satellite dishes.

Mom drew every curtain in the house, and she hasn't opened them since. Recently, her neighbor passed by while I was visiting and said, "I remember when you first came home. I'll never forget the sound of the helicopters." I won't, either. Those first few days out of prison were a tumbling free fall that landed me in a world that was surreal and confusing and certainly not *home*.

I found my childhood bedroom strewn with flower petals. Upon news of my release, my friends had bought out a flower shop of everything they had. It was a beautiful gesture, like a scene out of a rom-com, but it also served to highlight how unfamiliar that room had become. It had been a long time since I had slept there—two years of college and four years in prison. It had become more a time capsule of me at seventeen than a room that felt like my own. My stepdad's dismantled drum set cluttered the closet. Boxes of prison letters spilled out from under the bed. Otherwise, everything was just as I had left it—the patchwork quilt I sewed as a teenager; the two tall bookshelves packed with novels, schoolbooks, and manga comics; the alcove with a few dozen of my stuffed animals; a poster of fairies and a clock I'd hand-painted in middle school hanging on the wall; and in the closet, so many clothes that didn't fit me and which I wouldn't wear even if they did. I noticed the green peacoat Mom bought me to wear to court the day I received my guilty verdict. I shuddered to imagine wearing that cursed garment ever again.

I could hear the October leaves rustling on the trees, the few remaining birds chirping in the boughs, but the moment I tried to peek through the blinds to see them, the cameras outside clattered like a swarm of locusts. Even in prison I'd been able to look out the window.

My claustrophobia was compounded by all the *stuff* around me. Stuff on top of stuff, stuff inside of other stuff, stuff behind stuff, and all of it supposedly *my* stuff. I took my feelings out on my room. Out with the stuffed animals, out with the old clothes, out with my beloved Pokémon cards and manga collection. I filled bags and bags to take to Goodwill, some of which Mom squirreled away in her own closet. It was rash, but also, it bothered me so deeply that all that stuff, everything that was "mine," didn't feel like mine at all. It felt like it belonged to the past, to my younger self who had no idea how cruel the world could be and how useless all this stuff was against a tidal wave of injustice.

I nearly took down that fairy poster, but found myself staring at its purples and greens, at the fairies and frogs balancing on mushrooms. And I suddenly recalled my childhood secret place.

I suspect most children have such places, the ones only they know or care about, where magic just might be possible. Mine was a narrow passage between the back of my house and the chain-link fence surrounding my neighbor's yard. The fence was overgrown with lilac bushes, which spilled over to create a small tunnel. Mom didn't mow back there because it was out of the way and the ground was uneven, so the grass stalks were thick, flat, and reached up to my waist, accumulating dew. Sometimes it was dark and spooky, filled with spiderwebs, and my sister, Deanna, and I dared each other to run in and retrieve handfuls of the leaves that looked like banana chips—we pretended to eat them. Other times, when the sun was at just the right angle to illuminate the tunnel, the air sparkled with spiraling motes of dust, and it felt like a place that belonged to creatures I'd read about and wanted to believe in—fairies.

Once, in the morning when the light was just right, I wandered in there alone. The silence was ringing. I really wanted something to happen, something like the beginnings of stories I'd read, a wardrobe full of furs opening up to a snowy wood. I wanted the fairies to recognize my childhood innocence and choose to reveal themselves. My steps were tentative, gently rustling the grass. And then, through the leaves of the canopy, a flash of light!

Of course I knew it could have been—most likely was—the sun. I knew I could have imagined it, even. I was just old enough to be aware that there were some things I knew to be true, some things I believed to be true, and some things I wanted to be true. I had realized by this time, for instance, that people believed in God, and that believing in God wasn't like knowing that three times three is nine by clustering dried beans on your desk. I also knew that Santa Claus was not real, but that my family pretended he was real because it was fun. So I wondered about belief itself, if I could believe something because I wanted to believe it, or because it made my sister happy to believe it with me, or because it made my family happy to think I believed.

I never told anyone about that flash of light, the fairy. Not even Deanna, whom I told everything to, especially this type of thing. I felt joy and wonder at what I had seen. I felt special. But I also worried I was pretending. And while it felt good to believe in something I wanted to believe in, I knew I couldn't hang the weight of examination and explanation on my pretend belief, that the real world would rip my fairy apart like tissue paper. So I let that flash of light exist as a private emotion in a warm place between make-believe and knowledge. A place for beliefs, fantasies, dreams, desires, and fairies, existing only so far as the edges of my heart, existing just enough and not at all.

As I got older, I carried that spark of wonder with me, that desire to believe in impossible things, even as I became a committed skeptic who held rationality as a prime virtue. That spark was kindled easily in the ancient city of Perugia, with its twisting cobbled streets, its colorful pastel buildings, the sounds of birds and bells and the dry scent of cypress and olive. Those first five weeks were magical, and I don't mean that like an Instagram hashtag over a vacation sunset. I felt the same childhood wonder generated by that flash of light. I was walking in the footsteps of emperors, saints, and Renaissance painters. My eyes were opened to a refreshing rhythm of life, where coffee was sipped and savored, standing up at a counter, not guzzled on the go, where fresh tomatoes and cheese were enough for a meal, where no day was too busy for a siesta, where even the most banal sentiments uttered in Italian fluttered off the tongue. And when I met Raffaele, our relationship, too, seemed both improbable and inevitable. My own sweet, shy, nerdy Italian boy to kiss and cook with and read beside. My life had never been so full of possibility.

And then those possibilities collapsed in an instant. The wonder that was blossoming in me inverted, taking on a frightening surreality. It was as if my life were on a stage, and the lighting technician had suddenly flipped a switch, bathing everything in eerie hues and shadow. Prison is an otherworldly space where you are forced to redefine your relationships with practically everything. Like doors—I didn't open one for years. They didn't even have handles, just keyholes, and the large keys Agente carried functioned as handles once inserted. Moving from one room to another required an escort, so I got used to waiting in front of them like a dog unable to manipulate the simple mechanism that kept me confined. The way the staff and volunteers moved through the prison, the way the doors opened for them, it was like they were made of smoke. To see my mom at visitation, I had to be strip-searched before and after. All your clothes off, spin around, squat and cough.

As horrifying as all that was at first, it eventually became normal. Prison, with its oppressive gray sameness, its arbitrary cruelty, its casual indifference, was a place designed to stamp out curiosity and to crush hope. Trying to keep any sense of wonder alive was like cradling a match under a torrent of rain.

I thought perhaps I had lost it forever. But this silly fairy poster brought it back to me in full. It was actually the second wave of wonder to hit me since my release. The moment I stepped out of the plane a few days prior, what the news media couldn't capture was how the scent of the rain and pine trees hit me like smelling salts. The Pacific Northwest had become such a distant idea, a faded drawing in an old book, as dusty as the bare stretch of field where Capanne was situated. I needed that smell to feel fully alive.

A week out of prison, I managed to escape the media surrounding my house and met up with my Italian professor, who took me into the woods to forage for chanterelle mushrooms. The spongy bed of pine needles on the forest floor, after years of standing on nothing but concrete, felt like it might spring me into the air. I was an astronaut bounding on the moon.

The stillness of the forest was medicine. Anywhere else, no matter how slowly I moved, everything around me was buzzing. I was surrounded by frantic hummingbirds. I wasn't just reconnecting with loved ones, many of whom I hadn't seen in years; I was also meeting new people—lawyers, investigators, and supporters who had stood by my family. Meanwhile, the rest of the world was pressuring me to tell my story "before it was too late." All the different news networks gifted me DVDs of their coverage of the case. Phone calls and letters flooded in—movie and book pitches, interview requests. *Why haven't you answered my email?* Not to mention fantasy love letters, gifts of lingerie, death threats. Everybody knew me, even when I didn't know them. Sometimes they came up to me in the grocery store, sobbing with joy. *I'm so glad you're home.* Sometimes they stared at me from across the street with a dark look in their eyes.

The circus died down after a few weeks, but I still couldn't go to the store or walk the dogs without being followed and photographed. Mom urged me to take things slowly, but I wanted a room that felt like my own. Through four years of prison, my friend Madison and I had written letters back and forth about moving in together when I came home. We found a tiny two-bedroom apartment in Seattle's International District. My family advised against it. "It's not safe," they said. "The building has no security." It was true. Anyone—unscrupulous paparazzo, unhinged killer—could easily slip into the building and walk right up to our apartment door. But the last thing I wanted to hear after so much time had been taken from me was that I needed to wait even longer. No. I was done waiting to be allowed to live my life.

So I did the opposite. I rushed into things. We moved into that cheap apartment, and the wonder spun me dizzy. The keys were impressively unremarkable, but they were mine, and they felt weighty and huge in my hand, like they could open the gates of a city. I had almost forgotten what it was like to be the keeper of a key, the master of a door, even if that door led right into a tiny kitchen. There was no living room, just the kitchen, my room (which was actually smaller than my prison cell), Madison's room, and the bathroom. It was a fourth-floor walkup converted from a turn-of-the-century hotel room. We paid a combined $788 a month for that tiny slice of freedom.

Walking down the streets in my new neighborhood, I felt like the new girl on the cellblock, like everyone was sizing me up. And like the new girl on the cellblock, I kept my head down, my gaze averted. My acquired sense for imminent danger tingled across the back of my neck every time I walked out alone in public. Out of the corner of my eye, I'd see the lumbering shape of an inmate I knew and I'd jump, only to realize it was just some stranger walking along, minding their own business. I'd cross to the other side of the street anyway.

I was more vulnerable there than I had been at my mom's house, but rushing into that space had been worth it. I was in the thick of city life, surrounded by people who, for the most part, didn't recognize me. The food was incredible. The grocery store, Uwajimaya, where I had purchased manga comics in high school, was a culinary paradise. For a few splendid minutes each day, I was a queen and the produce aisle was my kingdom. I was within walking distance of the Goodwill, which I routinely visited to purge my wardrobe of court and prison outfits, replacing them with clothes full of fun colors and patterns. Our apartment was near Pioneer Square, the oldest neighborhood in Seattle, now full of art galleries, boutique shops, and hip restaurants. It was also home to one of my favorite independent bookstores, Arundel Books, which specializes in used and rare volumes. When I first walked in, I felt like Aladdin in the treasure horde. I put my nose in the books, I caressed their spines, I bought as many as I could carry at a time.

I was on my own again, always a little anxious, always a little confused, but my curiosity was blazing. Things I had not imagined for myself were suddenly possible, magic had tumbled back into my life, and who knew what strange surprise lay around the next bend? But as the days passed, I began to feel that I was living someone else's dream, a dream I couldn't manage to wake up from.

Self-Help

YOU WOULD THINK THAT AFTER everything I'd been through, I would be a therapy junkie. But you'd be wrong.

Mom was convinced, even before my acquittal, that I would need therapy, and lots of it. Therapy would be essential to my healing after years in prison, and she was not shy about telling me that repeatedly when I got home. I replied: "*Or*, I'm fine."

"That's impossible," she said.

"*I'm FINE*," I told her, sounding exactly like a person who was fine.

I didn't like the idea of talking to a stranger who had no clue what I'd gone through. I'd been pressured to go to therapy in prison. There were a couple of psychiatrists occasionally available to "help" the prisoners, but as far as I could tell, their job was to prescribe medication. You say you're depressed, you get antidepressants. You say you're having withdrawal, you get some methadone. I saw the results of their "help" all around me in the medicated stupor of cellmates who had drugged themselves numb to get through the day, the week, the years. I refused to see them.

It was only after I was convicted, when I cut off all my hair, that Agente forced me into that psychiatrist's office.

"So, you wanted to see me."

"I didn't want to see you."

"Okay, well, they brought you here to see me. What can I do for you?"

"Nothing. You can't do anything for me."

"So you're fine?"

"I'm fine."

"I see you cut your hair off."

"I'm allowed to cut my hair."

"I don't think that means you're fine."

What did it mean? The women around me went to great lengths to care for their hair however they could, using olive oil to condition it, combing and braiding it. For a while, I did, too. A part of me held on to my long hair as a link to the outside world. One day, I'd get out of prison and I'd want my long, beautiful hair.

But when I was convicted, my hair suddenly felt like an absurd, even grotesque form of vanity. I wasn't going home. I was a prisoner. What the fuck did I need pretty hair for? The prosecution and the media were calling me a seductress. Cutting my hair off was a big middle finger to those accusations, and a stark look in the mirror of my reality.

"You can't help me," I told the psychiatrist. "Can I leave now?"

That's the interaction I thought about every time Mom brought up therapy. I tried to brush it off, but Mom is stubborn. She found a trauma specialist at the University of Washington and begged me to go. I agreed, if only to prove to her that I didn't need it.

The office was in a building just off campus on the Ave, the strip of bars and restaurants that usually buzzed with student activity. It was a cold winter day, around five p.m., and already dark outside. I knocked on his office door. He called me in, and I found him already sitting behind his desk. His office looked like a stock photo of a professor's office. Books, framed degrees, some photos on the desk, a plant. He, too, was nondescript in his blazer, glasses, and gentle "trauma specialist" demeanor. He disappeared into his dark hair. I told him I didn't really know what to say. "That's okay," he said. "Just have a seat." I sat awkwardly for a moment. Then he said, "So, how are you doing?"

And my chest collapsed. That was supposed to be a softball question, but it felt like the hardest question in the world to answer.

Not being okay was not an option. In prison, I *had* to be okay to survive. Anything else was vulnerability, a weakness that would be used against me. In freedom it felt the same. But paradoxically, I also felt that if there ever was a time I should have been *not* fine, it was when I was stuck in a cell, and now that I was out, I should have been okay. After hanging on for so long, ever the survivor, I *deserved* to be okay. I wanted that to be true so badly.

I was now fully sobbing in front of this stranger, and with each gasping breath, my mind flitted back and forth between being angry at myself for proving Mom right and angry at Mom, because I had been holding it together just fine until she pressured me into this room. Before Italy, I was gregarious and unfiltered and an avid people-watcher. In high school I had frequently visited the Pike Place Market on the way home and meandered its labyrinthine passageways just for the pleasure of immersing myself in a world of bustling strangers. Now, I didn't talk to strangers. I didn't trust people. I assumed everyone was trying to take advantage of me. Even if this therapist had the best intentions, he had no fucking clue what I'd gone through, what I was still going through. No one did. Other people couldn't help me; they only made things worse. They only served to remind me that I no longer belonged anywhere or to anyone.

I gasped, "I'm sorry. I can't do this. I have to go." The professor didn't even have time to say goodbye. I was gone.

Okay, maybe I wasn't okay. A little while later, also at Mom's urging,

Free

I tried therapy again. I found a woman who charged three hundred dollars an hour, and I paid for it in cash—I didn't want it to be traceable. I was paranoid about being betrayed and sold out to the tabloids. I filled the hours talking, waiting for some breakthrough. I assumed this worked for other people, but it never came for me. It was just another way I didn't belong. I quit after two months.

It was then that Madison convinced me to attend a Vipassana silence retreat. It was just the thing for me: meditative, quiet, peaceful, and healing. The administrator called me ahead of time to ask about my history with meditation. "This is intense," she said. "It's ten days without talking, meditating for hours on end." I told her I'd sat in a prison cell for four years. I figured if I could do that, I could do this.

My stepdad dropped me off at the retreat center. It was nothing special, a few unremarkable buildings in a field. It didn't strike me as a particularly beautiful or peaceful place.

The first morning was awkward. They had us watch a two-hour video where a guru explained the meditation process, along with a bit of metaphysical nonsense. I hadn't realized I'd signed up for ten days of indoctrination. We then had an hour-long walking meditation in the field. The last time I'd had to walk in a circle like that, over and over, was in the prison yard. I tried my best to let that thought drift away. At lunch, we had lentils in the cafeteria and were instructed to avoid eye contact and not to talk to each other. A part of me liked that, because I didn't want to be recognized, but it was also exactly how I'd behaved in prison, keeping my head down, avoiding eye contact, trying to be as small as possible in the hope that people would leave me alone.

They sent us back to our small dorm rooms for three hours of meditation. I sat there for thirty minutes before the claustrophobia overwhelmed me. I went back out to the field and tried to do walking meditation, but a moment later, an administrator approached and told me I had to go back to my room. I tried to explain, but they insisted. So back I went, feeling reprimanded. A few minutes later, the panic attack started. I burst back out of the room in breathless sobs, and they brought me to the office of the lead instructor.

I told her I couldn't do it, that everything was reminding me too much of prison, that I had to leave. She held me there for another thirty minutes, trying to gauge whether I really needed to leave or if I just needed a moment to calm down. "I have to be able to go," I said. "Even this, right now, in your office, I can't, I just can't."

I didn't even last a day. That afternoon, I grabbed my things, called Mom, and asked her to pick me up. The ride home was excruciatingly quiet. Once again, I felt like I'd proved them all right, that I was a wreck. Once again, I felt that incoherent anger: *They have no idea what I've been through or what I need, and I was doing just fine until someone pushed me into this.*

I eventually realized that these mental health care attempts failed because I was trying them for the sake of others—for my mom, for my friend—not for myself. But even as I resisted therapy and traditional meditation, I did find ways to process my trauma. I spent a lot of time alone, walking or riding my bike, just thinking. For hours and hours. I would walk through the stacks of the library. I would walk five miles from the International District to the University of Washington. I'd wander the massive Goodwill aimlessly. I was taking in the sights, both large and small, as if everything—a skyscraper, a ladybug on a rhododendron leaf—carried the same cosmic weight. I felt like a drifting ghost, unattached and insignificant. Haunted, and haunting. For a time, it brought relief. I didn't talk about my trauma as much as you might imagine. I hadn't yet learned that it could be useful, not only to me, but that it could help others, that there was something uniquely healing about finding a purpose in that pain.

Free

In prison, standing up for myself wouldn't have worked. It would have meant violence. So I put up with a lot of shit, and I got smaller and smaller. In freedom, I thought I'd be back to just my size, but I wasn't. The gaze of the world was constantly on me, looking for anything it could possibly find to vilify me, and I still felt unnaturally small.

Back at Mom's house, I saw an old photo of myself as a teenager, posing in my soccer uniform, a naïve smile, a face that trusted in the goodness of the world. The girl in the photo—*she* was fine. Me, not so much.

Public Property

THE FIRST TIME ANYONE SAT me down and explained what it meant to be a "public figure" was in early 2012, a few months after I was released from prison. By now, I had grimaced through all the DVDs the press corps had gifted me, and I was coming to better understand the many faces of this cartoon character, Foxy Knoxy, who stood between me and my successful reintegration into free society. How the media had both dissected and distorted me, it felt...criminal. So I met with two lawyers in Seattle, and they gave me an assignment: watch the made-for-TV Lifetime film *Amanda Knox: Murder on Trial in Italy*, where I was played by Hayden Panettiere, and make a list of every fact the filmmakers got wrong. The film had aired while I was still in prison, appealing my conviction, and I'd successfully sued them back then to remove a dream sequence where the Amanda character murders Meredith. But beyond that, perhaps there was a case for libel.

Now, as I pressed play on the DVD they had given me, I tried to settle into the same state of numbness I had forged in the courtroom, where I spent hundreds of hours sitting silently, listening to people expound on theories, dissect gruesome facts, and quibble over insignificant details to determine whether or not I was a monster.

The film was full of errors, both big and small. I hit pause every few seconds to write them down. They portrayed the Seattle coffee shop where I worked like a Starbucks, when in fact it was a quiet mom-and-pop shop with a fine wine selection. My coworker referred to me as "Foxy Knoxy," but no one in college ever called me by that childhood soccer nickname. Hayden Panettiere, who was dressed around her cleavage, portrayed me to be a connoisseur of drug dealers. She smiled and waved for the television cameras.

Little details like these, some pulled straight from the tabloids, sent my heart racing. I had to take breaks to stay calm, but eventually, I came back to my lawyers with a long list and the disconcerting realization that this was what most people thought had happened. This was who most people thought I was.

I figured we had a good case to sue Lifetime. Besides the trivial things, the film made serious factual errors, like having Raffaele call the police to report the break-in *after* they had already arrived, which made him look like a liar trying to cover something up. In the movie, detectives informed me that I was a suspect during my interrogation, when in reality I was told that I was just a witness, and refused a lawyer. They didn't show when a detective hit me on the back of the head, or when I recanted the statements implicating Patrick Lumumba that I'd been coerced into signing.

My lawyers agreed that these were serious factual errors. But there was a problem. Factual errors weren't enough to make a case for libel. As a public figure, I had to prove that the filmmakers *knowingly* misrepresented these facts *with malicious intent*. We would have to submit a subpoena for their records, which could take months and turn up nothing, and in the meantime, "Foxy Knoxy" would make headlines all over again.

I objected. How was this fair? I didn't choose to be a public figure, to be "the girl accused of murder." But I knew my objections were feeble;

I had already lost this battle many times before. And anyway, Lifetime wasn't the worst out there by a long shot. But it rankled me that, once again, people who didn't know me were defining who I was, the truth didn't seem to matter, and I was powerless to do anything about it.

There is no statute of limitations on public figuredom. Nor is there a line demarcating what parts of a public figure's life are public and which are private. As a public figure, I had no legal recourse when the paparazzi followed me to a waltz class, and the tabloids wrote a story with insidious framing suggesting that I might as well have been dancing on Meredith's grave. Without any outright lies, and without proof of malicious intent, I was forced to let this misleading and salacious coverage ricochet through the media ecosystem. One tabloid would print such a story, another would pick it up, and another, until more reputable outlets like NBC saw the click-and-cash opportunity and put out their own more sanitized version that nonetheless retained the disparaging frame of the original article—and all of this mutating through the distorted gossip network of social media.

Can you believe the Halloween costume she wore? She's out singing karaoke? You know who will never sing karaoke again? Meredith. Any attempt to defend myself merely resulted in accusations that I was a narcissist hungry for the spotlight, a liar, and, of course, a killer.

It's often hard for people to understand what this feels like. Even my own family didn't. I learned something about my family while I was on trial: they would go to the ends of the Earth for me. They were unshakably loyal, even when the hate was so intense and so widespread that it spilled off me and onto them: "Foxy Knoxy, the girl who had to compete with her own mother for men"; "Foxy Knoxy's sisters posing happily for 'macabre' photos at the house where Meredith Kercher died." They sacrificed so much to save me, putting their own mental health, their own relationships, their own finances second to their one, all-consuming mission: *save Amanda*. I was allowed six hours of visitation a month in Capanne, and for four years, they made sure that someone was always there to see me. They never missed a single one of those precious hours.

When I was finally free, acquitted, and back home, they wanted to return to the lives they'd had before, and I wanted that for them, too. They deserved it. For them, the nightmare was over, and they could go back to prioritizing themselves, resuming hobbies and passions they'd set aside, the habits of their old selves. But I couldn't. The media was not done with Foxy Knoxy.

I felt like I was in a lab—a re-creation of freedom surrounded by one-way mirrors hiding men in white coats with clipboards. Imagine for a moment that you're having coffee in a café. Your friend comes back from the bathroom and reports that a man in the corner has been taking your photo with his phone. He's writing about you in his notebook: what you're wearing, the way your face looks, what he thinks you're thinking, whether you like rough sex or hard drugs. Do you carry on as if he's not there? Live your life? Or do you get the hell out of there? Do you report it to the police? Everywhere I went, everything I did, there were people observing me and speculating about me in just that way, and I was powerless to stop it.

Our ears are wired to burn when someone is talking about us, whether it's a newspaper across the ocean or a creep across the room in a café. I wish I could say that I somehow triumphed in spite of this ever-present spotlight, but I didn't. That judgmental lens made me awkward, too cautious and withdrawn sometimes, too suggestible and eager to please at other times. Perhaps my rejection of therapy, my insistence on being fine, would have worked if I'd been able to immerse myself in the rhythms of a normal life. Instead, I was immersed in a world so warped that it was near impossible to process and integrate the challenges and traumas of my life in a healthy way.

But that problem was my own. Other people had written a story around me, and I had mistaken it for my story. I was fighting to change who I was in that story, but I was still operating within a context I didn't want to be in. I didn't feel like the author of my own life; I was the villain in someone else's tale. I quickly learned that reacting to the falsehoods was a losing game. But I couldn't just bury my head in the sand and pretend the last four years hadn't happened. It was becoming increasingly clear to me that I couldn't ignore how my experience had changed me. Like in Capanne, for better or worse, I had to engage, in my life and work, with what it meant to be wrongly accused. I had to process that experience. But unlike in Capanne, where there was nothing I could do to alter my circumstances, to unlock a barred door from the inside, where I just had to accept things the way they were and make the best of them, now it felt like I had in front of me a nebulous opportunity, a duty, even, to intervene on my own behalf and alter my fate. It might take me years, decades, maybe even the rest of my life, but I had to try.

I was also deeply in debt, to my family, my lawyers, and the many people who'd volunteered their time and resources to save me. I wanted to make them all whole again, and the best opportunity I had to tackle both these goals—to process my experience and pay back my family—was to write a memoir. That would mean opening myself up to the world. It would mean becoming as large as I could be, taking up as much space as possible. And I knew the larger I became, the bigger a target I would be.

Defensive Maneuvers

I'D FELT SO SMALL FOR so long, voiceless while a cacophony of strangers debated who I was, what I'd done, and what I deserved. I thought that by writing a memoir, I'd finally be adding my voice to the fray, and by standing up for myself and what was true, I'd finally find my place in this new world.

Writing *Waiting to Be Heard* turned out to be more difficult and more cathartic than I'd imagined. In recalling small details about Capanne—how the warden had balked at my dismay after being shown Meredith's autopsy photos, how other prisoners had bullied me and gossiped behind my back—rage flamed up in me, and I had to get up from my computer and go on emergency walks around my block. I hadn't allowed myself to feel angry for years. But recalling those moments was a way to process them, even though I often felt utterly wrung out at the end of the day.

By the time the book was finished, I was coming around to the idea that this might be a real turning point. I might finally be recognized for the person I really was and be able to move on with my life and leave this tragedy behind. But if I wanted anyone to read it, I'd have to promote it, and that would mean stepping right into the glare of the sensational and judgmental spotlight I'd been trying to hide from since I got home.

I had not given a single interview, and I'd been hoping that when I did, the suspicion I was always faced with would have finally morphed into understanding. But just over a month before the memoir's publication date, on March 26, 2013, Italy's Court of Cassation overturned my acquittal and ordered a retrial.

To say I was shocked doesn't begin to convey the utter panic that swept over me. What did this mean? I had known for months that the verdict that released me would have to be rubber stamped by the Court of Cassation, Italy's version of a Supreme Court, and my lawyers had told me that my prosecutor, Dr. Giuliano Mignini, was deeply upset by my acquittal and that the state would appeal the verdict. But I had been under the impression that this was mostly a formality. I thought my innocence had been clearly established when the appeals court had hired two independent experts who debunked the DNA evidence on the supposed murder weapon, the only link between me and the crime. The day they presented their findings there was uproar in the court. The independent experts had demolished Dr. Mignini's case. It would not have been possible for me to take part in a vicious death orgy and leave zero traces of myself at the crime scene. I had assumed that was the final word in this saga—*how could you argue with that?*—so I was not at all prepared to be back in real danger again. And yet, here I was, suddenly on trial yet again, for the very same crime.

I began talking with my lawyers about extradition treaties and the possibility of mounting my defense in absentia, but in the meantime, my memoir was about to be published. It now felt like, more than ever, my voice and my perspective had to be out there. Of course, I wanted the book to succeed. I was also contractually obligated to promote it. Every journalist in the world had wanted a piece of me since I had come home. But now, on trial again, there would be no softball, sympathetic interviews. Anyone I spoke to would want to grill Foxy Knoxy, on trial for murder again, not Amanda Knox, who had spent four years in prison for a crime she didn't commit. Even journalists who presented themselves with more professionalism, with a desire to rectify misinformation, still saw me as a valuable "get." I was a commodity.

My lawyers narrowed it down to Matt Lauer at NBC, Diane Sawyer at ABC, and Oprah Winfrey. I met with Matt Lauer in New York. He seemed friendly enough...but I was tired of being grilled by middle-aged men, and I felt much better about a female interviewer. I chatted with Oprah on the phone, and she was both warm and wise. I could tell she got it. I told my lawyers that she was my pick, but there was a wrinkle. If I were to choose Oprah, my interview would air just after her interview with recently disgraced Lance Armstrong. My lawyers didn't love the optics of that. So they urged me to choose Diane Sawyer at ABC, instead.

I remember walking through the quad at UW beneath the cherry blossoms, keeping my head down to avoid being recognized, making this decision on a phone call with my team in the few minutes I had between classes. I hadn't had a chance to speak with Diane Sawyer, but ABC had done decent coverage of my case, and Nikki Battiste, a journalist who had grown close with my family during my imprisonment, would be a producer on the hour-long special. To this day, I regret not choosing Oprah.

ABC rented a loft in lower Manhattan for filming and put me up at the Waldorf Astoria in what felt like an enormous room—I was still used to the size of my cell and my tiny apartment back home. I didn't get much prep for this first, all-important interview. Tina, my book publicist, took me to J.Crew—a far cry from my favorite retailer, Goodwill—and bought me an outfit. My lawyers told me to remember to say the title of my book as many times as I could during the interview. They even showed me a video of Hillary Clinton doing just that, working in her book title, *Hard Choices*, every other sentence.

"Diane is going to ask you some tough questions," they said, "but you've answered those questions many times before. Just keep your cool."

Diane was friendly but distant. I didn't feel any personal warmth from her. The vibe in that room was professional—she was doing her job, and so I should be doing my job, which was to answer her questions. That attitude left me resigned to the fact that I was essentially on trial again, that I would have to answer, for the millionth time, the question: "Did you kill Meredith Kercher?" When I said "No," the world would analyze my facial expression for signs of deception. Even asking the question presented it as an uncertainty, presenting me as a figure to be doubted. And that was all Diane was interested in: doubting my innocence. She had so little empathy for me, she actually asked me if I enjoyed my notoriety.

The interview went on for seven grueling hours, though Diane herself left at some point and had another producer finish up the last couple hours of questions. And, of course, when the interview aired, they'd cut my seven hours down to ten minutes and filled the rest with Diane's own presentation of the case.

As my face and my trauma and my reputation played on prime-time television and across the mega screens in Times Square, as my innocence was debated in every rag in the checkout line, and through countless tweets and posts, I felt uncomfortably large, so big, so public, as if every person on the street was in the jury box.

A week later, I went to my publisher's office and spent days answering the same questions over and over again from a parade of print and radio journalists. *Did you kill Meredith Kercher?* No. *How do you feel about being back on trial?* Devastated. On a live radio interview with an Australian outlet, they started hammering me about Patrick Lumumba. *Why did you falsely accuse an innocent man?* I didn't have the language then to explain the complicated dynamics of police coercion, how they had systematically broken me down over fifty-three hours of questioning, how they had threatened me, hit me, and gaslit me until I was pliable enough to sign an incoherent statement they authored. I described the interrogation as the scariest thing that had ever happened to me, but the interviewer kept pressing. I looked helplessly at Tina, and she just grabbed the phone and hung up.

The Chris Cuomo interview came up last minute. In the makeup room at CNN, Chris came in and said, "I'm going to ask you some tough questions, but just so you know, I'm only doing it so you can answer them. A lot of them will seem like dumb questions, but they're the questions people are asking, and I want to give you a chance to confront those things head on."

We sat on a raised dais, with dramatic lighting and big screens behind me to show crime scene and courtroom footage. He nudged me through the interview, like he wanted me to give snappy objections to the litany of absurd accusations. "What about this mop I keep hearing about?" He was referring to a mop that I had brought from my house to Raffaele's the morning Meredith's body was discovered. It was to clean up leaked sink water in Raffaele's kitchen, but Dr. Giuliano Mignini had initially pointed to this as potential evidence that I had cleaned up the crime scene. There were no signs that the crime scene had been cleaned, though, and the mop had no blood or DNA on it. Chris knew that, and eventually he said as much. We moved on to the next irrelevant but damaging question. "Were you into deviant sex? Insensitive question, but hey, we gotta get to what it is. This fuels the doubt."

To this day, Chris Cuomo seems to think he was doing me a favor there. He said so on Twitter multiple times. He didn't seem to consider that *he* was in fact *fueling the doubt* about my character by asking such questions.

At the end of the interview, he asked, "What would you say to those who continue to doubt your innocence?"

"Speculation convicts me," I said, "but evidence acquits me."

My lawyers, and Tina, my publicist, were thrilled! *Who told you to say that?* "I just thought of it," I said as they gave me high fives.

But that line ended up on the cutting room floor. Ultimately, it didn't matter how well I made the case for my innocence during these interviews. It would all be edited and reshaped to fit the perspective of the journalist and the network, who put out whatever version generated the most clicks. The image CNN left viewers with was one of desperation. Cuomo asked me, "Five years from today, what do you want in your life?"

"I hope that I will be definitively found innocent," I said. "I don't know how long I can hold it together. I don't know how long I can defend myself. And the idea that I'm going to have to be defending myself against accusations of murder for the rest of my life, it is impossible."

Then Cuomo closed out the program by saying, "We may never know exactly what happened in the villa on the night of November first, 2007," and that despite the lack of evidence against me, "Amanda Knox's behavior and her incriminating words remain around her neck, like a noose."

Back in my hotel after this marathon week of interviews, I felt that tingle of panic. I took a bath, attempting to soothe myself, but it didn't work. By the time I was in bed, utterly exhausted, my breathing raced out of control, my body reflecting my inability to control my life. The interrogations never seemed to end. Would I forever be on the defense, forever forced to deny absurd accusations? *Why was this my life? Why was this my life? Why?*

I knew my advocates, my publicist, my lawyers, they all would have leapt in front of a bus for me. And yet *they* had pushed me into this media nightmare. That was just how things were done. They were in an ecosystem that had its own rules. And no one ever thought to say, *Actually . . . these rules are going to cause more trauma.*

The problem was the frame. Everyone was still turning to me for answers the same way Dr. Giuliano Mignini had. They were asking me questions about a crime scene I'd never even seen in person—I was not present when Meredith's door was kicked down, and I never saw into her room. They were asking me the questions they should have been asking Meredith's killer, Rudy Guede. Had I known then what I know now, I would have said, "Look, if you're here to ask me questions about Meredith's murder, I know just as much as you do. I don't have special answers for you. What I can tell you is what it feels like to be minding my own business and then get yanked out of my life and put in prison for something I didn't do. I can talk your head off about that!"

But lacking that language, I simply gasped for air. I was being judged on my answers to a test I couldn't possibly know the answers to. The test was predicated on the idea of my guilt, that I deserved to be judged. *When did you stop beating your wife?* I was still trapped, not in a cell, but in my own life.

I cried and heaved that night until I passed out from exhaustion. My panic came from a rising certainty that this was never going to change. My book didn't matter. It wasn't a turning point. Nothing I would ever do or say would cut that noose from my neck.

Just Ignore It

THE FIRST DEATH THREAT WASN'T even for me. It was for my mom. I had only been in Capanne for a few weeks, and I was already a magnet for hate. I read that letter in my cell, and at the end of a long screed, this stranger said he knew where my mother was staying in Perugia and that he would kill her to punish me. I immediately told Agente. "You have to do something! My mom needs protection!"

"Just ignore it," she said.

The next threat came, and the next. Over four years of prison, I stopped counting how many people wished me dead. It just became a part of my reality, a part of it that was so...unreal. As far as I knew, no one was actually stalking my family and friends in the apartment they rented on the outskirts of Perugia. The biggest physical threats to my well-being were inside Capanne's walls: Vice Commandante Argirò, male agenti, the occasional unhinged cellmate. I naïvely hoped my acquittal would put an end to all these threats.

But as I tried to rebuild a semblance of a normal life back home, the threats and harassment continued, and they only swelled once I was put on trial again. They arrived in the mail at my mom's house, and in the comments on the blog where I posted official statements when there was a development in the case. Amidst kind messages from supporters, there were always the ones wishing me dead, the ones describing how it would happen. This only got worse after the publication of my memoir, and those prime-time interrogations. Some threats were recurrent, the same twisted mind progressing further and further in their fantasy of murdering me. One dedicated death-wisher sent me a note describing how he would show up one day in an unmarked van and abduct me in broad daylight because he didn't care if he got caught. He would take me someplace where no one could hear me scream, and he would carve Meredith's name into my body. He would hook me to a car battery and electrocute me, delighting in my agony. He would torture me until I begged him for mercy and, slut that I am, attempted to barter sex to end my torture. He would refuse. Only when I begged for death would he finally kill me.

I turned to retired FBI Special Agent Steve Moore for advice. He had helped arrange and execute my heart-racing escape from Italy. Now, he connected me with the local FBI field office. They were able to track down the man who'd sent me those explicit threats. He was Canadian, so they contacted the Royal Canadian Mounties, who paid him a visit. I imagined Dudley Do-Right showing up at his doorstep on horseback. Word passed back through the FBI, and I learned that he was an older man who worked as a security guard. His wife was apparently as shocked that he was sending those messages as I was to receive them. The Mounties passed along a stern warning from the FBI, but that was as much as they could do. Unless he took concrete steps toward carrying out his threats, like buying a plane ticket to Seattle, there was nothing else to be done.

Perhaps unexpectedly, the darkest stuff hurt me the least. It was easy to see that man in Canada as mentally ill, and that *I* just happened to be the focus of his illness. But people like him were comparatively rare next to the torrent of casual hate on social media aimed in my direction. What both groups had in common was that they were righteous; they were vigilantes giving me what I deserved.

Everyone I knew—my friends and family—had already embraced social media. Even Oma was on Facebook. But I knew what would happen if I exposed myself to that world, so while I made Facebook and Instagram accounts, I kept them private—just for close friends and family. But that didn't protect me against seeing the cruel commentary whenever there was a development in my case and my name was thrust back into headlines, or someone posted yet another YouTube video interpreting my handwriting, hand gestures, or facial tics in the worst possible light.

When I tried my hand at making a public post, it always seemed to backfire. In the lead-up to the retrial, I posted a picture of myself holding a handwritten sign that read "Siamo Innocenti"—*We Are Innocent*. Italians responded by posting copycat images of themselves holding signs that read "Perugia Vi Odia"—*Perugia Hates You*, or by photoshopping my message so that it read: "Cercasi Coinquilina"—*Roommate Wanted*.

All of this gave me an insight into how toxic the world of social media was long before the rest of society started coming to terms with it.

The novel attributes of the online world—anonymity, immediate contact over vast distances, cultural echo chambers, virulent misinformation—had created a unique set of challenges for countering abuse and antisocial behaviors. While such platforms would attempt to limit online hate by filtering out keywords, in my case it has proved incredibly easy for targeted harassment to slip through the algorithmic abuse filters. I routinely get targeted with messages like, "We know you did it," and, "How do you sleep at night?" Or even just, "Meredith." Recently, a troll tweeted pictures at me of the house Meredith and I lived in. That's a deep cut in the world of harassment. To the algorithm, it's just a picture of a house, but I know, as does the troll, what that house—and crime scene—represents.

I know my case is extreme, but I also know that this kind of thing is happening at a lower volume all the time, everywhere. I know it because, in addition to death threats, I also receive messages from people, primarily girls and young women, who report being habitually denigrated and harassed in their social circles and online. And I remember well how the boys in my high school speculated openly about me and the other girls—"Is she an S? No, maybe she's a T? I think she's an F." We were mortified when we discovered they were talking about our pubic hair, whether we were shaved, trimmed, or had a "forest." If teens are clever enough to objectify and demean one another in front of teachers, it's all the easier to do so through social media. And it's the specific, targeted harassment that hurts the most. I once had an embarrassing menstrual moment in algebra class. When something like that happens to a teen today, how easy it is for a cruel classmate to slip through the social media abuse filters with a targeted phrase like "seat stainer."

There are discussions to be had about how to stem the tide of online hate, bullying, and harassment through altered incentives, regulations, better algorithms, and artificial intelligence. But from a personal standpoint, what do you make of the fact that someone hates you, wishes you dead, or wishes your mother dead just because she raised you?

At first, I didn't know how to process it. It wasn't at all comforting to know that what I was up against was different in degree, not kind, from the grueling uphill battle all women wage just to have a voice, a presence, on the internet. And I wasn't at all satisfied with the predominant advice from the people in my life who genuinely wished me well. From the men, usually it was: "If you can't take the heat, get out of the kitchen." From the women, it was: "The block button is your best friend." For a long time, I tried my best to just ignore it—as Agente told me when that first death threat arrived in prison—and I often failed. A death threat or even a cruel comment online would ruin my day.

What helped was to remind myself, over and over again, that none of these people actually hated *me*. They hated an idea of me. Which meant that I was lucky, in a way. The hate was so extreme, so widespread, so irrational, and based on such an outrageous pack of lies, that I was gradually able to divorce myself from the object of that hate. I learned not to take it personally. At least, most of the time. Sure, the thing they hated looked like me, it shared my name, and I would bear the downstream consequences of that hate in the practical realities of trying to build a life for myself, but *I* was not hated.

This realization cuts both ways, though. It also means that the praise people showered on me—and they do—often isn't really about me, either. Again, it's about that idea of me. In my case, the lack of overlap between me and that avatar is extreme, especially on the negative side. The criticisms of Foxy Knoxy have almost nothing to do with me, and though I like to think the praise has a lot more overlap with who I really am, the more important reminder is that I am not "Amanda Knox," the public figure.

This disjunct between how you feel yourself to be and how others perceive you is an opportunity to take stock, recalibrate, and better articulate who you actually are. It can also be an effective means for understanding the stories other people are telling about themselves, because so often they are merely using you as a prop. We naturally define ourselves in opposition to others, just as black goes with white, on with off. Labeling someone else as the bad guy is what enables us to sit safely in the circle of the good guys. I know it doesn't feel that way. It feels like the judgments we make of others are essentially about them, but such judgments are at heart ways of seeing how we measure up.

This insight helped me understand why the authorities responsible for my arrest and conviction could never admit fault, going so far as to try me for the same crime twice. Acknowledging their mistakes wouldn't just be acknowledging an incorrect judgment they'd made, it would compromise their own self stories as competent purveyors of justice, forcing them to reckon with a new identity as people who commit harm.

In time, I taught myself to see each new barb of hate, each threat, as a reminder of who I really was and who I wanted to be: a person who would try her damnedest not to get sucked into false beliefs, and to forever be on guard against the lure of that righteous feeling, that vigilante impulse, because it's so easy to harm others while believing ourselves to be champions for justice. I'm generally against vengeful thinking, but there's one kind of revenge I've learned to cherish: the revenge of becoming my best self.

The Bunker

AS HARD AS IT WAS to adjust to the surreal world of freedom and try to remake a new life, as hard as it was to accept that I would forever be a target of judgment and scrutiny and hate...those were all psychological problems. I was confident that I'd figure them out eventually. But Italy wasn't done with me.

The second trial, which began on September 30, 2013, was even more absurd than the first. The forensic evidence that led to my initial acquittal was not disputed. There was no bogus DNA trace to hang the narrative of my guilt on. So my new prosecutor, informed by Dr. Giuliano Mignini's work, argued a case based solely on indirect witness statements and behavioral evidence, twisting tiny moments out of context to again paint me as a drugged-up, sexually deviant femme fatale. It felt like the trial wasn't even concerned with whether I was guilty or innocent of the murder itself, but rather, whether I was a guilty or innocent *person*. Would an innocent person kiss her boyfriend outside of the crime scene? Would she falsely accuse an innocent man? Or was this the behavior of someone who clearly had *something* to do with the crime, even if we can't say for sure what it is? As Dr. Mignini said in an interview, "How can you separate the slander from the murder?"

I'd heard this argument before. It was a favorite line of reasoning for the trolls online who were outraged by my acquittal. It also happened to be the most common answer to that haunting *why* question: *Why was I wrongly accused in the first place?* Even many of the people who believed in my innocence thought that I had brought it upon myself. Because even though I was innocent, I *acted* guilty. There was something uniquely wrong with *me*.

Being blamed for my own wrongful conviction and scrutinized in the worst possible light made me anxious, of course, but even so, the case was so vague, so flimsy. I was optimistic. Then on January 30, 2014, Raffaele and I were found guilty once again. This time, my sentence was raised from 26 to 28.5 years in prison.

It was one of the most shrill, tense phone calls I'd ever had with my attorneys. "How is this even possible?" I screeched. "How could they convict me on NO EVIDENCE?"

Carlo Dalla Vedova, my attorney based in Rome, was like the Italian version of my dad. He was handsome, charismatic, a straight-shooter, dignified and professional but also warm, and a family man. One of my favorite memories from one of his visits to Capanne was when he tried to convince me, with a wink, that gelato counted as a balanced meal. Now, his voice was strained and muted. "It's not over. We can still appeal to the Court of Cassation."

"The Court of Cassation that OVERTURNED MY ACQUITTAL?!"

It didn't feel real, especially because this entire trial had taken place more than five thousand miles away, without my direct participation. I'd seen the updates on the local news. It was like hearing gunfire on the television, then looking down to find myself bleeding from the abdomen. I wondered bitterly if the Perugia police were celebrating, high-fiving each other like they did right after they coerced me into signing false statements. I wondered if my prosecutor, Dr. Giuliano

Mignini, felt as vindicated as I had the day I was released from Capanne.

The fact that I had one last chance to appeal to Italy's highest court meant that Raffaele and I were not immediately thrown back in prison. But once again, officially, we were convicted murderers, now living in limbo.

With nothing I could do in the meantime but wait, I tried my best to carry on as usual, but the threat of extradition loomed heavy in my mind. It felt like an axe was perpetually poised over the back of my neck, and my paranoia about paparazzi and stranger-danger deepened. I wasn't serving time, but I wasn't free, either. I couldn't plant roots of any kind. Now, there was an expiration date on any relationships I formed, on any career I might start. I'd thought my life had been derailed for four years, and that I was finally getting the chance to catch up to where I should have been at twenty-four. Catching up made no sense now. I had to prepare for the worst. I had resumed taking classes at the UW, but would I ever graduate? I didn't have the bandwidth for such questions. I was talking to my lawyers about reaching out to renowned DNA scientists and false confessions experts who could make the case that my conviction was unsound. Even then, I was lucky by comparison. Since our joint acquittal in 2011, Raffaele had been traveling the globe, looking for somewhere, anywhere outside of Italy, to settle. A friend of mine once half joked about marrying him to help him become a U.S. citizen. It had actually crossed my mind more than once; it wasn't his fault that his own country had turned against him. But it might not even help. I was separated from the nation trying to throw me back in prison by an ocean and by the U.S. government, but that was no guarantee I wouldn't be shipped right back if I lost my appeal. I was just one citizen, and the United States had long-standing economic, political, and military ties with Italy. If my appeal failed, my lawyers told me that the chances were slim to none that the U.S. would flex any political muscle solely to keep me out of prison. Italy was a sovereign country with a legitimate legal system, and maintaining diplomatic ties meant respecting their own rule of law, however flawed it seemed.

If I was found guilty again, I'd almost certainly end up in a cell. But maybe it didn't have to be in Italy. The American lawyers who negotiated my book deal offered to represent me pro bono if it came to an extradition battle. We made plans for how I would turn myself in and beg the U.S. government to arrange for my sentence to be served in an American prison, where at least my family would be able to visit me without an intercontinental journey.

While I was facing this harsh reality, my family was mulling another, riskier option. At dinner, someone would drop a hint. "We know someone who knows someone. They have a basement."

"What are you talking about?" I asked.

"It's well stocked. Enough for a short-term stay. From there, you would cross into Canada on a boat. You'd head north, far north."

"Who are these people?" I asked.

They would never name names. I don't think *they* even knew. "Supporters" is all they would say. People willing to help, even though it would have been a felony. Who would accompany me on this journey to the far, icy reaches of Canada? "No one you know" was the answer. If I did this, I'd have to be untraceable. The most high-tech thing I could take with me was a pencil.

To this day, I don't know how serious those plans were. But I understand why my family would have made them. And I would be lying if I said I didn't seriously consider running. And I'm a terrible liar. In a way, that's part of what dissuaded me from this path. I didn't consider it a stain on my integrity to run. I didn't owe Italy my life just because they wouldn't accept that the man who actually killed Meredith Kercher was already in custody. Why didn't they care about Rudy Guede? His thirty-year prison sentence for rape and conspiracy to commit murder had been reduced to sixteen years on appeal. If anything, the utter madness of going after me a second time while reducing his sentence made me consider running more seriously. Why bother negotiating with people who aren't playing fair to begin with?

And yet, as I imagined what that life would entail—taking on a false identity, living alone in some bunker or basement hundreds of miles away from anyone I knew, dyeing my hair, maybe working the register at an antique store in Yellowknife on the northern shore of the Great Slave Lake, falling in love, despite myself, with a quiet man, only to leave him in the middle of the night for fear that he'd finally recognized me, or that the truth would erupt out of me spontaneously—as I imagined living that lie, that endless series of lies, I knew I could never do it.

What I could imagine was killing myself. I'd had those thoughts in prison—drinking bleach, swallowing glass, a garbage bag and butane stove. At the time, I'd decided against it because I couldn't do that to my family or to myself—where the last thing I'd see in this life was a prison cell. Now, facing potential extradition, I was attracted to the idea of going out on my own terms, standing my ground so that I could avoid ever being forced back into a cell again. Entertaining the thought became almost mundane. A friend and I even discussed it while rifling through clothes at the Goodwill, of all places. "I've thought about it," I said, "and I think I've decided. I'd rather die here than die there." She tried her best to convince me that it was worth living through another appeal, even another guilty verdict. "I'll help you," she said. "I'll get you whatever you need to do it, but not now. Only if you have no other choice, only if you end up back there."

I pushed through those dark moments, because even while I thought about it seriously, somewhere deep inside I knew that killing myself would have been its own kind of lie. It would be a betrayal of everything I'd fought for, a betrayal of the self I had been in Capanne, trapped and yearning for freedom, and the self I would become if I stuck around, no matter where she ended up.

My convictions for murder had turned my own name into a kind of prison; I was trapped in my identity. If I ran from that, I'd be letting them win. And it wasn't just me. My mother would still be known as the mother of a killer—people convinced of my guilt had tried to get her fired from the elementary school where she taught. If I gave up, I'd never get the chance to clear *her* name, either. It wasn't enough to escape that prison. I had to tear it down, which meant fighting, both in and out of the courtroom, for the truth. The problem was, after being tossed around now for two years in the unstable world of freedom, I had no idea who Amanda Knox really was anymore. And in truth, I wasn't strong enough to stand up for myself every second of this journey that seemed in perpetual limbo. So, for a time, I decided to become someone else.

Other people, normal people, had jobs. I needed a job. I know that sounds a little like cracking open a new novel as your plane is going down, but there was still the chance that I'd be acquitted, and in the meantime, I had bills to pay and days to occupy. I received a hefty sum for the sale of my memoir, but after taxes and agent fees and paying back all my legal and family debts stretching back to 2007, most of that was gone, and I still had an appeals trial to mount. I didn't want my family to take on further debt if I wound up in an extradition battle.

So when the owner of the antiquarian bookstore I frequented asked me if I'd like to work the register, I said yes. I was already in there several days a week perusing the eclectic selection of rare and first editions, just breathing in the smell of books—my preferred aromatherapy. The store was below ground level in Pioneer Square, the oldest part of Seattle. It was cozy and tucked away, received little foot traffic—most of their books were sold online, I soon learned—and was perfect for someone like me. The last job I'd had before Italy was as a barista in the University District. That was face-to-face interactions all day long. I didn't dare apply for such a job now. Nor, I guessed, would many employers want all the baggage that came with hiring Amanda Knox. I knew Raffaele was having trouble finding a job in Italy for that very reason. I was a convicted killer, of course, so there was some measure of bad publicity a business would have to deal with if they hired me, but there were also issues of liability, given the stalkers, haters, and death threats.

Phil, who ran the bookstore, didn't seem to care about any of that. And he said that if anyone came in looking for me—and that did eventually happen—I could retreat to the back room and work on shipping, and he'd take over the counter.

The job brought a sense of routine back to my life, which I was grateful for. The only real downsides were that it paid minimum wage, which didn't quite cover my monthly expenses, and it wasn't the start of something that might become a career. That wouldn't matter if I was sent back to prison, but if—knock on wood—I wasn't, I hoped I could do more than stand at a counter for the rest of my life. I didn't know exactly what I was looking for, but it came at me from an unexpected direction.

A man named Patrick reached out to me on Facebook, introducing himself as an editor for the *West Seattle Herald*, the local newspaper that had covered my neighborhood for the last century—it was founded in 1923. "I would love for you to write for the paper," he said. I was immediately suspicious. *Of course* he wanted me to write for the local paper.

Free

My attorneys had warned me of supposed well-wishers such as this. He didn't know or care if I could write. What he really wanted was the attention my name in the byline would bring. I was not about to sacrifice myself on the altar of public shame for the benefit of my local newspaper.

"I read your memoir," he said. "You can write! We'd love to give you an opportunity to write more. You could cover the arts for us. You can even use a pseudonym if you'd like."

For all the stubborn insistence I'd felt about not changing my name—my name wasn't the problem—this offer was intriguing. He wasn't interested in exploiting the worst experience of my life to promote his newspaper? Phil from the bookstore aside, I thought that was the only thing any random stranger cared about when it came to me. Paradoxically, by his offering me a chance to write under a pseudonym, I actually felt appreciated for who I really was, not for what my name had come to represent.

This offer from the *Herald* gave me the chance to be creative on a regular basis under low pressure. It allowed me to further develop my writing skills. The pay was paltry, but it would supplement my bookstore income, and, more important, it was the beginning of a writing career I had thought was unavailable to me. Even though my memoir had been a *New York Times* bestseller, I knew it wasn't because of the writing; it was because of people's fascination with the case and with me. It hadn't felt like the start of something. Everything I had done thus far in my adult life was judged in relation to the accusation of murder. This job would allow me to produce work that would go out into the world and be judged on its own merits. I happily accepted.

You'd think I would have given a lot of thought to my pseudonym, but my mind went blank. It should sound like a real person's name, I thought, but also hold some meaning for me. I chose the name Emile, because it was gender neutral, and because it was the name of a character in Oma's favorite childhood novel. I chose Monte because I had a can of Del Monte peas sitting on the eye-level shelf in my pantry. And Monte was Italian for mountain, the symbolic mountain I had yet to climb. By assuming this false identity, I would take my first steps. Emile Monte it was.

I took to it immediately. I didn't have to go to an office. I corresponded with my employers over email. I could work while cocooned in my apartment. When I ventured out to report for the paper, it was to a darkened theater to review a local play. On those rare occasions that I interviewed local artists and authors in person, I always introduced myself as Emile. If my interviewees recognized me, they didn't say. I stayed professional and avoided eye contact. I was timid and a bit withdrawn, but I tried to be a good listener, treating people the way I wished I'd been treated in my interviews.

The *Herald* had a small, local circulation. The readership of my articles was as modest as the high school plays and independent theater company productions I was reviewing. But that's exactly what I needed after years imprisoned in the harsh glare of a global spotlight. Like my bookstore job, this one, too, felt like an act of charity. The editor at the *West Seattle Herald* didn't have to reach out; he didn't need my particular pseudonymous point of view. He just wanted to give me a shot at being a normal person. That wasn't possible for Amanda Knox. But it was for Emile Monte.

Which isn't to say that I've ever felt above criticism. I welcome judgment when it's based in truth. You can't improve if you're unwilling to face criticism. When people criticize you for something you truly could have done better, it is a gift.

The problem was, I was in an abusive relationship with criticism. I was being condemned for things I hadn't done and for traits I'd never possessed. And everything I did do was always viewed in the worst possible light. Judgment and criticism were so pervasive in my life that, even as I pushed back against the worst of it, I still couldn't help internalizing at least some of it, especially when it came to parts of my experience that I still didn't understand. What had happened to me in that interrogation room? What had four years of isolation and ostracism done to my personality? I desperately wanted to merely be judged for who I actually was, for what I'd actually done. But even I wasn't sure how much blame rested on the rest of the world, and how much rested on me.

It's natural to tie our egos to our failures and successes. We feel like champions when we triumph, and we feel like losers when we fail. And when you fail hard enough, or too many times in a row, or in a very public way, your self-image takes a hit. When that happens, you're not actually judging your own actions on their merits or even lack of merits—you are judging the kind of person who you imagine would make that mistake—*an idiot, a failure, a coward, an asshole*. Whenever I catch myself tying my mistakes to my identity, I think of Emile Monte, that faceless stranger, and I remember to judge the mistake on its own merits. Instead of allowing it to warp my sense of self, I just try to learn how to avoid making the same mistake again.

Strangely, by becoming someone else for a time, I started to see who Amanda Knox really was. Amanda Knox would never die by her own hand. Nor would she live out her days in a bunker, forever on the run. What would she do? What would *I* do? For better or worse, I couldn't help but remain optimistic, I couldn't help but see people as essentially good—that men like Phil and Patrick were the rule, not the exception. I couldn't help but dream that the world was a better place than it had seemed from inside my cell or inside the prison of my name. Dreaming, however, made me especially vulnerable.

Ex–Conned

IF I LEARNED ANYTHING FROM media, both traditional and social, it was that I couldn't trust strangers with my intimate life. Foxy Knoxy was catnip to creeps who enjoyed debating whether it was worth risking being murdered for the chance to fuck me, for those who propositioned me for murder-themed porn, for the reporters who continued to comment upon the state (waxing? waning?) of my sex appeal and posed to their audiences questions like: "Foxy Knoxy: Would Ya?" I wasn't about to make friends with anyone I didn't know from before Italy, much less *date* them. That's why when I joined social media, I steered well clear of anything remotely resembling a dating app. No way, OkCupid! *Tinder?* Hell no. Facebook? It's complicated.

Astonishingly, I still had a love life. I just didn't go about it like other people in their mid-twenties in the mid-2010s. And really, I didn't "go about" anything. I fell back into a relationship with James, an old college boyfriend. It happened almost immediately. We had been exchanging letters for years. His apartment was just around the corner from where Madison and I lived. The first few months of being home, I hung out at his place listening to him practice classical guitar for hours each day. He was a loner, and now so was I. We were hermits together, inseparable for two years. That is, until everything fell apart all at once.

Free

It was the spring of 2014. I was about to graduate from college. I know that for most young people this is a bittersweet time. You say goodbye to campus, to friends, to youthful liberties and indiscretions. It's time to start a career and foster mature relationships and, you know, *be an adult*. But I had a special relationship with that campus that made it particularly difficult to say goodbye. It wasn't just because it took me nearly twice as long as everyone else to finally graduate. After prison, the University of Washington was the one place that felt familiar and safe to me. At least to a degree: I was still getting awkward looks from classmates, but at least the paparazzi couldn't follow me onto campus. Now, that was going away, too.

I didn't know where to go or what to do. Madison was moving across the country. James and I had just broken up. I had been re-convicted of murder, I was appealing a 28.5 year sentence, and I was facing extradition. The paparazzi were back in full force, and the tabloids were gleefully publishing headlines announcing that I was a "convicted killer" again. The year 2014 was not off to a great start. In fact, it was now competing with 2009 for the worst year of my life.

Madison wanted to take me out for a drink before she moved away. Except that was something I just didn't do. I didn't want to be recognized, to be ogled like a freak show, to be secretly photographed. But it wasn't just that—my lawyers had given me explicit instructions: *no bars, no karaoke, no parties*. Until my trials were over? For the indefinite future? It was not clear. My second trial had been all about character. The prosecution claimed I *acted* guilty, and a jury convicted me on spurious accounts of my behavior. The success of my appeal hung on appearances, as did any potential extradition battle if my appeal failed. It wasn't enough to be an ordinary twenty-seven-year-old woman. I had to be perfect, and invisible.

As lonely and on edge as I was, I should have insisted on staying home. Instead, I gave in to my longing to feel like a normal person. We went to a bar in the hippest part of town, a place I had never been. It was an underground dive beneath a burrito joint, and it was decorated with sombreros, luchador masks, and chintzy murals of Jesus. It was thrilling. I kept my head bowed, didn't make eye contact. I let Madison order for me. We nursed our whiskey sours and watched the crowd gesticulating in the red light over the too-loud music.

He came out of nowhere, a guy a little younger than us. He sat down at our table and asked, "What are you two talking about so intently?"

Madison took charge. "None of your business."

He didn't seem to recognize me, and his smile didn't slip. "No worries! Looked like you were having an interesting conversation. My buddy just got out of jail for something he didn't do, and I'm just trying to show him a good time."

We both perked up. *No fucking way.*

He called to his friend, a young Black man leaning forlornly against the bar. Let's call him Mike. Mike sauntered over and sat down across from me. He was fit, handsome. He seemed distracted and offered an aloof *hey*.

"So what happened?" Madison asked.

Mike's friend explained how he had been in jail for several months, but the charges were finally dropped, and he was let out. Mike rolled his eyes but smiled.

"Are you okay?" I asked him.

He nodded, looking away. "Yeah, yeah," but I knew—or thought I knew—that look in his eyes.

"I was in prison for something I didn't do, too," I blurted. Madison glared at me.

Mike finally met my gaze. "For what?"

I hesitated. "For murder..."

"Holy shit!" his friend said. Mike just scrutinized me.

"I know what it's like when you first get out," I said. I told him how I was still hand-washing my underwear in the bathroom sink.

Madison and I ended up spending the rest of the evening tagging along with Mike and his friend. We finished our drinks at the bar, then wandered to a café to hear some amateur hip hop. We walked through the park and mostly talked about Mike's plight: his "crazy" ex who'd accused him of (unspecified) things he didn't do. He was in jail for months. He still had to report to a parole officer. He'd lost his job. He was broke. His family couldn't help him.

My insides squirmed. So many people had helped me when I got out. My family had received me, given me a place to stay. Supporters cobbled together two thousand dollars to help me get back on my feet. I felt so fortunate compared to Mike; no one was helping him.

I decided I wanted to pay it forward. We met up a few times over the next few weeks, went for walks and talked. Eventually we hooked up. Was I his lover or mentor? Was he my partner or project? It was a blur. I thought I'd finally met someone who could truly understand me. But beyond that, Mike also gave me the opportunity to distract myself from my own problems, trick myself into thinking that I was better off than I truly was. Caring for somebody else, somebody with tangible challenges, like getting a phone or getting a job, the kinds of problems that I had already solved for myself and could immediately help address—it was a relief. It made me happy. It made me blind.

It wasn't long before Mike asked me for money. He'd been ordered by the court to pay for his own psych evaluations, he said, but he couldn't afford it. I gave him two grand from my savings—my ongoing legal fees fund.

A few weeks later, I introduced him to my family. I had finally graduated college, and in lieu of taking part in a public college graduation ceremony, my family threw me a barbecue to celebrate. I invited Mike. Immediately, my family members got bad vibes from him. One of my friends even pulled me aside and said, "Watch out. He's a snake." Frankly, I couldn't believe that my own friends and family were writing off another wrongly accused person like this, that they wouldn't give him the benefit of the doubt. Didn't he deserve that? Didn't *I*?

Not long after that gathering, I found myself planning for a cross-country move. It was another impulsive decision; Madison was moving to New York, and I decided to follow her. We got apartments near each other in Harlem. That was the extent of my plan. I showed up one day at my publisher's building and asked them for an internship. They offered me some freelance work reading manuscripts from the slush pile. As with my other jobs, the pay was paltry, but it was a start. I was in the Big Apple, and I had my foot in the door of a career in the arts. I remained a convicted killer facing extradition, but—or, perhaps, because of this—I had to stay positive, even force enthusiasm. I dreaded my own powerlessness. I was afraid of falling back into that state of numbed sadness that I knew all too well. It was a strange, overwhelming cocktail of emotions.

And in the midst of all this, Mike arrived on my doorstep. He kept running into roadblocks back in Seattle, so I'd invited him to start over with me in New York. I offered to let him stay with me until he could get a job and an apartment for himself.

But Mike made no effort to get a job. He took the money I lent him to buy professional clothes and bought himself a Game Boy instead. He lay on my couch playing *Pokémon* all day. Madison, who'd been skeptical of Mike from the start, began urging me to kick him out. She looked into his arrest record and found out that he'd been accused of domestic violence and breaking and entering. She planted the seed of doubt: Had he actually been wrongly accused? Or was that a lie?

Free

A few days later, I met up with an old friend from school who'd moved to New York years ago to pursue a music career. Mike came down from my apartment and saw us chatting on the sidewalk, and he walked right up and slapped my friend across the face. It was like he slapped me, too. In that moment, I realized how bad I had fucked up.

I marched Mike back up to my apartment and demanded that he pack his things and leave. He said no. I insisted. His friend, the one who had introduced us, was now living in D.C. "Go stay with him," I said. I gave him two hundred bucks for a train ticket and said goodbye.

Two days later, I came home from work and found Mike sitting on my bed. He had climbed the fire escape and broken into my apartment.

I screamed.

He grabbed me.

I twisted out of his grip and ran.

He chased me down four flights of stairs and into the street.

I dove into a taxi, pleading, *"Go! Drive anywhere! Please!"*

I couldn't go to Madison's apartment. It was too close by, and Mike knew where she lived. I was in a state of panic. I'd fled, leaving the door wide open, and I was worried that my two cats had escaped. The darker side of my imagination worried that Mike would harm them to get back at me. I talked with Madison, and she urged me to call the police, but I was terrified of what would happen if I did. I called my lawyers instead, explained the whole situation, and they confirmed my fears. They were firm: *Do not call the police.* If I did, the tabloids would find out, and it would be international news that I had shacked up with a guy who'd done time for breaking and entering and who'd been violent toward women. For some reason, it wasn't until they spelled it out that I realized who Mike truly was. He was not someone who had been victimized by an overzealous justice system, like me. He was a criminal, a con man, a burglar, a liar...just like Rudy Guede.

Every hair on my body stood on end. If anyone found out about this, it would be a devastating blow to my appeal and any hope of fighting extradition to serve out that 28.5 year sentence in the U.S. I needed help, and I didn't know what to do. So I called my stepdad back in Seattle. I sobbed into the phone, overwhelmed with shame, but he snapped into action and promised to be on the next red-eye to New York City.

When he arrived the following morning, we went back to my apartment together. Aside from my cats who, thankfully, hadn't escaped, it seemed empty. But then we heard a creak when we walked into the kitchen. We spun around and there was Mike, hiding behind the door. It all happened in a matter of seconds. My stepdad stared him down—*"Get the fuck out of here!"*—and Mike fled. We hurriedly packed up my things, and I hopped on a plane back to Seattle, my tail between my legs.

On the flight home, I felt such deep shame at how stupid I'd been. I hadn't seen the warning signs. I'd ignored my family. I'd put them in the position of having to save me, yet again. My new adult life in New York was over before it even started. My internship at the publishing house, that door to a literary career, was closed. Whatever optimism I'd kindled in the chaos of my life was snuffed out. I'd wanted so badly to see the good in people, to find a way to make my suffering useful for someone else, and it had only made me a target.

For years I tortured myself over this incident. My family, graciously, never rubbed it in my face. But I did it for them. After everything that had happened to me, after all the ways I'd been exploited, I should have known better. I hadn't learned yet that my naïve optimism, however vulnerable it made me, was a strength, nor that we all make mistakes when we are under pressure, and that when we feel lost, we often can't see what is right in front of us. And I had never been so lost.

Free

With the world still telling me that my wrongful conviction was my own fault, I started to think maybe it was true after all. I was a stupid girl who made stupid choices, who walked right into dangerous situations, putting myself at risk, derailing the lives of those who cared about me in the process. Maybe I *did* deserve this wreck of a life that no one in their right mind would choose.

Not Alone

Io Lo So Che Non Sono Sola Anche Quando Sono Sola

We Know

LONELINESS COMES IN MANY SHAPES, and I have known more than a few of them. There is the quiet and almost comforting loneliness of living in a book. On summer afternoons as a kid, I liked to climb the tree in my backyard, straddle a branch, and stay there for hours reading *Harry Potter*. There's the exciting loneliness I felt in Perugia, going on long walks, discovering new shops and viewpoints, thrilled to be on my own in a foreign place, and yet aching for the familiar even as I knew I couldn't have both at once. There is the loneliness of feeling tiny and anonymous, a speck of no consequence, that eerie rush you get in a planetarium when the lens zooms out and the Earth disappears into the Milky Way. And then there is the loneliness of abandonment. I saw it first when I was fifteen, walking in one day on my oma weeping hysterically into the phone, begging her husband to return to his family after having left her two years prior. And, of course, loneliness was my constant companion in Capanne, where I was stripped of life as I knew it and surrounded by strangers from walks of life previously unimaginable to me.

When I came home, I craved the familiar. More than anything, I wanted to go back to the life I was living before I was wrongly accused of murder. So I did the only thing I could think to do—go back to school and immerse myself with my peers.

But the University of Washington wasn't how I remembered it. All of my friends had graduated. I was now much older than most of my fellow students, with a *lot* more life experience, but without the wisdom that comes from processing it. I felt like the new kid on the cellblock again, unnerved and awkward.

Like in prison, I stayed mostly to myself. Get in, get out. Ever the teacher's pet, I raised my hand and participated in class, but as soon as the bell rang, I bolted. No getting lunch in the student hub, no lingering around campus at the end of the day, no extracurricular activities, no friends. Google Alerts informed me when my classmates took surreptitious pictures of me in the lecture hall and posted them to social media alongside captions like, "Foxy Knoxy…👀" or "Look who's in my math class! What should I do? My plan is to try to pee in her butt, but y'all got any other ideas?"

In Capanne, I had signed all my letters with the phrase "Io lo so che non sono sola anche quando sono sola." *I know that I am not alone even when I am alone.* It was a phrase I had picked up from an Italian rap song by Jovanotti. It became a mantra, helping me to feel connected to my family and friends and the life I thought was waiting for me on the outside.

But the mantra stopped working in freedom. Even though I had my family and friends to lean on, my loneliness pulsated inside me, deeper than I ever could have imagined. My identity, a home I had inhabited all my life, had been condemned, deemed unfit for me to live in. At family gatherings, I couldn't sit ten minutes through a casual conversation without becoming irritable and snappy, or deeply sad and withdrawn, triggered by some off-the-cuff observation or bit of celebrity gossip. Before Capanne, everything just rolled off my back. Now

I was a land mine: hypersensitive, prone to going off and then completely shutting down. Over and over again, my mom watched me flit from one extreme emotion to another—outrage, despair, apathy—over seemingly small, random things, like being cajoled to drink a cocktail I didn't want or seeing someone reading a mostly benign tabloid like *People* magazine. My mom wanted to help, but she and the rest of my family—they didn't get it. They couldn't. They had been shaped by their trauma in different ways than I had. They had learned different lessons. I felt like I was moving through the sea of humanity in a scuba suit, an alien life form not adapted for the environment. Who could possibly understand what I'd been through?

Then I found myself sharing two classes—a poetry writing class and a literature class on Shakespeare—with the same girl. Even from across the room, I felt an immediate kinship with her. We both gave detailed feedback in our writing workshop and fully embodied our characters while reading Shakespeare passages aloud.

Eventually, she made the first move: "Want to meet this weekend to talk poetry?" I was hesitant. I was still hearing whispers behind my back in class and being stalked by paparazzi outside my apartment, but she didn't seem to know who I was. I took a risk and said yes, suggesting an out-of-the-way café in my neighborhood.

The Panama Hotel and café is a historical monument south of downtown Seattle, on the edge of the International District. During World War II, Japanese Americans hid their belongings in the basement before being taken to the internment camps. The hotel is still operating today, though I've never stayed the night. Instead, I spent inordinate amounts of time in the ground floor café. It had a wide selection of tea and espresso, but best of all, it was quiet, and packed with an eccentric collection of tables, desks, chairs, and couches, perfect for withdrawing into a nook with your laptop. It was my sanctuary, and I invited my classmate in.

For several weeks we met every Saturday morning to talk about class, reflect on each other's poetry, and just keep each other company as we wrote. Our poems were abstract and emotional. I wasn't writing explicitly about prison or being wrongly accused, but those themes were inevitably coming to the surface in the metaphors I chose without me even realizing it. And for whatever reason, my poems seemed to resonate with her, as hers did with me. We were both trying to navigate something in our writing, trying to find meaning through the feeling of being trapped and helpless. I had even cautiously, tentatively, in that fanciful manner of daydreams, started to think that she was becoming my friend.

But then, one Saturday morning, she plopped down next to me and announced, "You're Amanda *Knox*."

My heart plummeted. My throat went dry. Oh, no, what had she Googled? What did she think she knew? What would she do to me now that I had been so intimate and open with her? Would she sell me out to the tabloids the way one of my neighbors had? Would my mediocre poems end up in the *Daily Mail*?

She saw my stricken face and touched my arm. "Wait. Sorry. I just meant, I get it now. I understand why we get along."

"What do you mean?" I asked.

She leaned in and stared at me for a moment, gathering her words. Then, in a low voice, she said, "I was raped when I was a teenager. By two guys I thought were my friends. That feeling of utter helplessness that keeps coming up in your poetry... I know what that feels like."

My heart started beating again, and a warmth spread through me. In an instant, she had revealed to me a life-saving truth: *you don't have to experience the same trauma as someone to understand and connect with them.* A small part of me started to wonder if perhaps I was not doomed to loneliness after all.

Meanwhile, my mom had not given up on me. When I was at my lowest, re-convicted and facing extradition, she saw the despair coursing through me like a sickness she didn't know how to treat. But someone else did. One day, the director of the Idaho Innocence Project, Dr. Greg Hampikian, reached out to her. Greg had become invested in my case early on, and after independently reviewing the evidence, he'd published an amicus brief—an expert review of, in this instance, the DNA—and helped advocate for my innocence to the American public. But Greg wasn't reaching out about evidence or legal matters this time. He told my mom that there was a gathering in Portland happening later that month, the Innocence Network Conference, an annual meeting of all the Innocence Projects throughout the country. He said bringing me there would help. Mom was convinced, but I was skeptical. The last place I wanted to be was in a room full of hundreds of people who would recognize me instantly. I was frankly terrified of the prospect. But Mom insisted. So we hopped in the car and drove three hours down to Portland on a Friday afternoon in early April 2014.

The event was held in a hotel conference center, in the same featureless rooms that no doubt hosted real estate conventions and antique shows on other weekends. We followed signs to the main ballroom, pausing before the double doors. I stared down at the gaudy carpet. I was sweating through my shirt and shaking so badly I had to clench my teeth. I was ready to turn right around and drive three hours back to Seattle, but Mom opened those doors and gave me a gentle nudge inside.

It was a large room filled with banquet tables and lots of people, mostly men. They were smiling and laughing. I felt like I'd stumbled into someone else's family reunion. And then they spotted me: a lanky black man with short dreadlocks, and a muscular white man with a military haircut. They walked right up to me. They could see the fear on my face. Legally, I was still a convicted killer. They had to know that. They had to know that I didn't belong in this room full of lawyers, scientists, and exonerated people. They were smiling, but still, I almost backed away. Did they want something from me? Then they reached out and hugged me, one at a time. And seeing my bewildered face, one of them said, "You don't have to explain a thing, little sister. We know."

The tears came suddenly. As we settled at a nearby table, Antione Day and Josh Kezer told me their stories. They each had spent over a decade in prison for crimes they hadn't committed. And they, like so many of the dozens of exonerees I would meet in the coming days, had followed my case religiously—just not in the way I had come to expect. They were rooting for me, many of them from inside their own cells, and they had cheered when I was released. Because, as one exoneree told me, if a tame little white girl from the suburbs could survive prison, well, so could they. And now, maybe people would finally start paying attention when police coerce innocents into implicating themselves and others behind closed doors, when they lie on the witness stand, when prosecutors make their cases on junk science and character assassination.

In an instant, I was delivered another life-saving truth: *my trauma was not unique.* There were people I didn't have to explain myself to and who didn't have to explain themselves to me. I was a drop in a bucket, a tiny speck in the universe—but also, I *mattered*.

This community embraced me, but they *really* embraced my mom. The second day of the conference, she was talking with a man named Johnnie Savory who'd been in prison for thirty years, and when he told her that he'd never seen the ocean, she said, "Well then, let's go! Right now! Why not?" She grabbed him by the arm, drove him out to the Oregon coast, and they ran barefoot into the Pacific together.

By the end of that weekend, I had a new family. A family largely made up of men, disproportionately men of color, most of whom had lived hard lives even before their wrongful convictions. Some of the exonerees I met had been on death row. Almost all had spent far more years in prison than I had. They'd lost loved ones while locked up. They'd emerged into the free world with little time left to find companionship or start a family. I suddenly felt so lucky. At least I was free now. I'd only spent four years inside, and I still had a chance for an appeal.

I left that weekend feeling alive, ready to fight for my innocence, and most of all, like I'd found somewhere I belonged. I also had a new purpose. I don't look like most exonerees. I'm an outlier in so many ways. I'm young, female, college educated. Before I was wrongly accused, I never gave the criminal justice system a second thought, because I belonged to a class of people who didn't have to. I went to school to study a foreign language, thinking I'd be a translator. And eventually, I became one, just not in the way I expected. I now translate this experience—felt acutely by many members of our society—across the cultural and economic divide.

Since that first Innocence Network Conference, I've traveled to dozens of local innocence projects from Alaska to Florida to tell my story, raise awareness, and help fundraise. And what I tell them is this: I'm not special. You don't have to be especially weird or especially unlucky to wind up wrongly convicted. You don't have to be especially smart or especially strong to survive it and come out the other side believing in the goodness of the world. The same is true for cancer, assault, bankruptcy, you name it. Part of being human is confronting tragedy and getting through it. It's easy to think you're alone when you're in the thick of it. Loneliness is essentially a feeling of separation from everyone around you, a separation that comes from feeling like you're uniquely cursed or blessed (fame and fortune can be lonely, too!). The mantra of the lonely becomes: *You don't know what it's like.* I can't tell you how many times I said that to myself. And with each repetition, the crack between you and the world widens. In that divide, loneliness grows like a weed that keeps returning no matter how many times you try to pluck it by the roots. But the weed shrivels when you recognize that other people do in fact know what it's like, that you're not unique in the hand life dealt you. However much it may feel that way, you are not, in fact, alone.

When well-intentioned people come up to me and say, "I can't imagine what you've been through," I simply say, "Try." We're all going through something, we're all carrying something, and the gulf that separates us from one another is bridgeable through empathy. Empathy is a tool of the imagination. You may not have lived someone else's worst moment, but you've lived your own. One of the greatest gifts I've been given is the feeling of being truly seen for who I am, what I struggle with, and what I've strived to accomplish despite those struggles. My exoneree family gave me that gift, and so had the girl from poetry class, who became my first true friend in freedom, and who remains a close friend to this day.

But I also know that to receive this kind of gift, you have to be willing to be seen, you have to allow people into your intimate world. For a long time, that was a risk I wasn't willing to take. No wonder I'd felt so alone. How many offerings had I missed, how many opportunities for real connection had glanced off my suit of armor? Strangely, when I started taking risks again, making myself vulnerable, when I exposed my loneliness, my mantra regained its power.

Io lo so che non sono sola anche quando sono sola.

Sisterhood of Ill Repute

BEFORE ITALY, I WAS ONLY vaguely aware of that ancient stereotype that all women secretly hate one another, that we are incapable of true friendship. Some call it "venimism"; others refer to "mean girls." In 1893, the Italian criminologist Cesare Lombroso wrote that, "Due to women's latent antipathy for one another, trivial events give rise to fierce hatreds; and due to women's irascibility, these occasions lead quickly to insolence and assaults." The source of our latent antipathy? Sexual jealousy, of course. We hate one another because we are ever competing for male attention.

I always thought this misogynistic myth was obviously false. I had lots of girlfriends, from school and soccer; so did my sisters, my mom, pretty much every girl I knew. But then again, I also thought my innocence was obvious... And clearly, the stereotype found its way into my courtroom, where a cross hung on the wall and my devoutly Catholic prosecutor accused me not merely of being a murderer, but of being a dirty, drug-addled, woman-hating slut.

"Meredith was astonished that Amanda had started a relationship with a boy after just arriving in Perugia...that Amanda owned condoms and a vibrator," explained Dr. Giuliano Mignini. "It is possible that Meredith argued with Amanda...because of her habit of bringing strange men into the house.... [So,] under the influence of drugs and probably also alcohol, Amanda decided to involve Meredith in a violent sex game.... It was her opportunity to take revenge on that British girl who was too serious and 'moderate' for her tastes, whose clique of English friends always excluded her, who openly accused Amanda...of a lack of cleanliness and excessive 'friendliness' with men. For Amanda, the time had come to take revenge on that 'simpering goody two-shoes'—so she must have thought."

With these words, which echoed out through the global media, Dr. Giuliano Mignini inducted me into a not-so-secret society of women. You know who I'm talking about. The women who've been the subject of *TMZ* headlines, *SNL* skits, and David Letterman's Top Ten Lists. The women who've been turned into Halloween costumes and found themselves referenced in rap lyrics. The women we treat like punching bags and punch lines. The women whose broken bodies, broken relationships, most vulnerable moments, and worst experiences we consume like candy. I call us the Sisterhood of Ill Repute. I didn't even realize I belonged to this club until I met another member: Monica Lewinsky.

It was shortly before my first ever speaking event in January 2017, at a private conference in Seattle. Monica was one of the other speakers. I had an hour to fill, and I was terrified. After crafting and polishing my talk, I'd rehearsed a half dozen times leading up to the event. I knew that to really tell my story, I would have to break my own heart in front of the audience, so I went to the places that still hurt. But saying those words in my living room was nothing like standing in front of a crowd of hundreds who might believe all sorts of falsehoods about me.

Before the event, Monica invited me up to her hotel room to chat.

She had gone through the gauntlet of public shaming in the worst possible way when I was just a kid. I remember eating dinner with my family and listening to them discuss the news. It was the first time I'd heard the term "oral sex," and when I spoke up to say that I couldn't understand why everyone was so upset about people saying sexy things over the phone, my entire family keeled over with laughter. In the years after that, I, too, casually absorbed the image of Monica presented by the tabloids. I didn't dig into the story, I didn't educate myself, and if you'd asked me about it in high school, I probably would have said, "Oh, yeah, Monica. The blow job lady." I had yet to discover what it truly meant to go from anonymous to "public figure."

But after getting the tabloid treatment myself, I humbly withdrew the conviction that I could ever trust the image presented to me by the media of who any person really is. And when Monica gave her TED Talk, "The Price of Shame," she opened my eyes, and many millions more, not only to who the real Monica was, but who she had always been. I'd followed her closely since then, reading all her writing for *Vanity Fair*, feeling utterly validated when she described her experiences of being ruthlessly shamed in the press, humiliated and demonized for the sake of other people's entertainment and political gain.

I expected to be starstruck when I walked into that hotel room. Instead, what I found, almost immediately, was a big sister.

From the first moment, she was warm and kind. She made me a cup of tea. We sat by the windows, overlooking downtown Seattle, and we talked about my speech. She gave me some invaluable pointers about mental preparation and self-care, but most of all we talked about processing trauma. How you're never really done with it, and how talking about it publicly is both triggering and healing. She gave me the run-down of which kinds of therapy had worked for her, which hadn't, and why. (I have yet to meet anyone more committed to therapy.) But perhaps what struck me the most was what wasn't said. *You're that girl from Italy! What was prison like? What's it like to be famous?* All those conversational notes, ranging from cringey to offensive, that popped up whenever I met a stranger who thought they knew who I was because they'd absorbed a decade of media coverage, were absent. And it wasn't because Monica had been unaware of all that. She'd read about Foxy Knoxy just like millions of others, but it was Amanda she'd invited for a cup of tea.

I walked away from that meeting feeling truly seen. It was akin to what I'd experienced with my poetry friend, and at the Innocence Network Conference. Here was someone to whom I didn't have to explain the trauma of prolonged, widespread public shaming. I had been grappling with my status as a public figure since I came home—the invasion of my privacy, my impotence to fight slanderous statements in the press—and seeing her surviving it, and thriving even, gave me hope that I could as well. A strong sense of empathy can form a bond between people with vastly different life experiences, but it's a lot easier to make such connections when the other person has been in your shoes. That's why support groups exist, and it's why I left that meeting inspired to connect with other publicly shamed women.

When I was producing a podcast called *The Truth about True Crime*, I did a live episode with Lorena Bobbitt (now Gallo) at a true crime convention in Washington, D.C. Like Monica, Lorena had been ducking her head for twenty years in the face of reputational damage that could never be undone. But she agreed to meet me on a stage and talk in front of a live audience about how we've lived our lives in the crosshairs of public shaming. Most people remember the castration of John Wayne Bobbitt, but they forget that Lorena was a victim of domestic violence and marital rape, and that her own violent act was done in a moment of mental instability. That doesn't excuse her actions, but it is crucial context that is often left out.

The morning of that event, Lorena and I met up at a local TV news station to promote it. I got there early, and I was in the green room waiting for Lorena to arrive, when a comedian from New Jersey came in. He had just finished his on-air segment, and we chatted briefly. When he asked what I was going to be talking about, I told him I was interviewing Lorena, and he said, "What about? Which knives are best for slicing sausage?"

"No," I said. "Actually, we'll be talking about how people still reduce her to a penis-chopping joke when she is in fact a complex human being who advocates in support of victims of domestic violence."

To his credit, the comedian replied, "Oh, I get it. She's not the monster. I am!"

But as much as we are all responsible for the media we consume, I don't want to demonize the audience, the millions of us who casually absorbed skewed and incomplete stories about Lorena, about Monica, about me. Such stories are designed to appeal to our worst impulses. Judgment will always come more easily to us than mercy, understanding, forgiveness, and a nuanced acknowledgment of the complexity that underlies nearly all serious harms. It feels good to hate "bad" people, and there's a special kind of hate reserved for "bad women." The narrative of the "mean girl," the "homewrecker," and "girl-on-girl" crime is titillating precisely because it confirms the stereotype that women are secretly one another's worst enemies. *Amanda vs. Meredith.* It distracts from the actual crimes committed against women by men, and even validates them, giving tacit permission for men to hate women, too.

We've advanced far beyond the days of Salem, 1692. Now, we're all experts at witch-burning. Social media enables us to single out targets in a flash, to dox and shame and deplatform without due process or any sense of proportional sentencing. And we are all at risk, because we are all, myself included, converting our meals and our hikes and marriage proposals into public content. We make that choice every day without a second thought. I never asked to become a public figure, but I did make a Myspace page in high school, a Facebook page in college, and when I was put on trial, my social media profiles were mined for material that could be used to vilify me. It's where the tabloids discovered my soccer nickname, "Foxy Knoxy," and where they sourced a photo of me at a war museum pretending to fire a Gatling gun. If Monica was patient zero of the twenty-four-hour news cycle and internet shaming, I was patient zero of social media cancellation.

The social media algorithms, which amplify outrage, are a big part of the problem, but we also need to demand higher standards from our traditional media, which so often fails in how it frames a story, even if it is accurate at the level of individual details. This is something that really hit me when I viewed my own story next to Monica's. It matters what you call a thing. For years, the series of events that resulted in President Bill Clinton's impeachment were referred to as the "Lewinsky scandal." But who actually committed adultery, and lied about it? Who was exploiting whom, and why? What about Ken Starr, for that matter? Calling it the "Lewinsky scandal" and not the "Clinton affair" or the "Starr investigation" erases these men's responsibility and culpability. The same can be said when people call those events in Perugia that derailed my life the "sordid Amanda Knox saga" instead of "the murder of Meredith Kercher by Rudy Guede." Such framing has reputational consequences for all parties—it cements the idea of me as guilty or guilt-adjacent, lets Rudy Guede off the hook, and erases Meredith as a victim.

I can only do so much to rectify these misleading frames, but my powerlessness to do so, and to stop the attacks on my reputation from traditional media and the chattering crowds online, has been an unexpected blessing. My reputation, my public self, I've realized, doesn't really belong to me. Legally that is true, but it is also true socially, and it always has been. My reputation and public identity are property of the commons. So is yours. That doesn't mean it doesn't sting when someone attacks you publicly, when they shame or disparage you. We care deeply about our reputations, because losing the trust or faith of your tribe is tantamount to a death sentence. Being recognized as honest, reliable, safe, friendly—all that matters immensely. It matters the way your bank balance matters. It shapes your possibilities in life. But it doesn't say anything about who you really are. And ultimately, your reputation doesn't fully belong to you. It can be shaped and altered or demolished with impunity by the actions of others.

Dwelling on what people thought of me made me miserable, so I learned to detach myself from those judgments. This came into stark relief for me when Netflix released the documentary about my case and chose to advertise the film with a campaign where they showed two photos of me, with the word "monster" on one and the word "victim" on the other. These ads were everywhere online, and on giant billboards in L.A. and New York. I remember standing in Times Square underneath those giant photos of my face, pedestrians passing by me, none the wiser.

It helped me to see that my public identity was like a piñata in the shape of me, and I was watching from the back of the crowd as people gleefully took swings at it. The real me wasn't hanging there in the spotlight. The real me was a sister, a daughter, a lover of foreign languages and dancing, a Renaissance nerd and theater geek; the real me was devouring an heirloom tomato and licking the plate. The real me was untouchable.

It was the real me that Monica had seen that first time we met. People have asked me what's it like to be friends with Monica Lewinsky. It's like having a true friend. It's like having a big sister. The only difference is that our past traumas and ongoing challenges—a cruel news story, a development in my legal saga—are public. Beyond that, you know exactly what it's like. On more than one rough day, I've received a text from Monica checking in, looking after my mental health when I've been too busy battling my problems to step back and breathe.

I wasn't the first woman to be slapped with a scarlet letter, and I know I won't be the last. I take comfort from the view inside my Sisterhood of Ill Repute. From here, it's easy to see how the impulse to crucify others for their misdeeds, whether real or imagined, says more about the shamer than the shamed. And it leaves me optimistic that we might all become a little more hesitant to piñata-fy our fellow citizens. It once seemed unthinkable that smoking would be almost universally reviled as a toxic and disgusting habit. After all, doctors once smoked while examining children. We see the same shifts happening with sugary sodas, and now even with alcohol, thanks to Gen Z. We have it in us as a society to recognize behaviors that harm us and others, and though we will likely never eradicate them entirely, we can push them to the fringes and replace them with healthier alternatives. Shame-fueled media is no different. And I see the changes happening already.

A few years ago, I gave a talk to a group of lawyers in Kentucky. Afterward, a woman about my age approached me. She was sobbing, and it took her a moment to get her words out.

"I'm so sorry," she said. "I'm sorry I treated you as entertainment."

I hugged her for a long time. So much for women hating women.

Just Amanda

WHILE MY PEERS WERE IN their prime dating years, I'd been literally walled off from the world of flirtation and romance and sex. When I got home, I was rusty at all forms of social interaction, but in the romance department, I'd been a rookie even before they locked me up. Not to mention that after being imprisoned for a sex crime, known the world over as a rapist and killer, figuring out a healthy romantic life in freedom was...a challenge. I didn't know whom I could trust, who might sell intimate details about my life to *TMZ*. Raffaele made that mistake and ended up going on a date with a girl only to discover the next day that she was actually a writer for an Italian tabloid.

After my encounter with Mike in 2014, I was deeply shaken. I had allowed someone I didn't know into my intimate life because I'd imagined that he was like me, that his challenges were my challenges, and we could take on the world together. My desperation to be understood made me the perfect victim for a con man. I was humiliated and frightened. And I no longer felt I could trust my own instincts. I was beginning to think that romance just wasn't in the cards for me. I'd almost forgotten what it was like to feel pretty in a cute sundress, to make eyes with a guy across the room at a party, to navigate the awkward, exciting, and sometimes upsetting dance of sex. But most of all, I missed companionship.

Enter Colin. Colin and I were friends from middle school, though we'd lost track of each other during college. He'd gone off to New York to pursue his dream of becoming the next David Bowie. I'd stayed home in Seattle, and then left for Italy. We didn't really know each other as adults, but when we reconnected, I recognized that sweet, smart, safe person I'd known for years.

Adult Colin was handsome, thoughtful, and fun. But the fact that he was safe was the biggest thing that attracted me to him. I saw in him a person who would never exploit, betray, or abuse me, and though I didn't recognize it then, I felt like that was the best I could hope for as "the girl accused of murder."

Our relationship blossomed while I was in the midst of crisis, in late 2014, when I was having all those conversations with my attorneys about turning myself in and fighting extradition. Colin was there for the ride. He had followed the case closely from afar, and as the tabloids kept painting me as a killer, he reacted by holding me up as a patron saint of injustice, a martyr for the wrongly accused.

After a few months of dating, he proposed, and I said yes. It was almost a form of magical thinking, as if grasping onto this symbolic tie to my home life as I faced extradition might somehow ensure that I didn't wind back up in an Italian prison. But even as I said yes, a part of me felt squeamish. Colin told me that he imagined me as the reincarnation of Joan of Arc, and I started to wonder if Colin knew me as well as I'd imagined he did. I was not a femme fatale, but I also wasn't a saint. I was a regular girl who wasn't perfect, who could make mistakes. Just as I didn't want to be defined by the worst thing that had happened to me, I also didn't want to be burdened with the weight of quasi-religious iconography.

Free

I was facing an extreme version of a challenge we all face when looking for love. It starts from the moment you see someone across the room or when you swipe right. You start crafting an image of them in your mind, imagining all the ways they might satisfy your desires. And in those fluttery early days of a relationship, confirmation bias takes hold: you see what you want to see, magnifying the importance of that shoulder rub he gave you in the park, ignoring the way he was rude to that waiter at dinner. You build an idea of a person and fall in love with that idea. And when the stubborn reality of the person finally shatters that idea, you find yourself disappointed. *You've changed. Where's the person I fell in love with?* you think, not realizing that person never existed. You break up, you meet someone new, and the cycle continues.

Colin and I had each fallen into this trap. He'd fallen in love with a martyr who didn't exist. I'd fallen in love with a man who I thought knew me because he'd known me since childhood, but who, in reality, barely knew me at all.

All these misgivings were below the surface, and whenever they bubbled up, I shoved them back down. I told myself I was lucky to have anyone, that I could be back in a prison cell the next week. Colin was by my side on March 27, 2015, as we awaited the verdict in my second appeal. I was still bracing for the worst, that they would uphold my conviction, and that the next morning I'd have to say goodbye to my family. I didn't dare imagine what actually happened: that the court would definitively acquit Raffaele and me, finally ending our legal nightmare once and for all.

It took me months for this legal freedom to really sink in. As it did, and my possibilities in life slowly blossomed, my incompatibility with Colin became more apparent. But rather than call off the engagement and break up, which would have been better for both of us in the long run, I clung on because I *did* love Colin, and I told myself that I couldn't expect a relationship that fulfilled me more deeply. It wasn't Colin's fault. It was my own for getting suckered by the Hallmark fantasy of love.

And then a strange twist of fate: I had been writing for the local newspaper for more than a year, and was finally using my byline post-exoneration, when I was asked to review a novel called *War of the Encyclopaedists* co-authored by two local writers. It was moving and hilarious and so smart and so dumb in all the right ways. I wrote a rave review and submitted it to my editor, and that was going to be the end of it. But then I walked out of my apartment and saw a poster in a diner window for a book launch party for that very novel, that very evening, and at my local bookstore! Years of being hunted had conditioned me to stay away from public events, but it was so serendipitous, I felt like taking a risk.

The reading room at Elliott Bay Book Company is in the basement underneath the bookstore, and I dipped in a few minutes before the event was set to start, thinking I'd be able to watch from the back of the room, quietly and anonymously. What I found was not a sober literary reading but a bubbling crowd of more than a hundred people cramming that room to capacity, the wine and beer flowing freely. It was festive and electric, and there were no available seats except at the very front.

The whispers started almost immediately. I could see people pointing, staring, and I started to feel trapped, but that feeling vanished as soon as the reading began. There on stage were the authors, and they were quite the odd couple. One was some kind of hipster Elton John, and the other was a stocky, bald Army veteran. They were best friends, and their chemistry was palpable.

I was too bashful to ask any questions during the Q&A or to wait in line to get my book signed, but I decided to reach out to them afterward for an interview.

I met up with Chris Robinson and Gavin Kovite at Chris's apartment the following week, and what began as a professional interview about the intricacies of co-authoring a novel and navigating that blurry line between memoir and fiction gradually transformed into a scotch tasting. After a tangent about space travel all of a sudden we were watching an episode of *Star Trek: The Next Generation*. Before I knew it, we were simply hanging out. It felt natural and comfortable, which was *very* strange, because I did not know these two guys at all.

As the evening came on, I had many opportunities to excuse myself and head home, but I found myself lingering. Gavin was going to meet up with a woman he'd met on OkCupid, and Chris, who had a serious girlfriend, was tagging along to keep it light and casual. I tagged along as well. The four of us hung out in a stately mansion on Capitol Hill where the woman was house-sitting. That whole evening had a dreamlike quality: the intimate yet anxious feeling of being in someone else's house, examining their things, the feeling that I was spending time with old friends who had earned my trust, having conversations about art and literature and philosophy, being just Amanda, and not "the girl accused of murder."

I took some photos that evening, capturing Chris and Gavin in silly poses. We drank wine and invented funny stories about the people who lived in the mansion. As Gavin directed his flirtation at the other girl, Chris and I ended up in deep conversation. Chris was witty and quick to laugh, but he was also introspective, erudite, vulnerable, and he had no interest in small talk. At one point, he asked me how I felt about my engagement to Colin. Was I ready? Was I nervous? I hadn't been asking myself these questions, though I should have been, and it suddenly hit me that I didn't know the answers. It struck me that not only was I *not* ready, I wasn't even sure if I was on the right path. I was honest with Chris about my uncertainties, and he opened up to me about a period of depression he'd gone through a few years prior, his fixation on the idea of suicide, and how he remained a nihilist at heart, but a capital-R Romantic nihilist. "Life has no inherent meaning," he said, "but there's still beauty, and that's enough." He recited poems by Wallace Stevens. He quoted Wu-Tang Clan lyrics. He asked about my life and family, my dreams and goals, but never once did he ask about Italy or prison.

Sometime around midnight, we parted ways on the street outside. Gavin gave me a big bear hug, and Chris reached out and shook my hand. "This was so much fun," he said. "We should be friends." In the instant he let go of my hand, I experienced a flash of premonition. As I walked through the warm summer night back to my apartment, I felt a strong assuredness, the very same confidence that I felt about the sun rising in the morning: *I could love that man.*

To be clear, I didn't fall in love with Chris that night. I barely knew him. I was still engaged. He had a serious girlfriend who was lovely and whom I'd met at the reading. I fully expected that our lives were on very different tracks. But I knew deep down that, were circumstances otherwise, in some alternate universe, Chris and I might be madly in love.

The other thing I walked away with that night was a feeling of blessed and unexpected normalcy. It was the first time since emerging from my mental state as a prey animal, hunted down by forces so much bigger and stronger than myself, that I thought, *Wow... Can I just make friends now... like a normal person? Not just those rare trauma bonds like with my poetry classmate, but anywhere, and with anyone?*

Over the next six months, Chris and I kept in touch, but we didn't really see much of each other. He and Gavin left town to spend a month in Detroit researching their next novel, *Deliver Us*. As they did, Colin and I drifted further apart. Chris's girlfriend broke up with him while he was in Detroit, and when he returned to Seattle, he was deeply sad. I offered a shoulder to cry on. That fall, Chris and Gavin left for two months to attend a writer's retreat called Yaddo in Saratoga Springs, New York. Around that time, Colin and I broke up. Not because of Chris, exactly. Rather, Chris revealed to me the possibility of finding a kind of connection that felt exciting and forward looking, rather than safe and reactive. That possibility was the last straw among many that caused my relationship with Colin to collapse. When Chris returned from Yaddo, a new novel draft completed, he'd pulled himself out of his post-breakup funk.

He invited me over to his place to cook dinner and watch a movie I'd recommended to him. He cooked up an artichoke risotto—I had no idea he was a great cook—and then we watched the film. About halfway through, Chris put his arm around me, which was a welcome surprise. I bent my arm up to hold his hand, and in what remains the most restrained yet sexy moment I've ever experienced, he gently stroked the inside of my palm with his finger.

Chris and I started dating in earnest, and six months later we moved in together. I knew even then that this man would be my husband and the father of my children. From the first moment we met, Chris had given me a gift I thought I'd never receive. He didn't care about the tabloid stories. He wanted to know me on my own terms. Meanwhile, everyone he knew would ask him, as soon as they found out he knew me: *Do you think she did it? Is she weird?* And he rebuked that dehumanizing attitude and made what in this day and age is a radical decision: he decided not to Google me, not to read anything that had been written or said about me by the media. He hadn't followed the case, but he knew there was a deep rabbit hole of information and misinformation about the evidence and the controversy. He didn't want that lens distorting or mediating his view of me. He also never pushed me to talk about the case or prison, though he engaged thoughtfully when I brought it up. After years of feeling trapped in my own life, trapped in the idea of me that was out there for public consumption, he gave me the gift of letting me just be myself. Not an icon or a target, not a celebrity or a villain, just Amanda.

Punching Down

I DON'T OFTEN ENCOUNTER SOMEONE who is cruel to me in person. In fact, I somewhat pride myself on the fact that if someone meets me in real life, they come around to seeing me as the person I really am. Negativity usually comes at me from a distance. The tabloids disparage me for clicks. Haters I've never met release their rage into the comments section. I delete and block like a game of Whac-A-Mole.

On good days, anyway. But I'm not always my best self. It got to me when the *Daily Mail* ran a story about how crass it was that I'd given a talk to some law students. They got the Kerchers' lawyer on the line to say that the very idea of me giving a talk was offensive. Even as I raised awareness about criminal justice reform, I was the villain.

Against my better judgment, I found myself dwelling on this as I arrived at a comedy club to celebrate my little sister's birthday. We all piled into a booth at the back of the room to watch her favorite comedian perform. The first comic warmed the crowd up nicely, closing with a line about how he couldn't be happier now that both white girls and Black girls have big butts. I found myself laughing in spite of my bad mood and the crassness of the joke. I sipped my glass of chardonnay, letting the tension go. *This will be fun*, I told myself. Who knew I needed a night at a comedy club? There was one more opener before the headliner, another local guy, and when he took the stage, I felt a glimmer of recognition. Where did I know him from? Then, a few jokes in, he said, "Have you ever been in a room with a famous person and you didn't realize it?" The back of my neck started tingling, and I broke out in a cold sweat.

I'm often recognized. People come up to me in airports, at the grocery store, in restaurants. Without context, people often can't place me. "Did we go to high school together? You look so familiar." Sometimes I tell them who I am; sometimes I don't want to deal with it. "Just one of those faces," I say. When I have a chance to be anonymous, I often take it.

I like it when the focus isn't on me, so I was thrilled when, a few months before this night at the comedy club, Chris was invited to be interviewed for a podcast hosted by two local comedians to talk about his novel. I tagged along to the recording session and sat quietly in the corner. I'd brought along a cross-stitch project I was working on for Chris's birthday: a scene from *Super Mario Bros.*

At the end of the interview, one of the comics took Chris down the hall to show him where the restroom was, and I chatted with the other comic, showing him the gift I was working on. He didn't seem to recognize me. To him, I was just the girlfriend. He thought my cross-stitch project was cool, and we had a pleasant chat for a few minutes about video games.

When Chris returned, we packed up and left. It wasn't an impactful moment, chatting with that comic, but it was pleasant enough. A friendly bit of small talk, the kind of thing I don't get to enjoy when the conversation veers into "Holy hell, you were convicted of what?" I probably would have forgotten all about it, but the comic on stage certainly hadn't.

"Have you ever been in a room with a famous person and you didn't realize it, and you only find out later? I was interviewing this guy for my podcast, and his girlfriend comes along. She's like knitting in the corner the whole time."

My breath was quickening, and I could feel a panic attack coming on. Even so, I really hoped that the joke he was about to tell would somehow not be at my expense. A small part of me was enjoying the irony that he had unwittingly re-created the setup of this joke. Here he was, in a room with me without realizing it, *again*.

"Afterward, my buddy says, 'What did you think of Amanda?' I'm like, 'She's hot, sure.' But then he says, 'Dude, you didn't recognize her? That was Amanda *Knox*.'"

At this point, my three sisters turned to me and my ghost-white face. We were the one table in the room that had fallen dead silent.

"I'm like, 'You left me in a room with Amanda Knox?! She had knitting needles! She could have killed me! That's like leaving me in a room with O. J.!'"

Laughter erupted from every other table in the room. I sat there paralyzed until the end of his set, trying to get control of my breathing and keep from exploding into sobs. Two of my sisters tried to comfort me quietly. One of my sisters—the birthday girl—was furious. She left the table, and five minutes later, called me out to the hallway. She'd managed to shit talk her way back to the green room to demand that the comic come out and apologize. It was the last thing I wanted, but she was angry, it was her birthday, and she wouldn't take no for an answer.

I found him near the entrance to the club, a forlorn expression on his face. My sister let him have it. He offered a weak apology, tried to explain that comics look for material everywhere. "It was just a joke. I make jokes about my autistic cousins." I felt stuck inside myself, not knowing what to say.

My sister demanded that he cut that joke from his set—there was another show that night a few hours later. When we got back to our seats, the tears burst out of me. Staying for the headliner was not an option.

That night, we heard from my sister's friend that the comic repeated his joke in the second set and went on to make fun of my little sister. How many times, I wondered, had he told that joke before? At how many open mics in my own hometown had he honed his wording? I eventually calmed down and spent the next few hours trying to figure out why his joke had bothered me so much. Plenty of comedians had joked about me before. Bill Hader had even impersonated me on *SNL*. None of those jokes were kind. I'd thought this kind of thing was water off my back.

I found myself feeling sad more than anything else. What this episode revealed was that I was wrong to assume that a pleasant face-to-face interaction would mute the Hitchcock soundtrack playing in people's heads whenever they heard my name. I also knew that this wouldn't be the last time the worst experience of my life would be the butt of someone's joke. I'd never escape being a Card Against Humanity, or an option in a game of Fuck, Marry, Kill: *Casey Anthony, Jodi Arias, or Amanda Knox?*

I've always loved comedy. I know the job of the comedian is to test boundaries, to walk right up to the line, which inevitably means stepping over it at times. As strange as it's been to find myself in the unenviable position of having jokes made at my expense, I understand why comedians often think making the worst experience of my life the butt of a joke is totally acceptable. They're suffering from a condition that is so common we don't even have a name for it. I call it 2D-osis, the condition of seeing your fellow humans as cardboard cutouts in the shape of people. Our ancestors, in their small tribes, never had to interact with more than a few hundred people, so it makes sense that it's hard for us to conceive of those beyond our immediate families, friends, and colleagues as real. It's the same reason why it's so shocking the first time you encounter your elementary school teacher at the grocery store. She shops? And eats? How could she exist outside of the context of the classroom? And now, with social media, the vast majority of people we encounter on a daily basis are literally in 2D. They are pictures of people, ideas of people that we interact with superficially, parasocially, quasi-anonymously.

I know that for so many people, I still exist solely in the context of a tabloid murder scandal. That context is persistent because giving in to 2D-osis is a lot easier than imagining the full inner life of the guy who cuts you off in traffic—his extended family, his hopes and fears, and the sweet things he says to his daughter when he tucks her into bed at night. It's hard for me, too. Remembering that makes it easier for me to forgive the people who like throwing darts at a cardboard cutout of Amanda Knox.

And it helps me to poke fun at myself. In the tense final hours of the Biden versus Trump election in 2020, I tweeted, "Whatever happens, the next four years can't be as bad as that four-year study abroad I did in Italy, right?" Tens of thousands of people liked it, but plenty of others called me crass and insensitive. "Please delete this for your own dignity." "This is foul." "You absolute ghoul."

This kind of response happens whenever I joke about my wrongful conviction. I understand why these people are upset. For some of them, I'm guilty, and any comment I make about my experience is like O. J. Simpson joking that he got away with murder. For others, I'm innocent, but they associate my name with Meredith's murder, so they assume I'm making a joke at Meredith's expense. They don't recognize that the object of my jokes are my *own* experiences. I joke about being falsely accused and imprisoned. And I do so because after everything that was taken from me, my sense of humor helps me make sense of what I've lost.

This is one of the great powers of comedy, and that's why it's no accident that comedians tend to be people who've known serious loss. Comedy allows us to take ownership of what's been taken from us, and to give it a meaning other than crushing despair. There's a catharsis that comes from prodding your wounds and expecting a jolt of pain, but finding a pleasant tickle.

The best jokes reveal something true about life, and they offer a perspective shift that we can't get anywhere else. They dimensionalize rather than flatten their subjects. This is especially true when comedians self-deprecate. By unpacking their own flaws and failings and wounds, they become more human to us, and in recognizing ourselves in the pictures they paint, we too feel more seen. It's an act of service in a way. The comedian who rips into herself becomes a martyr, letting the audience know: *It's okay. Life is hard, and we're all in this together.*

So I'm leaning in. If people are going to constantly compare me to O. J. Simpson, I might as well joke about it.

What's the one thing Foxy Knoxy and O. J. have in common?

They both have the same birthday...

As Tom Hanks.

And *that's* why I don't believe in astrology!

Joy

WHILE I WAS IN PRISON and on trial, Chris was in grad school and traveling the country, moving from artist colony to artist colony, living the life of an untethered bohemian writer. His life was so, so different from mine...at first glance. But during those formative years in his twenties, he, too, was living a lifestyle far afield from his peers. He didn't have a steady job. He spent months at a time hundreds of miles away from his friends and family, in the company of strangers, or no one. He read as many books as I did from my prison cell over the course of four years, and while my writing energy had gone into countless letters to friends and family, he wrote several poetry collections, a couple novels, and dozens of short stories and essays. Like me, he processed his life through writing. And he, too, in the loneliest moments on his aimless, self-created, poetic pilgrimage, had grappled with thoughts of suicide.

I think this uniquely positioned Chris to appreciate the baggage I carried into our relationship.

You know the old joke about the fish who says, "What the hell's water?" For me, that was fear. I'd been swimming in it, and breathing it, for so long I'd stopped seeing it. If you'd asked me if I was afraid, post-exoneration, I probably would have said, "Of what? No one's hunting me down anymore." But after years of living under an unforgiving spotlight, where my every quirk was magnified out of proportion and infused with sinister meaning, I was still so cautious, so careful, so ready to be scrutinized. Was that merely rational, as I'd been telling myself, or was it a prison of my own making?

I found myself confronting this question directly when Chris and I started packing for Burning Man in the summer of 2017.

From the very beginning of our relationship, Chris and I *played*. For his birthday, I put together a cyberpunk live-action role-play scavenger hunt. For my birthday, Chris constructed an *American Gladiator*–style obstacle course at our local park. We looked forward to every opportunity to dress up in costume. When Chris's brother, who runs a sword-fighting theater troupe called the Seattle Knights, invited us to a Viking-themed party, we showed up as *Star Trek* characters. While everyone else was dressed head to toe in leather and fur, drinking mead from mugs made of elk horn, Chris and I went around scanning them with our tricorders.

With Chris indulging my silly side, I was rediscovering a part of my life that I was told, both explicitly and implicitly, was forbidden: *joy*. Then he got the idea to write a novel set at Burning Man and decided we had to attend as "research." I know what you're thinking: *Please don't tell me Amanda Knox "found herself" at Burning Man.* Don't worry, I didn't. But it did come, weirdly, at just the right moment on my journey. As they say, *the playa provides*.

We packed the essentials—gallons of water, food, sunscreen, sun hat, goggles, dust mask—and then Chris and I went to the local Goodwill to find our Burning Man outfits. He shopped in the women's aisle, finding some XL sequined items. I found a quasi-see-through leotard and hesitated. If wearing an "All You Need Is Love" shirt was enough to make the news media clutch their pearls, what would happen if someone recognized me wearing *this*? I nearly put it back on the rack, but then threw it in my cart when I realized I was just succumbing to my fear again.

Black Rock City transported me immediately. In the most mundane sense, it was merely an accumulation of 80,000 people in tents and RVs in the desert. But that description captured almost nothing of the magic of Burning Man, which was an otherworldly, almost mythic place that appeared out of nowhere for ten days only, then vanished without a trace, like one of Italo Calvino's invisible cities. There was no commerce, no money, no trade or barter. It was strictly a gift economy. Strangers approached me and offered a cooling spritz from a water bottle, a shoulder rub, some chilled homemade pickles, hot pho soup. Chris and I had gathered a few baskets of plums from our backyard and that gift—fresh fruit in the desert when most people were subsisting on dehydrated meals—brought unadulterated joy to people's faces.

Burning Man welcomed all types. I didn't do well in loud throngs of people dancing to techno, and I couldn't stay up late into the night—I've never been a night owl. Instead, I cruised the sleepy streets on my bicycle under the hot sun while thousands were sleeping off their nocturnal revelry, and I found plenty of delightful surprises.

I witnessed a parade of bunnies engage in mock battle with a parade of carrots. I relaxed in a spacious pillow-filled tent to watch cat videos on loop. I attended a two-hour Ask Me Anything offered by a physicist and a mathematician, and got to ask, "What the heck is time, anyway?" I wandered out of the hot sun into a camp that offered chilled chardonnay and art supplies. There, I meditated on the fear I was trying to let go of and let those emotions shape some watercolor drawings. Chris and I Lindy Hopped into the evening at one camp, then raced our bikes across the flat playa like tiny neon fish in an infinite abyss.

Three days into Burning Man, I was thoroughly dusty, exhausted, enlivened, and wonderfully bewildered. No one had recognized me. I was wearing a dust mask and goggles much of the time, and our friends had started calling me Domu, as if I were some kind of mysterious guide in a Miyazaki film. While my friends were altering their minds in various ways, I remained sober, reminding everyone to stay hydrated and guiding us through the dust storms back to camp.

Around me I saw people with way, way fewer inhibitions than I had. I walked by the Human Car-cass Wash, the only place to get clean at Burning Man: a group effort, where after becoming a human soaper, then scrubber, then rinser, then dryer, rotating your way through the carwash-like stations, you were allowed to strip naked yourself and walk through the cleansing gauntlet. By day four, I worked up the courage to try on that see-through leotard. It was tame compared to what many others were wearing, but for me, it was an act of defiance. As a kid, I'd felt no shame about my body, but the media had turned me into the kind of person who wouldn't dare be caught in a bikini at the beach. A part of me was always reacting to the imagined tabloid smear, thinking, *Do not give them any evidence to think you're a slut!* My inner voice was afraid, and I was tired of listening to it.

That day, I stumbled into a geodesic dome that was hosting an event called Slutty Storytelling, an open mic where people got up in front of the crowd to tell their most embarrassing, most depraved, most titillating sex stories. In a moment of panicked inspiration, I leapt up in front of the crowd and told them how I'd learned to masturbate in prison. Afterward, I felt my racing heart slow as a warm glow came over me.

Like the ever-present advertising and transactional relationships in our daily lives, judgment is one of the primary compounds of the air we breathe. (Incidentally, you can find these three elements all concentrated in the tabloids at the grocery store checkout line.) I was very much aware that Burning Man was a bubble within the larger capitalist world I inhabited every other day of the year, and that this place could only be sustained by a massive influx of time, energy, and money (tickets alone cost nearly six hundred dollars), and even then, it lasted just ten days, a shimmering ephemeral city that could never sustain itself. But the value of Burning Man, I was realizing, was in merely seeing, for just a few days, what a world without transactions, shame, or judgment was like.

And gnawing at me the whole time was the crystal of pain that had been lodged in my chest, its sides reflecting my anxiety, my sadness, my anger. I was free now, wasn't I? I wasn't trapped in a cell, and no one was trying to put me back inside. Why was I still afraid? At least back in Italy, the source of my pain was obvious. I was surrounded by it.

The stories-tall Man sculpture isn't the only structure that gets lit on fire at Burning Man. All throughout the week, thousands of burners make a pilgrimage to the Temple, wander inside, and leave mementos and tokens. There were countless photos of departed loved ones, letters, flowers, and a wide variety of small keepsakes—a pair of earrings, an old baseball mitt—items whose personal significance was known only to those who'd left them. I saw a hand-scrawled confession from a man admitting that he'd raped someone and that he felt like killing himself. A woman had nailed her wedding dress to one of the beams. I paused before a photo of a small child, wondering whether he'd died of some illness or disappeared from a playground.

I took the small watercolor postcard I had painted at the Art and Chardonnay camp and placed it in the Temple. It read, "Pain was simpler in prison." On Sunday night, it went up in flames with all the other sacred items, while the crowd, sitting in silence, wept quietly for themselves, for everyone, for the possibility of truly letting go.

Fear, especially fear of judgment, is poison for play. Play is a wiggly hand, not a clenched fist. It requires a looseness, a willingness to take risks. After Burning Man, as the year progressed, the more I let go of my fear, the more Chris and I played. We danced on subway platforms; we sang in the grocery store; our outfits grew more eccentric and fabulous and color-coordinated by the day.

Then one Sunday evening in the late fall of 2018, a meteorite crashed in our backyard. At least, it seemed that way. Chris couldn't keep a straight face; he was up to something. *E.T.* music tinkled to life from hidden speakers around the garden as I cautiously approached the smoking, glowing crater. Cradled inside the meteorite was a glowing slab of iridescent stone engraved with an entry from the *Encyclopedia Galactica*—about us, and our love, and our future together.

"It appears to be some kind of data crystal," Chris suggested helpfully.

I giggled. "It's a data crystal. Okay...What?"

"Oh my god," Chris said. "I had been thinking about this but...it's already happened...in the future? Which is...it's happening now?"

Chris got down on one knee. "Will you stay with me until the last star in the last galaxy burns out, and even after that? Amanda Marie Knox, will you marry me?"

It took a moment to sink in. I was dumbstruck. This whole scene, with the sci-fi special effects, the painstaking execution...*this was my person. This was the life I wanted.*

Finally, I sputtered, "Uh...yeah."

And in our usual spirit, Chris and I wrote the narrative of our wedding based upon the groundwork he had already laid. We envisioned it as part performance, part escape room. Our wedding would be a one-night interactive theater piece for two hundred people, a romantic live-action episode of *Doctor Who*.

After a year of building props and sets and puzzles, our time travel–themed wedding took place on a day outside the normal flow of time—leap day, February 29, 2020. The day before, as we were

Free

frantically assembling the scenery and testing out the AV, I was called into the office by the elderly man who ran the venue. "I think I made a mistake..." he muttered. "Some journalists just called asking if we were hosting a wedding tomorrow. I said yes. I wasn't thinking. I didn't say your name, but I'm afraid I might have given it away..."

I went cold inside. "Okay. Please don't say anything else to anyone," I stuttered. I returned to the wedding hall in a daze and approached Chris. "We have a problem."

I started to cry. I knew what was about to happen. Paparazzi would show up to get pictures of us. They might harass our guests or even try to infiltrate the wedding venue. Everyone was arriving in costume, dressed in their finery from time periods past and future. It would be easy for an uninvited guest to sneak in. And this is how they would frame their latest scoop: "Narcissistic Knox Holds Bizarre Celebration While Kerchers Continue to Grieve." It was always the same; everything good in my life was spun as some kind of obscene offense to the memory of Meredith. The message was loud and clear: *How dare I live when she is dead?*

And once again, my heart was a clenched fist. It wasn't just that other people boxed me in as a tragic figure and expected me to live in mourning for the rest of my life. It was also that a part of me, deep down, agreed with them. The part of me that felt guilty that I had survived my study abroad, and she hadn't. The part of me that blurred my identity with Meredith's, my tragedy with hers. The part of me that was still angry and hurt and deeply sad, because I could never go back to being that daring, silly, dreamy-eyed kid who boarded that flight to Italy, and neither could she.

I was hyperventilating. Chris took me in his arms. "We'll get wristbands and security guards, we'll check phones at the door, we'll solve this problem," he said. "But even if we don't, look at all this!" And we glanced around the ballroom that we'd transformed over the last week—there was the glowing time tunnel guests would enter through, the smoking regeneration canisters on stage we would emerge from in lieu of walking down the aisle, the dozens of wacky clocks we'd built adorning the walls, their hands spinning in erratic directions. "You deserve to enjoy this," he said. "You deserve to be happy. Don't let them take that away from you."

It's true what they say about weddings; they go by *really* fast. Our friends and family showed up in wild costumes from every conceivable time period—ancient Rome, sixteenth-century France, the Golden Age of Hollywood, the distant future...one friend even came as a dinosaur. There was a lightsaber battle, a frantic escape room puzzle hour, wild dancing, Prohibition Era cocktails, and Viking mead. And because our wedding took place right before the pandemic shutdown, it came to be known by everyone who attended as "the last fun thing."

As Chris and I collapsed in bed that night, exhausted from joy, I felt somewhat the way I'd felt in that safe house the night I was released from prison, afraid to go to sleep lest I wake up to find it was all a dream. I'd spent so many days and nights asking myself, *How is this my life?* And that question had always come with a miasma of despair. For the first time, that question hit me like a blessing.

Inferno

Abandon All Hope Ye Who Enter Here

The Only Way Out Is Through

IT IS A STRANGE COMFORT to always have your demons by your side. My demon is despair. It found me in my prison cell, in the hours after my conviction, and lay atop me like a lead blanket. As I worked to rebuild my life, my demon transformed, taking the more manageable shape of a shawl resting on my shoulders. On my best days, it is a ribbon in my hair. But it never leaves. And in the wrong circumstances, before I am even fully aware of what's happening, it can grow once again to smother me.

That happened in April of 2019, when Chris and I had just moved into our first house. We were busy unpacking and getting our lives in order when the Italy Innocence Project called. This fledgling organization, which only formed in the wake of my case and was staffed by just two people, was hosting its first ever justice conference, and they wanted me to headline it, speaking about "trial by media." The Italian minister of justice was going to be there. The head of the scientific police. All of Italy would be watching.

I didn't realize it until that moment, but in the back of my mind, I had been looking for the right way to return to Italy. People often assumed I would never set foot in the country again. They would even apologize for suggesting we eat dinner at an Italian restaurant. But I love Italian food and Italian culture. That's what brought me to Italy in the first place. Four years in Capanne hadn't changed that.

Italy and I had unfinished business. But the idea of actually returning, now that it was a real, tangible possibility, filled me with dread.

On the one hand, I wanted to tell my side of the story to the people who had imprisoned me and continued to view me as a guilty person who got off on a technicality or through political pull. I'd had trouble imagining how I would ever return (I couldn't just book a ticket and waltz back into the country), but here was an invitation to speak precisely about one of the major issues that had caused my wrongful conviction. I didn't think I would ever find a better opportunity.

On the other hand, I didn't want to keep rehashing the worst experience of my life, exploiting my trauma as my one pitiful resource, the only thing I had that anyone might care about. Even then, most people didn't. Did I have any wisdom, or was that just a vain illusion? Was I just fooling myself that I could help anyone? Who was I? Just a girl a terrible thing happened to, who would never do anything in her life that defined her more than an accusation of murder.

That was my demon talking. My demon wanted me to feel resentful and disconnected from the world, to ignore how confronting my trauma could help others and myself. It wanted me to feel impatient and aggrieved, exploited and exhausted. *Stop looking at my wounds, my eyes are up here!* It wanted me to feel like nothing I did was ever enough or would ever really matter.

The problem with this invitation was the event was only two months away, and with such short notice, Chris and I had no time to plan the trip the way it should have been planned: *very carefully*. I agonized over the decision and found myself panicking about private security. I had no idea how Italy would receive me. *Someone will try to shiv you in the street*, my demon said. It was hard not to listen to that voice when it could very well be right. The crowds in Perugia had chanted, "Vergogna! Vergogna!"—*Shame! Shame!*—when I'd been acquitted. A friend of mine had been punched in the face after leaving the courthouse. *The Italian police will arrest you for some bullshit charge*, my demon said. Again, not impossible. They'd charged me with criminal slander against the police for testifying that they'd hit me during my interrogation. My demon wasn't wrong. In telling my story, I *was* risking being charged and arrested again.

I asked all my friends and family, and the recurrent note was: *Don't risk it. You don't need to go. You can video call. You can record a speech. Why put yourself in jeopardy?* My lawyers were against it, too. It wasn't just the police they were worried about. Could we trust any hotel not to put hidden cameras in our room? Would an Airbnb host sell us out to the paparazzi? Chris was the only person who seemed to understand how important this was to me, even if I couldn't fully articulate it to myself. Though my mom didn't want me to go—she didn't understand why I wanted to—she said that if I did, she was coming, too. She wasn't about to let her baby girl set foot in Italy alone a second time.

Finally, I said, "Screw it, I have to go." We booked tickets, and then, in the midst of thinking through security and how to avoid getting torn apart by the Italian media—which was already frothing at the announcement that I would return—I had to figure out what the hell I was going to talk about when I stepped onto that stage under the glare of a spotlight, with hundreds of cameras and the eyes of Italy, and the world, scrutinizing me.

I didn't even know how to begin thinking about what to say. I had given talks before and told my story in interviews and essays. I'd written a whole memoir. But I felt like I had to start fresh. This opportunity deserved a blank slate, a radical rethinking of what had happened, what this meant to me, and what insights I could share. You get used to thinking about something using the same sequence of words, and you discover over the course of telling your story many times that you rely on those words. You feel safe in those words, which take you and your listener to a place that you have been before. We live in houses made of stories. And sometimes, you need to knock your house down and build it again from the ground up.

I knew that to genuinely convey myself to the Italian people, I had to do it with the strength and confidence that only comes through deep vulnerability. Which meant doing the hard emotional work of finding the right words. Not knowing how to start, I reverted to the form I felt most comfortable in. I'd gotten into the rhythm of writing letters in prison. I must have written thousands of letters. I wrote "Dear Italy," at the top of my notebook, and just the idea that I was speaking to *someone* kickstarted my mind.

Dear Italy,

There have been rare, rare moments in my life when I experience flashes of premonition. The first was on November 6, 2007. I was in the interrogation room again, which I didn't know was an interrogation room. I had been yelled at all night, slapped, and told I didn't remember, that I had amnesia, and I tried and tried to remember what I didn't remember, I tried to think of who murdered Meredith. And what did it really mean when my boss Patrick Lumumba texted me that night? And my mind was trying to make sense of why I was being pushed and bullied and abused, and as my interrogators leapt up and embraced each other for breaking me, as they scattered from the suffocating room, I had a flash of premonition. I was going to suffer. I was going to suffer long and hard. Something was terribly wrong, and I didn't yet know why or how, but I was going to suffer.

When I was stripped naked and photographed by police officers, I was too tired and scared to question them, to object when they examined my genitals for signs of sexual violence. When they put metal handcuffs around my wrists and drove me away in a police car, I believed them when they said it would only be for a few days, that I was an important witness, that I was being taken to a holding place for my own protection. I didn't know. I didn't know that this was just the beginning of my suffering.

I had another flash of premonition when I landed in Seattle for the first time after my imprisonment and I breathed in the fresh, wet, grassy air that I hadn't smelled in years. It came suddenly: I'm going back. I felt it more than I thought it, because I really didn't know if or how I would return to you. I only intuitively knew that our story wasn't over.

I looked over what I'd written. *It's shit*, my demon said. *Throw it out. Nothing you can say will ever be right. Why say anything? There's no point. No one is going to hear you.*

In the weeks leading up to our departure, Chris and I circled through a looping discussion as I tried to figure out why I was doing this and what I would say. As I drafted more material, I found that I was describing how I got fucked over; how a naïve twenty-year-old girl whose friend was murdered was then brutally interrogated, mentally shattered, thrown in a prison cell; how the whole world decided she was a monster; and how she found herself contemplating suicide thousands of miles from home. I got angry and sad thinking about that. But I knew it wasn't enough for me to return to Italy and say, "This is how you fucked me over." There had to be a *now what?* I had to find a way to make this story valuable to a potentially hostile Italian audience. I've never been one to prove people wrong on principle; that's a recipe for an unhappy and unproductive life. I didn't have to tell Italy that they were wrong to convict and imprison me to know I was right.

It's funny. I find myself most fascinated by stories that live in the gray space, in situations where it's unclear who's right and who's wrong. Should a murderer get sentenced to life in prison if they committed the crime as a seventeen-year-old, when their adult brain wasn't fully developed? Should drugs be illegal? They have a high social cost with overdoses and addiction, but so does the brutal and ineffective war on drugs. These are complicated questions to answer. That's partly why my own situation has always frustrated me. It's been treated, by the Italian courts, the media, and the general public, as this byzantine story, this uncertain gray space, when in fact it's a simple story, and one that's starkly black-and-white. I didn't kill anyone. I know that, Raffaele knows that, and Rudy Guede knows that. Everyone else has to deduce the truth from the evidence, but the evidence is also crystal clear. It solely implicates Guede, far beyond a reasonable doubt. And yet, everything has been muddled with one *unreasonable* doubt after another. *Why?* That was the question I needed to address in my speech.

As the days ticked closer to our departure, my speech took shape, but the voice of my demon grew stronger, and my own certainty about going wavered. The panic attacks returned. Chris found me sobbing in the closet on more than one occasion. I was about to return to the place where I'd lost nearly everything, where Meredith *did* lose everything. It was like going rafting on a river where you'd nearly drowned, or having a picnic in the park where you were raped. *And you have so much more to lose now*, my demon said. I had a house; I was engaged; I had friends; I was building a career telling stories that mattered; I was healthy and safe and happy. Why? Why would I go back to the place that took so much from me?

My demon had me cataloging everything stolen from me in Italy.

Even the small things. The police confiscated nearly all my belongings, and they were either destroyed, lost, or never returned. I didn't get my laptop back, nor my camping equipment, my clothing or toiletries or books. I lost my home, my privacy, my freedom, my anonymity, my identity, my roommate, and so much time. One thousand four hundred and twenty-eight days. I lost touch with my family. I was only able to see my sisters for a few hours every six months. They grew up without me.

I needed to listen to someone else, so I found myself perusing my philosophy books. The stoics would have me banish my demon. There was Marcus Aurelius: "Everything that happens is either endurable or not. If it's endurable, then endure it. Stop complaining. If it's unendurable...then stop complaining. Your destruction will mean its end as well." That was all well and good. And I'd found plenty of wisdom in Aurelius, Seneca, and the other stoics. But I also felt like I couldn't just dismiss my demon this way. It was a part of me. Perhaps in the way Carl Jung thought of the shadow, the blind spot of the psyche. "The shadow personifies everything that the subject refuses to acknowledge about himself," he wrote. In my case: self-doubt, feelings of worthlessness and powerlessness. Repressing this shadow, Jung argued, leads us to project it subconsciously onto our environment, distorting our perceptions and thinking. It's not something we can dismiss. Rather, the goal is to make it conscious. "Everyone carries a shadow, and the less it is embodied in the individual's conscious life, the blacker and denser it is. At all counts, it forms an unconscious snag, thwarting our most well-meant intentions."

The way to deal with your demon, or shadow, in Jung's view, is to assimilate it into your conscious self. It's like accepting that you're an alcoholic, or that you have a fear of commitment. There are great benefits for doing so. The shadow is also what Jung called the "seat of creativity." It doesn't just conceal our negative and shameful qualities, but all of our potential. "The shadow is a tight passage, a narrow door, whose painful constriction no one is spared who goes down to the deep well. But one must learn to know oneself in order to know who one is."

I'm not a scholar of Jung, and can't vouch for the validity of all his psychological theories, but this rang true to me. I couldn't banish my demon, my despair, but I could wear it like a ribbon in my hair, like my semicolon tattoo, given to me by a suicide survivor—a symbol for a dark moment that wasn't an ending, but a pause. If I could wear my demon that way, it wouldn't unconsciously distort my world, and it would be a reminder of how deep the abyss goes, and that I should be proud for every inch I move upward toward the light.

It helped immensely that Chris could see me wrestling my demon, and that he understood that I couldn't run from it. Each time the panic overwhelmed me, he talked me slowly back into breathing. Seeing me like that, anyone else in my life would have said, "You don't have to go. You can cancel the tickets right now." Chris never said that. But what he did ask me, repeatedly, was, "Why are you doing this?"

Articulating the answer to that question helped re-center me, even if my answer kept changing. I imagined this trip as an awkward dinner with an ex-lover I hadn't spoken to since the breakup. The relationship was horrible, the breakup was awful, but there was a reason I had started dating that person to begin with. There was a reason I chose to go to Italy of all places, and those reasons were still there, deep down inside me.

After Chris asked me for the hundredth time, I turned it around on him. "Why are we doing this?" I asked. He thought for a long moment, then said, "Because truly beautiful things come out of difficult places. And this is an opportunity to make something truly beautiful."

Climbing out of the pit of my life has often felt not just difficult, but impossible. And it surely was impossible to convince everyone in the world of my innocence. It was impossible to restore my reputation to its pre-Italy state, to recover my anonymity, to rewind my trauma, to bring my murdered friend back to life, to live those exciting years of being a young woman with a sense of adventure and exploration and jubilance. But I couldn't help dreaming. If I could just do one impossible thing, if I could cast one spell, lift one pebble with my mind, then maybe all those other things I faced that seemed impossible would transform into puzzles—difficult, yes, but at least *possible* to solve. Perhaps I could even transform my demon into a guardian angel. That was in fact what I was in the process of doing, learning to hear its voice as a pointer toward important information, an indicator of the fears I needed to conquer.

And when I thought of all the impossible things I was faced with, the one impossible dream I found myself returning to again and again was this: Could I somehow reach the heart of the man who sent me to prison? Could I get Dr. Giuliano Mignini, whose actions had derailed my life, irrevocably warped my image in the world's eye, and invited the demon of despair into my life, could I get *him* to understand me? To see the real me? Could I release my anger enough to forgive him?

These were such strange questions to ask myself, because they didn't sound pleasant or even healing, necessarily. It all sounded, well, *impossible*. But that didn't stop me from writing him a letter. Strangely, it came more easily to me than figuring out what to say to Italy. I simply told him that I wanted to meet him, human to human, and that was the key that unlocked the rest of my speech. I wasn't returning to Italy just to confront my trauma, to stand up for my innocence, or to raise awareness about the causes of wrongful convictions, but to extend an olive branch, not just to the people of Italy, but to Dr. Giuliano Mignini.

When I told my family I was reaching out to him, they were shocked. "Why on earth do you want to talk to that monster? After what he put our family through?" They called him an asshole, a criminal, a delusional maniac. But while they were insulting him, what I heard was directed at me: *What is wrong with you, Amanda?* I love my family, but I knew they were speaking from a place of hurt and judgment, and that if I gave in to those impulses, I'd remain forever stuck in a prison cell of grievance.

"I have always hoped to have the opportunity to get in touch with you outside the interrogation room and the courtroom," I wrote to him, "where we were forced into the adversarial roles given us by the judicial system—prosecutor and defendant. I always suspected that this, above all, made it impossible for us to see and understand each other."

I had no idea if he would ever respond, but I knew that reaching him, however impossible that seemed, held the possibility of redefining the boundaries of my own life and what I could achieve. It would expand my sense of freedom in a way nothing else could. And I was not content to let my freedom be impossible.

In Bocca al Lupo

THE ITALY INNOCENCE PROJECT ANNOUNCED their conference and speaker lineup about a month before the event, and from that day, hundreds of interview requests flooded in, from small-time podcasts to major newspapers and prime-time news programs. I declined them all. What I had to say I'd say in Italy.

We landed in Milan two days before the conference. Modena was a two-hour drive away. I hadn't announced my arrival plans, and because Modena was about equidistant from Milan, Florence, and Venice, I was hoping there was a good chance no one would know exactly where to look for me, and that I could avoid the paparazzi as I entered the country.

But as soon as I saw the look on the customs agent's face as he examined my passport and heard his subtle radio message to another agent, I started to worry. My hosts met Chris and me on the other side, but when we exited the airport terminal into the parking lot, we were swarmed. Dozens of cameras and microphones were shoved in my face as Chris and I and the Italy Innocence Project lawyers fought our way through the gauntlet. The questions rattled over each other: "Why did you come back? How does it feel? What about the Kercher family?" The media rarely depicts its own worst tendencies honestly, and so, of course, a moment like this is referred to, even in the most reputable papers, as "Amanda Knox is approached by journalists." Or as the *New York Times* put it, Amanda Knox "engaged in a familiar and uneasy tango with the news media." This was not an approach, it was not a tango, not a consensual dance or interaction of any kind. It was an assault. My trauma response kicked in. I kept my head down, barely walking, as my hosts guided me to the car. As soon as the door shut, I started hyperventilating. We were able to lose the paparazzi on the freeway, and I calmed down. I had worried that my hosts would underestimate the media problem, and our airport arrival was not a good sign. They had failed to grasp the rapaciousness of the media appetite—my return to Italy was front-page news all over the world.

There was a cocktail hour for the conference attendees in an outdoor courtyard at the venue. My hosts wanted me to go, but when they said media would be allowed in, I balked. "We have to give them something," I was told. It was like they were being extorted by the mafia. *If you don't pay the protection money, it'll only be worse.* They convinced me to attend, provided that the paparazzi were cordoned off behind a rope thirty yards away. I felt like a zoo animal as their telephoto lenses captured thousands of photographs. I knew they'd select the most awkward images for the papers, and sure enough, in the photo they ran, my mouth was open wide, mid-laugh, making me look like a flippant psycho, treating this whole trip like one big party.

Mom arrived that night and met us at an Airbnb we'd reserved in her name—our backup plan if the lodging the Italy Innocence Project had arranged was discovered. The next morning was the first official day of the conference, and my speech wasn't until the following day. There were other speakers I wanted to see. My friend and fellow exoneree Peter Pringle was going to be telling his story. Justin Brooks, director of the California Innocence Project, was giving a talk about ending the

Free

death penalty. I wanted to support them, just as they were supporting me. Chris and I had been keeping to the privacy of a few isolated back rooms at the conference venue, but we decided to try sneaking quietly into the auditorium during one of these talks. The cameras started snapping immediately.

There was a circular balcony above us, with a horde of journalists stationed on it, preparing to cover my speech and looking for any sign of me in the meantime. Suddenly, a spotlight fell on me in the darkened auditorium. Mark Godsey, director of the Ohio Innocence Project, was on stage presenting his talk, but now all the attention was on me, sitting in the audience. I felt terrible for Mark, and I could sense a panic attack coming on. Chris ushered me out of the auditorium to the chattering clicks, and I collapsed in a stairwell, struggling to breathe.

My hosts met me there, gave me some water, and one of them grasped me by the shoulders and gave me a pep talk. "You are here and no one expected you to be here. We believe in you. We need you. You have to fight with us because there are many people like you," she said. "You have to be the person that shows them that life goes on. If you run away, these people like you will continue to say, 'My life is over, my life is over.' You have to help them. You have to keep your head high. Let them take their pictures. You look them in the face, and tell them to fuck off." She laughed, then added, "But with the eyes, not with words."

It was like she knew I'd been doubting whether anyone wanted me here. That was in part because I'd made the mistake of reading the flood of articles, and the comments, about my return to Italy. The news media was already feasting off me before I'd even given my talk. Under photos of me, head bowed, assaulted by the paparazzi as I arrived in Milan: "She wouldn't keep her head down if she wasn't ashamed." "Guilty as sin." "She'll do anything for attention."

Reading the commentary about my trip felt like a relapse into a behavior I'd mostly cured myself of. I knew it would only depress me, but that part of me that hoped for the impossible couldn't resist seeing if anyone had anything positive to say.

What I found instead was the narrative that somehow my very presence in Italy was deeply offensive to the Kercher family. Piers Morgan tweeted, "Out of respect for Meredith Kercher's poor family, Amanda Knox should stop her self-pitying 'all about me' victim tour—and shut up." This was the same guy who in the lead-up to my trip to Italy had begged me to be interviewed on his program, an offer I declined. Once again, a maddening accusation that I was somehow responsible for the media's fixation on me, and that I was an attention whore for speaking about the issues that had derailed my life, in the hope of changing things for the better.

It didn't help that the Kercher family's lawyer, Francesco Maresca, spoke out upon my arrival in Italy, telling the *Guardian* that my involvement in the justice conference in Modena was "inappropriate," and that I was only appearing "to keep the attention on [my]self." Never mind that I'd been invited to speak about trial by media. Never mind that I'd declined hundreds of interview requests, and that I would have banished the paparazzi to another dimension had I the power.

Maresca had always been a jerk. He once said of my gentle demeanor in court, "Prison has been good for her." If prison had had its way with me, I would have been a snarling dog, kicked one too many times. I don't blame the Kerchers for the attitude of their lawyer. Like many grieving families in such cases, they were told a comforting lie by the prosecution and their attorneys, which was repeated ad nauseam by the media, but then that lie was overturned when Raffaele and I were acquitted. What grieving family wouldn't find it difficult to relinquish their sense of closure? And so Maresca repeated to the *Guardian* what has been the official stance of the Kercher family since my release:

"The murder is a tragic memory for the Kercher family; they lost their daughter and sister in such a terrible way. It's also an injustice for them as they still don't know the full truth."

This was a veiled way of saying they believe that Raffaele and I were somehow involved and were unjustly acquitted. The "full truth" is there for all to see. But the lie of a conspiracy, of multiple attackers, of Raffaele and me somehow being involved, had been so stamped in by a decade and a half of misinformation that they remained closed off to the complete truth that was already available to them. If Maresca really wanted to talk about closure, he should have been focusing on the fact that Rudy Guede was serving a reduced sentence that did not fully account for his crimes. He was never recognized as the person wielding the knife that ended Meredith's life.

It was extremely frustrating to be yet again accused of traumatizing the Kercher family by speaking about my wrongful conviction and trying to use my experience to bring attention to issues that affect tens of thousands of people; according to Innocence Project estimates, there are anywhere from 20,000 to 100,000 innocent people in prison just in the United States. We should have been allies, the Kerchers and I, both of us victims of Rudy Guede and the Italian justice system. I wrestled through my fear and anger and frustration, realizing it reminded me of why I was in Modena at all. The media was still, even on the eve of my talk about *trial by media*, engaging in the same outrage and clickbait-inducing behavior that had affected my trial, distorted my character, imprisoned me in a false narrative years after my acquittal, and overshadowed Meredith's victimhood.

Mom saw the stress racking my body and wanted me to turn around and go home. "I can book a ticket right now," she said. "This isn't worth it." I love my mom, but I knew she was wrong. I could not back down and fly home early. What I had to say mattered, but even more so, the fact that I was willing to say it here, in person, in front of a potentially hostile crowd, mattered. For once, people might actually listen. This was a test of my own courage. I'd climbed all the way to the top of the highest diving board. I was standing on the edge. If I let fear of judgment send me slinking back down that ladder, I might as well still be in prison. It wouldn't be me making the decision, steering my life, but some other force that was more powerful than I was. Even as I understood this, though, even as I felt a growing sense of determination, I was an emotional wreck and worried about my safety.

The Italy Innocence Project arranged a former special forces carabinieri officer as a private security guard during my stay in Modena. As you can probably imagine, I have trust issues when it comes to Italian police, but he surprised me. The night before my talk, he drove us to a small agriturismo an hour outside of town to meet up with the other conference speakers for dinner. Agriturismos are kind of like vacation rentals made out of old or sometimes still-operating farms, and they're everywhere in rural Italy. It was the only way to avoid the paparazzi. By the time someone recognized me way out there and relayed word to any journalists, we'd be back in the car speeding away again. On the dark, winding roads into the countryside, this Italian military police officer recited verses from Dante, and Chris gave him verses in English from Robert Frost, in Spanish from Borges, and even an Italian poem he'd memorized by Eugenio Montale. I felt genuine warmth from him, and I started to hope that maybe I could get through to the Italian people when I gave my speech the following day.

Before we got out into the countryside, I'd felt like I was fighting a battle that there was no possibility of winning. The press was as cruel as ever. None of the articles coming out by the hour mentioned that I was invited to speak, that I was doing so to raise awareness about problems in the justice system, and that I wasn't being paid. I knew the Italy

Innocence Project, whose phone was ringing off the hook, was delivering these talking points over and over again, but they didn't fit the story that I was exploiting Meredith's tragedy for attention. I felt more trapped in this narrative prison than I had in a long time.

But that dinner at the agriturismo was just what I needed: a warm evening in the country overlooking olive groves, a family-style meal in the company of friends with decanters of wine, homemade amaro, and bats flitting after insects in the twilight. It was exactly the kind of quintessential Italian experience I'd come to Italy for in the first place. It was the Italy I'd thought I'd never get back, and yet there it was—the food, the warmth, the wine, the companionship.

Later that night, as we were trying to go to sleep, Chris asked me what I'd say to my younger self about this moment. It came to me immediately: "I know it doesn't feel this way, but everything doesn't depend on whether or not people believe you, because the people who matter *do*." Chris, my mom, my family—I was so lucky to have them, because not everyone does. A part of me still thought that what happened *to* me in Italy was the only thing that would ever define me. But I also knew that no matter how it went the following day, I was so much more than the worst experience of my life. And that being in Italy was a way to actually *do* something, to reclaim some agency.

In that moment, I felt at peace, with myself if not with the world. Whatever inner turmoil had been roiling me for months leading up to this trip, it was gone. I knew that I was trying my very best and pushing myself to my absolute limits. I knew there was nothing more I could do. There was a kind of masochism at work, too, an inability to love and accept myself until I'd given everything. I didn't know how to change that dynamic, but I knew I had it in me to get up on that stage, more vulnerable than I'd been in a long time, and tell the truth to the Italian people, and to the world.

I didn't know how Italy would react to what I had to say. I stopped caring whether I'd be crucified or praised. The inscription on the gates of hell in Dante's *Inferno* reads, "Abandon All Hope Ye Who Enter Here." I always thought of that as a warning that hell is a place full of torment with no hope of escape. But, paradoxically, it's also a bit of wisdom, advice on how to survive. Hope, like fear, is a way of living in the future and ignoring the present. It's what keeps you from appreciating what you have—your house, your job, the sun on your face during an unseasonably warm day in early spring. It clouds your view of reality—in prison it had prevented me from accepting the fact of my circumstances, and in freedom, it had kept me in a dysfunctional relationship. I had to abandon hope. Without hope, without any expectation of how I would be received or what the fallout of my speech might be, I couldn't suffer. Without hope, I was invincible.

Coraggio

I HAD A PLEASANTLY DREAMLESS sleep, and I woke feeling hushed and solemn. I found it hard to imagine anything after the speech. I could barely even imagine being on stage. My mind had erected some wall just before that podium. I'd read aphorisms, from Nelson Mandela to Mark Twain, that courage isn't the absence of fear, but mastery over it, the judgment that something else is more important than the fear itself. That wall in my mind was preventing me from imagining how people would react to my speech, because that was my greatest fear—that I'd open my heart and be booed, have things thrown at me, be attacked, or, more realistically but somehow more crushing, be dismissed, remain unheard, my words twisted by tabloids to reaffirm the time-tested, money-generating narrative: Amanda Knox = Bad. It wasn't an unreasonable fear, and I discovered that even my hosts were worried about it as the lawyer who introduced me went on and on and on, speaking for nearly an hour justifying to the audience, and to the press, why they'd invited me in the first place, why my presence was not only fitting but important at a conference about criminal justice reform.

And then, finally, they said my name. A hush fell over the crowd as I approached the podium. Above me, my face was twenty feet tall on the jumbotron screen. I took a drink of water, a deep breath, and began speaking in Italian:

This is my third trip to Italy. I first came here when I was fourteen. My whole extended family piled into minivans and toured the Colosseum and the ruins of Pompeii. We ate snails on the Amalfi coast. I fell in love with Italy on that trip. And when I returned as a twenty-year-old, to write poetry, drink wine, and take siestas, I was met instead with tragedy and suffering. Despite that, or because of it, Italy became a part of me. The language and the culture shaped my mind. I have returned a third time because I have to, because I've been invited by the Italy Innocence Project, and because this beautiful country once felt like home to me, and I hope that it will feel that way again.

A lot of people think I'm crazy to come back. I've been told that it's not safe. That I'll be attacked in the streets. That I'll be falsely accused and sent back to prison. That even if I return home unscathed, it will all be for nothing.

To be honest, I am afraid. I'm afraid of being harassed. I'm afraid of being mocked. I'm afraid of being framed. I'm afraid new charges will be brought against me just for telling the truth here today. But most of all, I'm afraid my courage will fail me.

I know that despite my acquittal by the Court of Cassation, I remain a controversial figure in the court of public opinion, especially here in Italy. I know that many people think I'm a villain. That I don't belong here. Some have even claimed that just by being here, I am re-traumatizing the Kercher family, and desecrating Meredith's memory.

They are wrong. And the fact that I continue to be held accountable in this way—for the Kerchers' grief, for Perugia's reputation—shows how powerful false narratives can be and how they can undermine justice, especially when they are reinforced and amplified by the media. But the media can also reveal and amplify the truth, if journalists are brave enough to see it, and if the public demands it.

My voice was shaking, but I pushed through, telling the audience the tragic details of what had actually happened to Meredith, how we knew this with certainty from the evidence, and how attention came to focus on me instead of Rudy Guede. I choked up relaying the trauma of my interrogation and the coerced admission I was pressured into signing after being gaslit by authority figures for hours late into the night. That moment was crucial to understanding why this whole case went off the rails, why the Perugia police erroneously reported "case closed" after arresting Patrick, Raffaele, and me, all before any forensic evidence had come back from the lab. I went on:

This was a hasty and unfounded conclusion, a grave mistake. And this was the moment the media could have shined. Because the media is our first line of defense to hold our authorities accountable, especially when they wield their power to strip us of our freedom. It was here that journalists could have asked, "You've charged and arrested three people. Based on what evidence? You say the American girl confessed. Are her statements legally sound, coherent, reliable, and do they correspond with the evidence?" In so doing, the media could have incentivized the police to slam the brakes on an investigation that was veering wildly and blindly off the road.

Instead, the media pumped the gas. Without incriminating physical evidence, the police attacked my character, distorting my rather normal sexual history into deviancy so I'd fit into their "sex game gone wrong" theory. The media took this and ran with it.

On the world stage, I wasn't a defendant—innocent until proven guilty. I was a liar, a psychopath, a dirty, drug-addled slut so jealous of Meredith's purity that I raped and killed her—guilty until proven innocent. It was a false and unfounded story, but it sparked the world's imagination. It spoke to people's fears and fantasies.

I relayed how this fed back into the courtroom in a vicious cycle, corrupting the jury pool and any possibility of a fair trial. I brought the audience into prison with me, to feel the weight of that guilty verdict. I told them of my friendship with Don Saulo, and how he never judged me, never told me who I was, even as the world called me a monster. I told them how I felt supported by him in cultivating a mindset of compassion and empathy and gratitude, that it was this mindset that would allow me to understand what had happened to me.

It's not enough to get it right eventually. We need to get it right sooner, far more often than we do. And the media can be a powerful force in helping us do that. In those four years of prison, eight years of trial, and to this day, I have borne many costs for the mistakes of others. I want to share them with you, not to garner your pity, but to show you what happens when we get it wrong, in the hope that the next innocent person on trial suffers far less than I have.

I told them of my thoughts of suicide, the impact on my family, and I broke down in tears when I spoke about a time my father came to visit.

My family was only allowed to visit me for six hours a month. Once, my dad came, and I just couldn't hold it together. I was so tired of the fear and the uncertainty, the loss and the loneliness. I couldn't help it. I just started sobbing. And my dad held me. And I pleaded with him. I begged him to save me, even though I knew he was just as helpless as I was. And my dad had to tell me what my lawyers had told him: that it would likely be several years before I could expect another serious chance at freedom. And then he started crying. All he could do was cry with me. And that's when I knew how bad it was, because I had never seen my father cry before in my entire life.

I didn't have to bear these costs. They were not necessary or inevitable. The justice system and the media are tools, I said, not good or bad in and of themselves, but only as just as the people who wield them. So often our courtrooms are not like laboratories where competing information is boiled down to truth beyond a reasonable doubt, but more like battlegrounds where the most compelling story, not the most truthful, wins. In my case the media fueled the carnage on that battlefield. It could have done the opposite.

Then, finally, I turned to the subject of my prosecutor. I knew this moment would be controversial, that even my family wouldn't like what I had to say.

Recently, I've been thinking a lot about my prosecutor, Dr. Giuliano Mignini. For a long time, I've hoped for the chance to meet face-to-face with him outside the interrogation room and courtroom, where we were forced into the adversarial roles ascribed to us—prosecutor and defendant, good and evil. I've always suspected that this, perhaps above all, made it impossible for us to understand each other. Because to my twenty-year-old self, wrongly imprisoned and on trial, Dr. Giuliano Mignini was a nightmarish figure—a powerful and frightening man who had only one goal: to destroy my life.

I know that image of him is wrong. It is as flat and two-dimensional as Foxy Knoxy. It was the media who helped me to see that. In the Netflix documentary, I saw not an evil man, but a man with genuine, noble motivations, who wanted to bring justice to a grieving family. I would like to meet that man, the real Dr. Giuliano Mignini, one day. And I hope that when that time comes, he, too, can come to see that I am not a monster, but that I am simply Amanda.

I have the same hope in being here with all of you today. That by having the courage to stand before you, and meet with you face-to-face, we can arrive at some kind of understanding and reconciliation between us. Because true justice happens when we see our fellow human beings with compassion, when we judge with restraint, and when we return to each other, after pain and enmity, with the courage of an open heart.

I said a few words about the broader innocence movement, my exoneree family, and gave my thank-yous. And then two unexpected things happened. The crowd rose to their feet in a standing ovation. They had been silent for an hour, listening intently, surprised I had chosen to deliver my speech in Italian. Even my hosts had assumed I would speak in English, but I had returned to Italy to connect with the Italian people, and I had to do so on their terms, in their language. No one had booed. Not a single tomato was thrown at me. Instead, I was met with resounding applause. I was still shocked when the security guard standing off to the side ushered me backstage, away from the crowd, and down a winding passageway to the basement, where I would be safe. He squeezed my shoulders, looked me in the eyes, and said, "Perfetto." *Perfect.* And I hugged him for a long minute, sobbing into his shoulder.

I didn't get to speak with the audience, but dozens of Italians passed notes back to me through the hosts. I cried again reading these messages, some of them directly apologizing for how they'd judged me.

Chris and I dropped Mom off at the Milan airport the next morning and then sped for the northern border in our rental car. We had booked ourselves a few days to decompress on the south coast of France. It was there, looking out over the Mediterranean from a medieval hilltop village, that I received some shocking news. Over the last few months, I'd sent two letters to my prosecutor, Dr. Giuliano Mignini, one through Don Saulo, and one through an Italian journalist I trusted. I was told that he had refused to even read them. He didn't think it was proper. But my speech had changed that. He had heard what I'd said in Modena, and now he felt compelled to respond.

Purgatorio

You Won't Find the Way Forward by Looking Back

Dear Giuliano

IN EARLY AUGUST 2019, AFTER I had returned home from Modena and allowed my nerves to calm down, my dialogue with my prosecutor began in earnest. You might be asking, "Why on Earth would you want to talk to this man who painted you as a sex-crazed murderer, imprisoned you for four years, and put you on trial for eight?" One answer is: I wanted to know *why. Why had this happened to me? Why had he believed I deserved that? Why couldn't I let it go?* Those questions continued to haunt me. If speaking at the Italy Innocence Project event was an act of courage, then seeking this dialogue was about curiosity.

I knew that the enemy of genuine curiosity was judgment. Judgment is like a fog that clouds our vision; we see reality more clearly when we refrain from casting it. We see people for who they are, flawed and complicated. Seeing this also takes away the power from those who judge us. If I wrote Dr. Giuliano Mignini off as an evil, corrupt man—as most of my family, friends, and supporters had—I would learn nothing. Yes, he prosecuted the wrong people, flattening me into a cartoon villain for the world to judge. But I knew how wrong people were in their judgments of me, and I didn't ever want to be that wrong about another person. Especially him. A part of that impulse was rebellious and contrarian, a way of rejecting my status as a victim. If I did the expected thing—fear and avoid him—it was like my actions were still a product of his mistakes, but if I did what everyone least expected of me, I was shaping my own destiny.

It felt both noble and almost juvenile, the way a teenager might buck against their parents by forsaking the family business to become a competitive Ping-Pong player. The world is a richer place because of such mutinies. For me, living in a world of relentless judgment, my rebellion was curiosity, and compassion. Refraining from judgment had become a way of life for me. Call it radical empathy or extreme benefit of the doubt.

In his first letter, Giuliano wrote to me at length, taking the liberty of using the informal "tu" form, as I had with him. He found common ground with me over our shared trauma from the media. His character and actions had been distorted by the press, too. He said he was moved by my speech, and especially what I'd said about the visit from my father, a man he saw as respectable, stoically suffering in silence. But he also maintained that he had done nothing wrong, had never acted with hostility toward me, and was merely doing his job. He signed off by calling me "a happy surprise."

I took me more than a month to respond. The surreality of being in dialogue with this man was hard to wrap my mind around. When I did write him back, always in Italian, of course, I said, "Part of me is relieved to know that you never felt hostility toward me and that you never considered me a monster. Another part of me despairs that there is no easy answer to why you saw in me guilt that was not there." I told him more about my experience of being brutally interrogated by the police, and that I planned to eventually appeal to overturn my slander conviction for the statements I was pressured into signing, and that I hoped that if we should meet in court again in the future, it would not be as adversaries, but perhaps as allies in service of the truth. I also told him I desired to meet face-to-face, discreetly, without the presence of any media.

Two months passed before his response. Then his letters kept popping into my busy life a little like ominous messages from an oncologist: *Your results are in. Give me a call to discuss.* So I would turn my attention away from my work, or making plans for Christmas, and immediately enter into Trauma Land. I couldn't leave Mignini's words sitting there unread for more than a minute, even as I knew it would hurt to read them.

There was longing for connection in his letters, which surprised me. He told me that I'd helped him rekindle his friendship with Don Saulo, whom he had known for decades and who had once been his parish priest. He spoke wistfully, the way many aging men do, as their sharp corners get sanded down by time. He told me that he often looked at photos from the trial, and a few in particular where the two of us were in the same frame. He noted my pained expressions and how I looked toward him plaintively, as if I wanted to talk to him. He wasn't wrong.

Still, he lamented the final ruling from the Court of Cassation. He was hung up on "procedural matters," upset that they hadn't followed precedent by remanding the case back to a lower appeals court, instead issuing a definitive acquittal for Raffaele and me. He told me that our acquittal had unleashed a wave of attacks on him in Italy, and that in the midst of all that, his beloved dog Arlo, with blue eyes that reminded him of mine, died in his arms.

It's hard to feel angry at a man cradling his dying dog. Perhaps he knew that. But I also knew it must be hard to feel angry at a scared young girl, stuck in a cell and crying for her mom. I had introduced the rules and the goal of our correspondence: *See the humanity of the other person.* He was trying his best. He was being honest with me about what rankled him about the past: how the interrogation I was put through by the police was attributed to him, even though he only came in at the end; how the "case closed" comment uttered by the police chief was attributed to him, even though he called out his colleague for making such a flub. He even dared to conjecture that, had he been present during my initial interrogation, perhaps things would not have turned out as they did.

He spoke about his role during the investigation and trials in the lofty terms of logic and deduction. "The investigator must reconstruct a past event which he did not observe," he wrote, "a bit like a historian." To arrive at the truth, a good investigator must be equipped with "curiosity, intelligence, attention to all details, complete absence of prejudices and conditioning, logical rigor and extreme humility. He must follow his hypothesis, but he must be ready to review it when he realizes that his 'assumption' is arbitrary and not proven."

The cognitive dissonance made my jaw drop. This was the man who had wildly conjectured that I was "morbidly obsessed with violence and sex" and that I'd orchestrated an orgy-turned-murder with a young man I barely knew. And yet, he viewed himself as free of prejudice, utterly logical, full of humility, and willing to counter his assumptions.

But he said something else in his letter that left me even more flabbergasted. He wrote:

"Of course, in life one can make mistakes, and I could have been wrong and it is equally true that one thing is the official truth and another is the real truth. We must make sure that the two truths coincide. This is as close to my heart as you are." And: "You were all present, according to the verdict, but it is not possible to establish who killed Meredith. Anything could have happened, including that the guilty party, hypothetically, was only one person. It may be that the judges made a mistake, it is true, very true, but there is nothing we can do about it. The verdict is definitive."

He was not admitting fault, or wrongdoing, or even error, but merely acknowledging the *possibility* that he could have been wrong? And the *possibility* that Rudy Guede had acted alone? He was speaking in such careful terms, I wondered if he feared legal liability, for himself or his office. He remained stuck on the definitive ruling from the Court of Cassation which, in acquitting me and Raffaele, had also erroneously asserted that we were present at the crime scene that night, even if we were not involved in the murder. They did so because they took the unreliable confession evidence as fact: if I signed a statement saying I was present at the house that night, it could only mean I was present at the house. Even those comparatively wise judges who acquitted us were ignorant to the realities of coercive interrogations and false confessions.

If that tangled ball of sentiment sounds hard to process, it was even more so when he signed off with "Merry Christmas from your prosecutor." But when I started to get upset, I remembered that I hadn't been expecting him to take responsibility for his actions, to apologize, or beg forgiveness. I had to be content just seeing where this correspondence would take us. I'd learned from my trip to Modena that withholding expectation, abandoning hope of a preferred outcome, could open doors for unexpected, if complicated, blessings. Giuliano and I traded seasonal greetings on December 25 and January 1. Somehow, in this short time, he had taken on the role of some kindly, distant uncle.

I wrote him back in earnest a few months later, once the pandemic had arrived, apologizing for the three-month delay and explaining how bewildered and anxious I felt each time I saw an email from him in my inbox. Part of that was because it remained clear to me that he still didn't believe I was innocent. "I don't think I will ever feel at peace," I wrote, "even though I work every day to resign myself to the fact that I can never convince you and all the other people in the world that I was tried and imprisoned as an innocent person." But I also reiterated to him how precious this dialogue was to me, that it gave me courage and comfort to share even small understandings with him—what it feels like to be distorted and abused by the media—even if large and life-altering misunderstandings still lay between us.

He replied a week later. While casting blame on the police, and describing himself as "gruff," he also said he had a deep affection for people who had earned his trust. I had done so. My act of reaching out to him, he said, had moved him deeply. "I will never forget the grandness of your soul," he wrote. He told me of his love of Wagner and *Lord of the Rings*; "I am a Catholic of the 'chivalrous' variety, like King Theoden of Rohan.... You remind me of Eowyn." He said our correspondence made him feel as though we understood each other as few people do. I was skeptical, and yet, it was hard not to hope for a true connection, especially when he would say things like, "I'm happy for you." Could he really be happy that I was free? "I tried to do my duty," he wrote, "and I may have made a mistake." He kept returning to this fine line of near-apology. And whenever he did so, I found myself yearning for him to finally come around to believing in my innocence and owning his mistakes. I had started this dialogue, but I couldn't control it. The best I could do was react mindfully and try to see clearly what was actually transpiring between us, and not become blinded by what I wanted to see. But then he would write: "It does not seem to me that I led those journalists in portraying you so differently from how you are, but if it happened, I ask your forgiveness." He even went so far as to say, "Today, I defend you always and everywhere."

Frankly, I was stupefied. If he was truly defending me always and everywhere, I'd have heard about it. It would have been international front-page news: "Italian Prosecutor Admits to Making Mistakes, Amanda Knox Is Innocent." Another part of me saw him truly struggling to get there, so close to accepting accountability. I sympathized with how difficult it must be for him. His entire identity was wrapped up in his role as a man of integrity. For him to acknowledge that, despite noble intentions, he had made a tremendous error that had deprived Meredith's family of true closure and caused grievous harm to Raffaele and me was far more than just admitting a mistake. It would force him to reconceptualize himself as a person who had steered justice awry instead of restoring it.

At the end of his letter, he urged me to watch an Italian detective film called *Una Vita in Gioco* (*A Life on the Line*), adapted from a French novel about a detective named Inspector Maigret. He said that in this film I would find the torment of the investigator after the end of a trial, a torment that he felt about me.

With the pandemic raging, he suggested that before we met in person, we should continue to get to know each other through our correspondence. He signed off, "A hug, Giuliano."

A hug from my prosecutor? What on Earth had I gotten myself into?

A New Life

FROM A YOUNG AGE, I'D always imagined myself as a mother. Having children wasn't even a question. But after my guilty verdict, I was facing the prospect of being released back into free society at age forty-six. If that happened, it wouldn't just be my freedom stolen from me; motherhood would likely be stolen from me, too. I barely knew who I was at that point, but what I did know was that I wasn't anything like the girl they were portraying in the media, and that at heart, I was a nurturer, a caregiver, a mom in waiting. I thought about my own mom, who had poured all her love into my sister and me, and I wanted to be just like her. Now where would I pour all my love? Not into a daughter of my own, but into the void of an empty future.

By the time I was definitively acquitted and free to start dreaming about something as audacious as starting a family, I was twenty-eight. It could have been so much worse. I've met other women through the Innocence Network who weren't so fortunate. A friend of mine was sentenced to life and spent more than fifteen years in prison before she was exonerated. She emerged into freedom at the very end of her fertility window, and after numerous fertility treatments, failed implantations, and a miscarriage, she gave up.

This is something that is not often acknowledged when women are imprisoned. Both men and women lose their most productive years to overly long and punitive sentences, but men's reproductive functions do not expire the way women's do. When a woman is convicted and given a long sentence, she is effectively sentenced not just to time but to infertility.

All of this was on my mind as I thought about having kids with Chris, and it made me feel so lucky. The possibility of motherhood had been taken from me, and now that it had been restored, I didn't have a second to lose! But that journey wasn't one I felt comfortable sharing with Giuliano—he was the one who'd nearly deprived me of it in the first place.

My mom was twenty-five when she gave birth to me. She got divorced when I was just one year old, while she was pregnant with my sister Deanna, and she struggled as a single mom working full-time as an elementary school teacher. She dealt with that trauma, half in jest, by making me promise when I was only seven that I would wait until I was thirty before getting pregnant. I even signed a contract we drafted together in green crayon.

But as soon as my legal jeopardy was over at the age of twenty-five, she started asking, "Where's my grandbabies?" I was thirty-one by the time Chris and I got engaged, and I was ready then, but Chris wanted to wait until after we were married. By then, the pandemic was in full swing. Toilet paper was out of stock at the grocery store, and society seemed more unstable than it ever had in our lifetimes. When public-facing events were canceled, a lot of our income evaporated overnight, and we were seriously worried about defaulting on our mortgage. Was this the right time to bring a child into the world? But as they say, there's never a right time.

I went to Planned Parenthood to get my IUD removed, excited to tell the women who had supported me for years in preventing unwanted pregnancy, "You know how you're called *Planned* Parenthood? I'm planning that shit."

As soon as we started trying to conceive, I began talking to my baby, recording videos he or she would see someday. Imagining how embarrassed they'd be was part of the fun. We took a video just after our first attempt, my butt propped on a pillow. I spoke to the camera, leaving a message for my future baby: "Hope you exist soon!" After years of having my life documented by judgmental lenses without my consent, holding the camera to my own intimate moments, creating these silly videos just for our own nascent family, was empowering.

That positive pregnancy test wasn't a shock so much as a joyous inevitability. And because Chris and I are both eager planners, we started putting the baby room together right away, painting a bright and whimsical mural on the wall, picking out our crib and changing table. It had only been a few weeks! We heard all the wisdom about not telling people until a few months in, but Mother's Day was around the corner, and it seemed like the perfect opportunity to surprise our moms. I cross-stitched an artful image of a fetus and made little framed gifts for all the moms in our lives, my mom and stepmom and Chris's mom. And of course, they squealed with excitement.

Unable to join me because of COVID protocols, Chris stood out in the hallway by the elevators and Zoomed into the first ultrasound appointment. I really hoped he'd be able to hear the heartbeat through the phone. Despite the awkwardness of COVID, and the annoyance of being separated from my husband, I was glowing as I walked into that eight-week ultrasound. After all the things that had gone wrong in my life, finally, something was going right.

I had my feet in the stirrups and a wand probing around inside me when the technician asked, "When was your last period? Are you sure about the timing?" She couldn't hear a heartbeat. "It's looking like you're early," she said. "Maybe you counted wrong."

The fetus was measuring six weeks, not eight. So they scheduled me to come back in a week to try again. Chris put a lot of faith in the idea that we probably just miscounted, but I had the dark, clawing feeling that something was wrong... and that the technician already knew and didn't want to tell me.

I called up my sister, Deanna, who had gone through some fertility struggles herself, and when I told her how the appointment went, she just said, "Oh." She wouldn't say anything more, but suggested we talk again after my next appointment. I began to feel like I'd stumbled onto some secret society that no one would even admit existed. It made me angry, and as that week stretched on endlessly, I felt more and more certain that the medical professionals, and even my sister, were keeping information from me until *they* decided it was my time to know. I'd had more transparency about my potential fate when I was on trial; my lawyers always gave it to me straight.

When we returned to that ultrasound room, the fetus hadn't grown, and they still couldn't find a heartbeat. How was I supposed to make sense of that news? How could my body not realize the fetus was dead? I'd never heard of a missed miscarriage. I thought a miscarriage would be obvious, that I'd start bleeding. Instead, I was pregnant with a baby that had just stopped... becoming. I didn't cry at this news; I was numb. "Your body will probably figure it out sooner or later," the doctor said, "but it could take weeks." *Weeks?* The idea was unbearable to me, so she prescribed me some pills to induce my body to purge the contents of my womb.

We stopped at the pharmacy, and I walked up to the counter in a daze. When I handed my prescription to the pharmacist, she read it, looked at me, and said, "I'm sorry." I muffled an unexpected sob and muttered, "Thanks," my verbal abilities suddenly reduced to single-word sentences. "Have you ever done this before?" she asked. I shook my head no. As she walked me through the process, I nodded silently along.

Back in the car, I said nothing to Chris. He held my hand as we drove. Before heading home, we stopped by my mom's house, finding her in the backyard chatting with Chris's mom, who'd stopped by to return some Tupperware. I'd given them those cute fetus cross-stitches on Mother's Day, revealing our pregnancy very early despite knowing this could happen, but Chris and I had figured it was okay to tell the people we were comfortable grieving with if something bad should happen. And a part of me wanted to do just that when my ever-bubbly mom said, "How'd it go?!" Both of our moms were smiling at me, but all I could do was shake my head. Then Chris's mom said, "Oh," tears filling her eyes. I could tell they both wanted to hug me, but I couldn't bear to be there a second longer. I felt so stupid, not for telling them, but for thinking that I was due a win here, that after everything that had gone wrong, that after all the ways that Dr. Giuliano Mignini and others had harmed me, I deserved for this most important thing to go exactly right. Who was I kidding? I was destined to suffer. I just turned and left, and Chris followed me back to the car.

I had already been talking to my belly. We'd settled on names for a boy and a girl, and I was using those names in my head. Each week, I'd been looking at the pregnancy app—*She's as big as a kiwi and her skin is forming*. But as we pulled into the driveway, that ultrasound image of a lifeless fetus stuck in my head, I just kept telling myself: *That wasn't my baby. It never had a name.*

I took the pills and lay on the bed waiting for something to happen. An hour passed, and the pain came on suddenly—sharp abdominal cramps like I'd never felt before. I was shaking and crumpled. Chris tried to cuddle me to keep me warm, and eventually he convinced me to take the pain medication the doctor prescribed, which I had resisted. It kicked in thirty minutes later, and the shaking stopped. But the physical pain isn't what stays with me from this experience. It was those long, recurrent moments of silence in the bathroom over the next two days as I birthed wads of blood. The biggest clump was about the size of a plum. And every time a new clump sloughed out of me, I looked in the toilet, wondering, *Is that my baby? Is that it?*

I felt like my own body had betrayed me. Then my anxiety kicked in and I started to wonder: *Is this just the beginning? Do I have bad eggs? Am I too old? Did the trauma of prison—the malnourishment, the weight loss, the lack of proper medical care—somehow affect my fertility?*

Giuliano was still writing me, sending multiple letters for every one I returned, and eventually he said something that made my skin prickle: "Excuse me if I say so, but I know I can speak openly with you. Have you ever thought about becoming a mother? It would be wonderful to know that there is a little 'Amanda' in the world besides the one so dear to me."

Una Vita in Gioco

WITHOUT THE PREOCCUPATION OF BEING pregnant, and looking for distractions, I found a fuzzy copy of that Italian detective film that Giuliano wanted me to watch on YouTube. The film follows Inspector Maigret after he arrests and convicts a man named Heurtin of a double homicide. Heurtin is sentenced to death. But Maigret is doubtful about Heurtin's guilt and fears he may have prosecuted the wrong person. So he arranges with a judge to let the condemned man escape. Maigret then trails Heurtin to see whom he interacts with, finally uncovering the evidence he needs to arrest the true killer, a man named Radek, and set Heurtin free.

Again, I was shocked. This story represented the torment Mignini felt about the case that defined his career and unjustly derailed my life? I honestly couldn't bring myself to believe it.

Mignini clearly identified with Maigret. There is even an uncanny resemblance. They are both large men who dominate space and command respect, who dress simply but professionally. They both smoke pipes. They are both driven by a moral compass that occasionally gets them in trouble with by-the-book authorities. Both see themselves as detectives in the spirit of Sherlock Holmes, solving cases through the meticulous collection and astute examination of circumstantial evidence. A leads to B, B leads to C, a cascade of logical deductions that inevitably reveals the truth.

But if Mignini saw himself as Maigret, did he see me as Heurtin, the wrongly accused, or Radek, the actual murderer?

Heurtin, the innocent man, is on death row not due to any obvious mistake on the part of Maigret, who investigated him, or the judge who presided over his trial. The whole process was by the book, and for that reason, the judge thinks Maigret is crazy to feel plagued by doubt and accuses him of being irrationally "in love with the idea of Heurtin's innocence." But, Maigret admits to himself, some aspects of the case remain clouded, some facts don't seem to fit, some evidence may have only "imagined significance." And to uncover all the facts and their true significance, he must employ unconventional methods.

It's a classic example of the Italian concept of dietrologia—that hidden realities lie under the surface, that the official explanation is rarely the full truth, that things are more than what they seem. Enter Radek, the young foreigner whose behavior is undeniably suspicious, but whose involvement in the murders remains tantalizingly obscure. The drama of *Una Vita in Gioco* unfolds through a cat-and-mouse game between Maigret and Radek.

One scene in particular took my breath away. Maigret is sitting in the back of a taxi reflecting:

Quando si sente di girare intorno una soluzione, e non si può afferrarla, si è veramente tentato di inventare, di costruire un colpevole. Ma nel momento in cui si riaprono gli occhi ai dati reali, diventano dati erronei.

In English:

When you feel an answer swirling around, and you can't grasp it, you're truly tempted to invent one, to create a culprit. But in the moment that you open your eyes to the real facts, they become erroneous.

Was this Mignini's indirect and veiled attempt at acknowledging his mistakes, the closest to a mea culpa I'd ever receive?

I took a month to process all this before replying. I began by writing about my family, my cats, the difficulties of isolation in the pandemic, and how not being able to celebrate holidays with my family reminded me of the loneliness of prison. I didn't mention the miscarriage. And I avoided digging into the trial. I told him I was moved by his affectionate attitude, and that "it makes me feel like the long nightmare is beginning to fade." Finally, I quoted to him the line from Maigret musing in the back of the taxicab, hoping he would elaborate.

He had given me *Una Vita in Gioco* as a window into his thoughts and torment around the case. I offered him a window into mine, urging him to watch an episode of *Star Trek: The Next Generation* called "Darmok." In the episode, Captain Picard struggles to develop a connection with a seemingly hostile alien captain whose language he can't speak. But it is in fact the "enemy" captain who puts them both into a situation where they must face a common threat, an invisible beast on a rocky planet, which leads to their eventual cooperation and mutual understanding.

If the two of us had a shared enemy, it was the false narrative exploited and promulgated by the media. As for the case, I limited myself to saying, "I think humans are less rational than we think we are. I think we are driven by instincts, and our extraordinary reasoning skills are used mostly to find reasons to justify our already predetermined beliefs, and not to challenge them."

I signed off, "A hug, Amanda," to the man who'd locked me in a prison cell for four years and would have seen me rot in Capanne for the rest of my life if he'd had his way.

In his next letter, he told me how moved he was by the friendship I offered him and how he, his wife, their four daughters, and his kitten, Guli, were surviving the pandemic. He brought up Maigret again, saying that he was drawn to the character for his intellectual honesty, and that Maigret had, in the end, become convinced that things were not as he had once thought.

I felt like Giuliano was dancing around the word "sorry," but that he couldn't bring himself to admit fault. I wasn't urging him to apologize, mostly because I knew that I couldn't force him to atone. It was up to him. All I could do was make an effort to see him and to create a space for an honest dialogue. "I acted in full honesty, believe me," he wrote. "I may have been wrong, of course, in whole or in part. Besides, I didn't know you. Today I know you. And I must say that, day after day, I am struck by your qualities."

He told me that Maigret followed his intuition, and that this was something he also trusted in himself. "I generally know immediately if a person is honest or not, good or bad, sincere or disingenuous. I trust my first impression, and especially body language." Of course, what he saw as a virtue, I saw as a critical flaw.

His gut instinct had led him to suspect me, and that instinct had been wrong. Perhaps it was due to cultural differences, conspiratorial thinking, or the many lost-in-translation moments that led him and the police to misinterpret my behavior and testimony in the early days of the investigation. Whatever the case, he went searching for evidence to confirm his first impression, a classic example of confirmation bias.

He found nothing but unreliable, circumstantial fluff. My lawyers had always argued that zero plus zero plus zero still equals zero. But for Giuliano, the evidence never seemed to contradict his early intuition. I realized that talking about the evidence would never alter that. He hadn't arrived at his conclusions through logic, so logic wouldn't persuade him out of them. Instead, my act of reaching out in a spirit of friendship had touched him emotionally, and *that* had begun to shift his intuitions.

Maigret had come to believe in Heurtin's innocence by studying the man, not the evidence. And so, even though Heurtin was present at the crime scene at the time of the murder, Maigret asked himself, "Could this man have committed this crime? Was he capable of it?"

As the pandemic stretched on, I learned that Giuliano's father had worked on behalf of prisoners. The women's prison was across the street from the house Giuliano was born in, and as a child, he could see from his living room into the courtyard where the female inmates were allowed yard time. Giuliano's father died in a car accident when he was only four years old, and his mother struggled to care for the family. The inmates, who had grown so attached to his father, sent all their sympathies to her. Those inmates who were mothers themselves even entrusted their children to her care, and young Giuliano grew up celebrating his birthday with the inmates' children.

I had not expected him to have such a deep connection with the humanity of the incarcerated, and it was difficult to square this with the fact that he'd tried to send me to a place like that for the rest of my life, knowing the very real suffering that prisoners endure. I could only conclude that this meant that, however wrong he was, he really, truly believed, as he was prosecuting me, that I was a dangerous person who belongs in prison.

He went on about his cats, and told me that he, too, likes the rain, and prefers the quiet intimacy of foggy and snowy days. I can't overstate how much these letters, on both sides, were filled with things like this: the low-stakes and banal yet very real stuff of actual friendships. Trading these pleasantries and getting to know each other on this level was as surreal as the things he was saying to me about the case and his "mistakes could have been made" take on my innocence.

His repeated refrain was that he didn't know me then, but he knew me now, "thanks to that outstretched hand of your first letter." But for me, that raised the inescapable question: why didn't he care to know me back then, when he was spouting baseless theories about me and my motives? His lack of acknowledgment of that dissonance was staggering.

As frustrating as this was, it was outweighed by the genuine desire for connection and reconciliation. Talking with him was a bit like going thrift-shopping. If you searched the racks at Goodwill looking for a very particular item—like a yellow sundress—you were bound to be disappointed. Success in thrifting comes from being open to finding something beautiful that you didn't know you were looking for—like a mushroom-shaped lamp. What I was finding was a man so unlike the dogged antagonist I'd encountered in the courtroom. "I would like the people of Seattle to know me for who I am after the hostility they showed me at the time of the trial," he wrote. And, "Amanda is an auspicious name. Do not forget. It is a good name. It means lovable. It is a challenging name." I think by "challenging" he meant that it was a lofty ideal to live up to. If so, he wasn't wrong. My mom's early encouragement to be kind above all else positioned me well to live up to my name, and yet so many millions of people still thought I was a monster not only unworthy of love but deserving of hatred.

"I never felt above judgment," I wrote him. "That's why I'd looked to you during the trial, not with hatred or anger, but with sadness. I thought you hated me, and I didn't know why...I just wanted to be judged for who I really am."

In early December of 2020, he sent me a photo of a rainbow that appeared in front of the terrace of his house, offering it as a sign of hope. The next day, Rudy Guede was released from prison.

Rudy Goes Free

ON DECEMBER 6, 2020, THE *New York Post* headline read, "Man Who Killed Amanda Knox's Roommate Freed on Community Service." It didn't name Meredith, the victim of the crime, and it didn't name Rudy Guede, the man who killed her. As always, it named the one person who should have been a footnote: me. As much as I had begun to accept that it was my fate to bear the infamy of Meredith's murder, the way this news was framed still got to me, and I felt anger leaping off me in sparks.

Rudy Guede was born in the Ivory Coast. He was taken to Italy by his father at age five and later abandoned. He grew up in a series of foster homes, using his charm to get by, until he was eventually adopted by a wealthy Perugian family. That family disowned him when he was a teenager after he repeatedly stole from them. By the age of twenty-one, he was spiraling out of control. The night Guede raped and killed Meredith was the climax of a month-long burglary spree. Just days before the murder, he was caught in Milan burglarizing a nursery school and was found carrying a knife. After he killed Meredith, he fled Italy for Germany. The evidence of Guede's guilt was overwhelming, as was the lack of evidence implicating any other suspect. And though he initially said to a confidant, unaware that police were listening, that I had nothing to do with the crime, he soon changed his story. Taking his cue from the prosecution and media, he took every opportunity to accuse me, and I assumed he would continue to do so upon his release. Whatever scrap of naïveté I had left was barely able to imagine that Guede might, in freedom, finally acknowledge his crimes.

Had they occurred in the United States, and had Guede been charged, convicted, and sentenced for aggravated rape and second degree murder, as he should have been, his sentence would likely have been life without parole, which is our federal mandatory minimum. In Italy, Guede was charged, convicted, and sentenced for sexual assault and conspiracy to commit murder. His sentence, after it was reduced on appeal, was sixteen years. After ten, he was allowed day release. Now, after thirteen years, he could serve out the remainder of his sentence in freedom. And, of course, Guede's name was not the one associated with his crimes.

I sat with my anger all through that day, trying to stay off social media, ignoring the flood of media requests for comment. After journaling and meditating and talking with Chris, I found some clarity. I was not upset that Rudy Guede was free. I was not even upset that the journalists who continued to vilify me were humanizing him, quoting his lawyers, who claimed he was "calm and socially well-integrated." I wasn't upset that he was being given a second chance. I believe, after all, that everyone is more than the worst thing they've ever done. Even Rudy Guede deserved a second chance. But I *was* upset.

So many people were harmed by Guede's actions. He created a constellation of pain that enveloped Meredith's family, me, Raffaele, our families, and the many who fought to clear our names. I didn't need to know what was going through his mind that night, but I did want to know if he cared now, if he cared about what he did to Meredith, what he did to me.

Free

With the news of his release, people kept asking me, "What should his punishment have been?" I thought of my fellow exonerees. They are disproportionately men of color, like Guede. My friend Juan Rivera was sentenced to life in prison for a rape and murder he didn't commit. He served twenty years before his exoneration. My friend Greg Mingo was sentenced to life in prison for a murder he didn't commit. He served forty years before he was granted clemency. The average amount of time wrongly convicted people serve in the United States before being exonerated is fourteen years, longer than Guede had spent in prison for actually raping and killing someone. Should he have gotten a life sentence? I had thought a lot about punishment and sentencing over the years, and had seen that the guilty and innocent alike are given draconian sentences to be served in places that do not rehabilitate them. Thinking about such things always brought me back to the Golden Rule: "Do unto others as you would have them do unto you." That ethic of reciprocity occurs in nearly every major religion. Confucius put it this way: "What you do not wish for yourself, do not do to others." I prefer to think of it in terms of giving people expectations to live up to. If you treat them as bad as you think they are, they will rarely surprise you, but if you treat them as good as you hope they can be, you set them up for personal growth. That had been my tactic with Giuliano, and he was definitely surprising me. It was incredibly difficult to apply that thinking to the man who'd killed my friend and blamed me for it, but I tried.

Rather than speak to the media, I wrote an essay conveying my thoughts. Here is how it ended:

> I would not wish an unreasonably harsh sentence on anyone. I would wish them only true rehabilitation. Guede's lawyers say he's well along that path. Maybe so. But I do know one thing:

so long as he refuses to admit his crimes, to show true regret, I will continue to unjustly bear his infamy, be held accountable for the Kerchers' grief, be shamed for not showing remorse for Guede's crime. He could end all that in a second. I doubt he ever will, but the day he does, I will celebrate his rehabilitation and wish him the best on a new and honest chapter of his life.

I shared my essay with Giuliano, and he replied on Christmas Eve. He, too, lamented Guede's light sentence, but he noted that it was Guede's legal right to request a fast-track trial. He did not approve of the law that allowed this process, he said, which resulted in reduced sentences for serious crimes, but he had to respect Italian law, even if he disagreed with it.

He wished me a merry Christmas and happy New Year.

An Uncertain Miracle

THE NEWS OF RUDY'S RELEASE pushed our correspondence back into the weeds of the trial. I found myself frustrated at how much Giuliano clung to the official legal narrative and how much he defended his actions. "What I did as a prosecutor is over and no one can take it back," he wrote. "At the same time, the affection that has been born in us cannot be erased. You ask what I would do today if the trial was still pending. I could not help but abstain because of the friendship that has arisen between us."

It was maddening! He would say something shocking, but go on to say, "You cannot think that twenty or more judges found you guilty without a reason, based on nothing. They may have been wrong, of course, but you cannot try a person in the absence of evidence!"

That was, of course, exactly what he'd done. But he also recognized how much it pained me to talk about the trial, and he said he didn't want me to suffer. "My task is not easy today. It's like taking a thorn out of your foot," he wrote.

I had to remind myself that the better I understood his beliefs, and how he'd arrived at them, the better I would understand why this injustice had befallen me, and the less these discussions would pain me. But until we could meet in person, I agreed with him that it was best not to dig too far into our disagreements about the case.

We were over a year into the pandemic now, my wedding anniversary came and went, as did Easter, each with a message of warm wishes from Giuliano. He informed me he was writing a book about the case, and that in it he would try to "reveal the real Amanda." I was feeling optimistic but uncertain about our relationship, which was exactly how I felt about my journey to motherhood.

After my miscarriage, I'd wanted to get back on track as soon as possible, but my period hadn't returned for months. When it did, it was one negative test after another. The first time around, Chris and I had been baby-making like bunny rabbits. Now, procreation became a second job. I started to feel like I was back on the track, sure, but my wheels were spinning on grease. We weren't getting anywhere, and I couldn't see what would change that. What was different this month than last month? Nothing. I was already doing everything they recommended. Why would I expect to succeed? Negative test, negative test, negative test.

I tried and failed to be at peace with each disappointment as my failure to conceive stretched into a seemingly endless future of failures. I was feeling alone again, even with Chris beside me. Then one day, on a whim, I reached out to my followers on social media and asked if they had stories about miscarriage or infertility they'd be willing to share. The responses flooded in.

I connected with dozens of women and men, and heard tales of miscarriage, in-vitro fertilization, polycystic ovarian syndrome, endometriosis, and adoption. I heard from couples who still hadn't given up trying after a decade, and from those who made the shattering decision to quit trying altogether after years of failure.

I was so moved by all this vulnerability that I made a miniseries about infertility on my podcast *Labyrinths*, where Chris and I tell stories about the many ways we can be lost and how we can find our way again. Against my will, I'd been inducted into another secret society of women—those who know what it's like to lose a pregnancy. I had gone through that ancient and private rite of shedding what could have been a baby. I realized, for the thousandth time—as I had when I first attended the Innocence Network Conference—that being alone in pain was a choice I'd made, one that society had encouraged me in—but it had been my choice nonetheless. And I could choose to share my grief with others, with total strangers even, to lift the burden of their trauma as they lifted mine. So often, we don't open ourselves this way because it seems like there's nothing we can do to solve someone else's private pain, but the very act of opening ourselves holds up a mirror and conveys: *you are not alone.*

That didn't mean I was ready to share myself this way with Giuliano. Being that vulnerable with strangers, and with listeners of my podcast, was one thing. With Giuliano, I already felt vulnerable just talking about my cats.

Eventually, I did get pregnant again, but after that first miscarriage, I celebrated much more tentatively—it wouldn't be real until I could hear a baby crying. Meanwhile, I don't know if every pregnant woman goes through this, but sometime around the end of my second trimester, I realized I had passed the point of no return, where the baby in my womb wouldn't fit through any of the holes in my body as I, up to that point, understood them. Supposedly women have been giving birth to babies through their vaginas since the dawn of humanity, but...*how?* Like, *really?* There was no way. *There was no freaking way.* All I could imagine was being split in half, cracked open like a gruesome egg. How could I possibly survive?

I spent the final months of my pregnancy convinced that I would die in childbirth. Or rather, I intellectually understood that I likely wouldn't die, given the blessings of modern medicine, but my body wasn't convinced. As I became more and more bloated, as the baby just kept getting unnervingly bigger and bigger, I wavered between giddy anticipation and morbid dread. It was not unlike waiting for a verdict.

It wasn't just my fear of dying in childbirth that made me anxious. After the emotional upheaval of having our wedding crashed and criticized by the tabloids, Chris and I were paranoid about keeping our pregnancy a secret. We couldn't bear the thought that pictures of my pregnant belly, and eventually our baby, might be used as a ploy to further vilify me. I struggled, more than ever, with the feeling of being trapped in the shadow of the worst thing that had ever happened to me. The last thing I wanted was for my future baby to be trapped in that shadow as well, and until we figured out how to build a life and raise her in such a way that she wouldn't feel that burden, we did everything we could to hide the fact of her impending existence, to protect her. That's what we told ourselves, but I was also having difficulty accepting that I deserved the kind of heart-exploding joy a child would bring. Life had conditioned me for disappointment.

I was trying to shake that conditioning by reframing what my past meant to me through my ongoing dialogue with Giuliano. I told him how my sister Deanna had recently given birth to a son. "I am happy for Deanna," he wrote. "I have very good memories of her. Even during the trial she was always kind to me." He went on to share his own good news, that his niece had given birth to a baby girl named after his own mother. "When I found out, I was very emotional," he wrote, "because it will be like filling the void left by my mother on April 23, 2012. The funeral was conducted by Don Saulo in the Santo Spirito Church where I was baptized many years ago." I intuited that it would mean a lot to Giuliano to know that I was pregnant, but I still couldn't bring myself to share that with him, because I couldn't bear to think of how it would feel to write to him if I miscarried again. *It's not real until I hear the baby cry.* Giuliano and I were getting close, but not *that* close.

As my belly expanded, I hesitated to go out in public. I was visiting my mom one day when her neighbors brought over a hand-knit blanket as a gift. We awkwardly thanked them and then shrank away, feeling less grateful than paranoid. *Who had told them?!* Had they just assumed, seeing me walk into my mom's house? They didn't know this was a secret. What if they told people? The rites of passage of many modern mothers—pregnancy glamor shots and Facebook announcements—were yet another small part of life that I couldn't take part in. Instead, I was constantly badgering bewildered family members not to post pictures of me to social media and not to tell even their closest friends the good news. If the tabloids found out, I knew I'd be hounded—paparazzi had already staked out my house once during the pandemic—and worse, I knew this joyous moment would be used to smear me: *You know who will never get to have children? Meredith.*

Despite all this, I was in a good mood in the final week. The day after my birthday, I put on a sundress, and Chris and I hopped on the ferry to head to my mom's house in West Seattle. It was a gorgeous day, and I was finally feeling that pregnant lady glow. I was staring out at the Puget Sound when, out of nowhere, my underwear was soaked. At first I thought I had peed myself. In a stall in the bathroom, I took off my underwear and smelled them to be sure. *No, not urine. But then, what?* There was no gush, as if my water had broken. I wasn't feeling contractions. Instead, I just felt...uneasy. *Was everything okay? What new thing might be going horribly wrong?*

Lying on the couch at Mom's house, I called my OB-GYN and we decided that, even though my water hadn't broken and I wasn't yet showing signs of labor, I shouldn't get back on a ferry to head home.

Instead, I should get comfortable and, in all likelihood, labor would come along within the next twenty-four hours.

I spent the day second-guessing myself, feeling embarrassed and uncertain. I didn't know what labor should feel like. Everyone told me that, like having your first orgasm, when you go into labor, you *know*. My water never broke, but suddenly, at eleven p.m., I was struck with abdominal cramps that rolled over me like waves. They were so painful, I struggled to breathe, and I emerged after the peak of each contraction gasping for breath. Yeah, I *knew*.

Poor Chris... all he could do was help me count the intervals. On the way to the hospital, he tried to crack jokes to distract me. I quickly informed him to shut the fuck up and just get me where I needed to go. At the hospital I was cared for by an extremely kind and competent nurse who eased me into positions that allowed me to brace for the pain and make way for the baby to come more easily. Soon enough, my mom arrived to provide emotional support.

Eureka Muse was born after only five pushes, six and a half hours after my contractions began. My first words to her, as the doctor laid her on my chest, were, "I'm sorry." She was screaming, and I already felt the impulse to soothe her, and the existential crisis of not being able to take her pain and put it onto myself. But I was so, so happy to see her. She was absolutely perfect.

Or was she? As I held Eureka against my chest, cooing at her, as the doctor pulled the placenta from my body and stitched up my vaginal tearing, Chris reached over and pointed to a patch of skin on Eureka's hand that was raised and white. "What is that?" he asked the nurse.

"Just the vernix. It will wipe off," she replied.

"It doesn't look like it will wipe off..." Chris insisted.

I felt a flash of annoyance. Why was Chris already finding flaws in our child? "It's nothing," I said.

"She's perfect," Mom echoed.

Chris demurred and went back to stroking my hair. But after we were moved to a postpartum recovery room, he took a closer look and again drew attention to the patch of raised, discolored skin.

"It's probably just a birthmark," I said.

But when the nurse took a look, she said, with a curiosity that was hard to place tonally, "Huh, I've never seen a mark like that. And look, it trails up her arm, too."

Sure enough, an archipelago of small, raised, discolored patches of skin trailed up Eureka's arm, and as we looked more closely, we saw further patches running down her torso and leg. When the doctor came in to examine her, Chris brought it up right away. I felt embarrassed. *My hypochondriac husband...* But the doctor paused when she took a closer look. "I need to get back to you on that..." was all she said.

My heart sank as she left the room. I looked down at my little girl, who was already doing so well. She latched onto my breast easily. She was sleeping peacefully. She only complained when nurses came in to poke her and draw blood. "She's so good..." I kept repeating aloud, utterly in awe. It was inconceivable to me that something could possibly be wrong with her.

When the doctor returned, she was calm but solemn. "The distribution of the patches on Eureka's skin follows what's called the lines of Blaschko," she explained. That is, the usually invisible pattern of how the skin develops across the fetus as it grows in the womb. "This suggests a genetic mutation and corresponding conditions." She wrote out the name of the likely condition on a white board near the bed: *Incontinentia pigmenti*.

"What is that?" I asked.

"It's a genetic disorder that affects the skin, hair, teeth, nails, and central nervous system," she explained.

"But we tested for genetic disorders..."

"Not for this one, unfortunately. It's exceptionally rare."

Why? Why couldn't I just have this moment of joy, cradling my daughter? Why couldn't she be perfect? I felt like I'd just come through a near-death experience intact. I needed quiet; I needed to just be present with my daughter. Instead, I was hearing the doctor explain the symptoms of incontinentia pigmenti in more detail, and I struggled to process the catalog of horrors: cerebral atrophy, severe intellectual disability, lifelong seizures, detached retinas, blindness, scoliosis, hypodontia (i.e., nightmare teeth). Eureka could have parts of her brain missing. Heart issues, kidney issues. Not to mention the raised, discolored patches of skin, which would eventually harden into aggravating, wart-like blisters... "We need to schedule an MRI and EEG immediately," the doctor explained, "before you can leave the hospital."

The next two days were a daze. We never left the postpartum room, and were visited by a parade of specialists who sat across from us and answered our endless stream of questions. Between visits, Chris dived deep, learning as much as he could about incontinentia pigmenti. It was rare, one in a million. It was a de novo mutation, which meant it didn't pass down from parent to child, but just occurred randomly. This was hardly reassuring, because even if I hadn't passed on the mutation, I felt stricken, responsible for passing on my bad luck. The skin lesions were the most obvious and common symptom among afflicted children, while the other associated problems with the brain, eyes, and other organs ranged from one in three to one in six. We kept thinking, *Does she have all her brain? Roll the dice. Will she be afflicted with seizures? Roll the dice.* I cradled Eureka, overwhelmed with both love and despair. This was not what I imagined parenthood would be like. Sure, we always knew there was risk in bringing a new life into being, but we had been so careful. We had taken every test, asked every question.

And now what? I saw our future unravel before my eyes. Our daughter would be a vegetable. Would one of us have to become a full-time nurse for our child? How could we afford that? Would we get help from the state? We would be caring for her basic needs our entire life... and then what? What would happen to her when we were gone? Would she even have a life worth living?

When we dared voice these thoughts aloud, I felt Chris dissociating, pulling away emotionally. I knew what he was thinking. I was thinking it, too. *Had our baby just ruined our lives?* She wasn't even a day old, but *would it have been better if she had never been born?* And that shameful, immature, and recurring thought: *Didn't I* deserve *a healthy baby? Hadn't I already been through enough?*

And yet, holding her, gazing at her, I still felt utter loyalty and love. There was nothing more important than her. Like my mom before me, I would be there for her no matter what. And so would my family. I'd been through enough crises to know that I had to fight through any instinct to isolate, that my loved ones would help me bear the weight of this pain. Chris was sharing constant updates over a text chain with our families. That had to be enough, because this was a problem we couldn't solve on our own, and one that may not even have a solution.

For two days, the doctors put Eureka through test after test. They took her from me and laid her in the cold metal womb of the MRI machine. They attached dozens of wires to her scalp and scanned her brainwaves. She barely put up a fuss. At the end of it, before they released us from the hospital, we knew at the very least that her brain was intact. But that's about it.

We returned home in limbo. And those first few months were a little like my first few months in prison. We were unsure of what was wrong and what that would mean for us. I wept while breastfeeding her. Chris held her and fretted that every twitch in her sleep was a seizure. We followed up with every kind of specialist—neurologist, ophthalmologist, cardiologist, dermatologist, geneticist...hoping for the best and fearing the worst. Slowly we gained pieces of reassurance: she wasn't missing any brain matter; her retinas remained attached; her heart, kidneys, and skeleton were normal; her lesions even subsided partially.

Meanwhile, Chris and I were debating how and when to reveal the birth of our daughter to the world. We couldn't keep her a secret forever. And we knew it was impossible to stop the birth of my first child from becoming a tabloid story. I had accepted that. We decided that, rather than let the tabloids be the only voice framing this personal development in relation to the long saga preceding it, at the very least, we would tell our own story on our podcast.

As we polished up those podcast episodes, I found myself thinking about Giuliano. I realized that though I had chosen to let this man into my life, a choice that affected me and Chris mostly, I would soon have to make a decision about whether to let him into the life of my child, and I could feel the decision coalescing.

A reporter named Jessica Bennett from the *New York Times* had reached out wanting to write a feature profile piece exploring the complicated ways that I remained trapped in a story despite my acquittal. I was glad to have the opportunity to show the world how long the shadow of wrongful conviction is, that life doesn't just revert to normal once they let you out of prison. That profile would come out in the fall, at the same time as our podcast series about my pregnancy. The world would soon know I'd given birth to a daughter. I couldn't say why exactly, but I knew that I should share that news with Giuliano first. Perhaps I was curious to see how he would react. Three weeks after Eureka's birth, and months before the podcast or the *New York Times* profile was published, I sent him a photo of me in the postpartum room, with Eureka bundled and nuzzled into my arm. I told him she was a secret and asked him to keep my confidence. I hadn't even given a photo like that to the *Times*.

Giuliano was overjoyed. "Finally, I see you happy without that shadow that you carry around," he wrote, "and I know that I have contributed to your happiness. What splendor! It is a sign of affection to allow a person to participate in your most intimate world," he wrote. "And I'm happy to keep this little girl's face a secret. I'll keep it to myself. This is your most effective 'medicine.'"

It was nice that he saw my joy, but also disappointing that he couldn't see that I was still under the shadow of what he'd done to me, that no amount of joy could simply erase that. And of course, he didn't know about the new shadow that had fallen over me with Eureka's diagnosis.

A few months later, the geneticist delivered some good news: Eureka tested negative for the dreaded incontinentia pigmenti. The bad news: they had no idea *what* Eureka's genetic mutation was, or what kind of symptoms she might exhibit in the future. It certainly wasn't nothing. And as it appeared along the lines of Blaschko, it was only similar to a few known conditions like incontinentia pigmenti and epidermal nevus. It might be merely a birthmark-like skin lesion for the rest of her life, or it could develop into something far worse.

Back in prison, I had to learn to accept uncertainty as a fundamental principle of my existence. Now, I was having to accept that all over again, but this time for my daughter, for my family. Once again, I felt unnervingly grateful for my experience in Perugia. And I used this to help Chris, my mom, and the rest of my family sit with the uncertainty as well.

Chris and I thought of creative ways to help Eureka frame her pathology in positive terms. She's part dragon! The raised patches on her arm were dragon scales. Who knew what magical powers she might develop one day? The part of me forever in search of silver linings saw this condition as a potentially helpful corrective for Eureka, because aside from this small patch of rough and discolored skin on her hand, she was absurdly beautiful. I could already tell she had the kind of beauty that would be dangerous for her own sense of self, and I hoped those dragon scales would help remind her not to place too high a value on her physical appearance. If those skin lesions were the extent of her condition, Chris and I felt completely equipped to guide her as she developed her self-image. If more serious problems developed later...we'd face them together as a family. Whatever came her way, we would be there for her. Just as my family had been for me.

Life Isn't Fair

DURING THOSE FIRST MONTHS TENDING to my potentially severely disabled but increasingly healthy and normal newborn, my correspondence with Giuliano slowed, but he made a point to reach out on the anniversary of my release, October 4. "For me, at the time," he wrote, "it was a defeat, but today I'm happy for you. A kiss to the baby and a hug for you."

"Every year, this is a day of reflection for me," I wrote back. "I recognize the good fortune of being not only free, but also alive. Now that I'm a mom, I know a new layer of pain—the pain of Meredith's mother and my mother."

My mom had given me such a happy childhood, so free of pain, that a few weeks into my imprisonment, after screaming repeatedly in the quiet of my own mind: *Why? Why is this happening to me?* I thought, *Is this my balance coming due? Having forgotten me for years, was misfortune now making up for lost time by subjecting me to twenty years' worth of pain in a matter of weeks?* This thought came long before I was convicted and sentenced to twenty-six years.

I wanted my daughter to understand that life wasn't fair, but also, that no one deserved the kind of trauma I went through, nor the fate that befell Meredith and what her family faced in the aftermath. No one deserves cancer, either, or to have their son or daughter die in an earthquake. We don't deserve the traumas we inevitably face, but we don't deserve the opposite, either—a life free from pain. Nothing is guaranteed. And because we don't deserve the tragedies or joys we face, I think that allows us to view compassion as something we *do* deserve. We're all struggling against the randomness of life. None of us choose our circumstances, our genetics, our talents and flaws. So let's cut one another some slack. That's something my mom taught me that helped me survive prison and helped me to see the humanity in my fellow inmates, to see the humanity of my prosecutor.

As I continued trading letters with Giuliano, I wondered how Eureka would learn about my past. I worried that, despite my best efforts, she would end up living in the shadow of my wrongful conviction, and that the media content mill that objectified me would objectify her. I wanted her to feel free in spite of my deep fear for her, fear shaped by my own trauma. I knew pain would manifest in her life—it does for all of us—but I hoped that when it did, she would not have to fight for her freedom, that freedom would be as natural as air. And as my own mother hoped for me: I wanted her to be kind, to herself and others, especially when life is unfair. I wanted her to grow up to be the sort of woman who would extend a hand to those who'd harmed her.

With the pandemic waning, I felt like it was time to set a date to finally meet face-to-face with Giuliano. I proposed June and said I would bring Eureka with me so he could meet her.

He agreed, and as the months passed, I continued sharing photos and telling him about my daughter, that she was learning to eat kiwi and peanut butter, that I read to her in Italian and German and was teaching her sign language. We talked about logistics into the spring of 2022, and Giuliano suggested something public, perhaps moderated by a journalist he trusted. I knew this meeting would be unlike any other in my life. I knew it would be rare, and tense, and that there would be value in it not just for me, but for anyone who felt like they were facing an adversary or a trauma from the past that was implacable and unshakable. If I could cross that precarious bridge, maybe others would follow. Most of us don't have prosecutors in our lives, but plenty of us have estranged relatives, exes, and unhealed wounds that throb when hearing a particular song or when passing by a certain restaurant. Giuliano clearly wanted our meeting to leave a mark beyond how it affected the two of us. I wanted that, too, but I also knew that the media could not be involved. Meeting in public, or having a journalist present, would fundamentally change the tenor of our interaction. I worried that Giuliano wouldn't be as fully transparent and honest with me if he was in front of an audience. And for that matter, I worried that I myself might freeze up in front of a stranger. I suggested that our meeting remain private—just me, Giuliano, and Don Saulo, who knew us both and who could help mediate if needed.

The moment I booked my ticket, I stepped back from the laptop and had to catch my breath. What had been hypothetical for so long had just become real. I was going back to Perugia to meet the man who'd imprisoned me. And I was bringing my daughter. I was hit with a flood of conflicting emotions. I was excited, scared, proud, and yet I also felt like I might be a little crazy. *What was wrong with me? Why did I care so much what Giuliano Mignini thought? Did I have Stockholm syndrome? Why couldn't I just let him go, let him be wrong on the other side of the world?* He couldn't hurt me anymore, unless I did what I was apparently doing, going out of my way to place my beating heart in his hand.

It didn't help that my entire family thought it was a bad idea, perhaps even a dangerous one. My stepdad sent me a video of a talk Giuliano had recently given in which he and a few other panelists, who were clearly invested in the idea of my guilt, called foul on the logic and legality of my 2015 acquittal. "They not only overstepped their boundaries talking about evidence, they even encroached on the jurisdiction of the courts of merits," he said. "It rather departs from the realm of lawfulness." There he was, saying things in public so different than what he wrote me in private, arguing that the Court of Cassation ruling that acquitted Raffaele and me was a miscarriage of justice, a violation of legal precedent that should never have occurred.

I started to panic. Could he really have been lying to me all this time? Which was the real Giuliano, the public prosecutor or the kindly uncle? My stepdad was convinced that Giuliano was luring me back to Italy to have me arrested again. I couldn't discount that possibility entirely. But none of my family had gotten to know him as I had. They'd been telling themselves stories about who he was and why he did what he did—*he's evil, he's corrupt, he's an idiot, and he's a coward*. They hadn't ever been able to truly see him, nor were they interested in hearing me relay what I had learned about him by listening. Listening to another person, truly hearing them, isn't just a kind thing to do; it's a great source of power, to heal and to harm. Those who know us best can hurt us the most. But they also know just where we hurt, and how they can salve our wounds. I knew this intuitively as a young adult, but I'd really learned how true it was in prison: *people will tell you exactly who they are if you just listen, if you stop telling yourself the story of who you want them to be.*

There was no turning back. I still didn't know why I was doing this, not exactly. I knew it felt important. It was scary, it was difficult, but knowing how hard it was, paradoxically, motivated me even more. Maybe I'm a masochist after all. As the meeting drew closer, I kept interrogating myself. *What did I hope to get out of this? An apology, a recognition of error, a commitment to defend my innocence?* All of those things seemed foolish and shallow. So why put myself in such a vulnerable position—psychologically, emotionally, even legally? What could I gain by taking such a risk?

As it turned out, I was asking myself the wrong questions.

Paradiso

Love, Which Moves the Sun and Other Stars

Preemptive Closure

I LIKE TO SOLVE PROBLEMS, check boxes, finalize plans, and as I counted the days until my meeting with Giuliano, I found myself spending a lot of time working through the logistical details: my travel itinerary, my packing list, emergency escape plans if my presence in Italy was discovered by the paparazzi. It was a lot easier to answer those questions than to address the Big Question at the center of it all: *Why sit down face-to-face with this man, my antagonist, who had, over the course of the pandemic, become... what? A friend? A confidant? An ally?* I couldn't find the right word to describe the relationship Giuliano and I had built. Perhaps it was not pushing that relationship to be any one thing that had allowed it to grow. But it had grown at a safe distance of six thousand miles, and I had no idea if it would crumble the moment I walked into a room with him. The anxiety felt familiar, that feeling of staring at the blank page in a notebook before you write a poem, or looking at an empty canvas, paintbrush in hand. I am not an accomplished poet or painter, but I've fumbled enough at both to know that art is impossible unless you're willing to start without a plan or coherent vision for what you hope to create. You just have to trust that something will arise from the effort.

I brought all of these anxieties with me to a speaking event, where

I'd been asked to tell my story to a private group of entrepreneurs and business leaders. I'd agreed a long while back, and I was somewhat regretting that as it came less than a month before my departure for Perugia.

I closed out my talk in a similar fashion to how I'd ended my speech in Modena, by talking about how I had learned to see Giuliano's humanity, and that I wanted to understand him beyond what he had done to me. Asking for confidentiality, I told the room I'd booked tickets and would soon be sitting down across from him. In a mess of tears, I said:

> *I don't know what's going to happen. I don't know what to expect. But the difference between me now and me then is that I can do something. Back then I was helpless. Now I have agency, and I can choose to do something that feels right. I'm trying to figure out the answer to a lot of really hard questions, in part for Eureka, because it's one thing for me to live in the shadow of the worst thing that I never did. It's another thing for her to. I know that up to this point, I haven't really accomplished much. But I have done the thing my mom asked of me as a kid. The thing that I can do is be kind. Because I can. I can be kind. No one can stop me! And so that's what I'm going to do, and that's the model I'm going to hold and share with my daughter.*

My host had advised me not to be shy about asking this group of successful entrepreneurs for help. I didn't really know what to ask for, but I said that if anyone had advice, I'd listen.

After the applause died down, a silver-haired gentleman with warm eyes stood for the first question. He said he was honored to accept my request for help, and that he was damn good at providing it.

Free

It was an emotional event, and Chris, Eureka, and I went home exhausted the next morning. I was ready to jump back into the logistical planning, answering those easy questions instead of figuring out the hard one, when that silver-haired man, David Zelman, followed up by email asking if he could visit me before my trip to Perugia. I was surprised, but we put it on the calendar. I had gathered that he was some kind of business coach, and I assumed he wanted to help Chris and me figure out how to make our writing and podcasting business actually profitable. But David wasn't interested in giving me career advice.

We picked him up from the airport, and before we even got back to my house, he said, "This is what I'm offering you: that by the end of this weekend, you can have closure about your prosecutor, about your trauma, about everything that happened to you in Italy. You don't need to go back to Perugia and meet him to achieve that. You can do it right now."

It was an audacious claim, and I was skeptical. Chris and I spent a weekend with David. We did a little hiking, we cooked dinner, but mostly we sat down and talked for hours and hours. David had gone through a personal transformation in his early life, became a psychotherapist, and wrote a book called *If I Can, You Can*. Now he spent his days coaching people, mostly business leaders, in personal development and well-being. I knew next to nothing about that world, nor about the thinkers who had influenced David's own practice, people like Werner Erhard and Byron Katie.

Erhard was an author and lecturer whose self-improvement method and training seminars came to prominence in the early 1970s. His insight arrived as an epiphany. As he told his biographer: "It was so stupidly, blindingly simple that I couldn't believe it. I saw that there were no hidden meanings, that everything was just the way that it is, and that I was already alright...I realized that I was not my emotions or thoughts. I was not my ideas, my intellect, my perceptions, my beliefs."

Byron Katie, whose self-improvement teachings gained prominence in the late eighties, also had an epiphany that allowed her to leave behind her depression and drug abuse. "I discovered that when I believed my thoughts, I suffered, but that when I didn't believe them, I didn't suffer, and that this is true for every human being. Freedom is as simple as that. I found that suffering is optional."

David had had his own epiphany, and he had his own way of phrasing these ideas. I didn't make the connection then, but what David was essentially offering me was the insight of Zen Buddhism. Erhard, in fact, had been close friends with Alan Watts, the rascally philosophical entertainer who popularized Zen Buddhism in the West in the 1960s. This was a growing area of interest for me. Chris and I had been using the Waking Up meditation app since the start of the pandemic, and much of that practice was about recognizing the character and qualities of consciousness prior to the occurrence of any thoughts or emotions, which arise and depart on their own. It is so much more than simply paying attention to the breath or "quieting the mind." The goal isn't to void your mind of thoughts, but to clearly observe how thoughts and emotions arise, without judgment, and to recognize that whatever you are is not synonymous with the buzzing swirl of anxieties, expectations, hopes, and fears that populate your mind.

David offered me two key insights over the course of that weekend. The first was that everyone has their own reality, and that you have to recognize how their reality differs from your own in order to act appropriately. If a child sees a snake and wants to touch it, you have to understand that in the child's reality, there is no danger. The danger exists in *your* perceived reality. Recognizing that pushes you to intervene instead of allowing the child to get bitten. As I prepared to sit down face-to-face with Giuliano, I would have to engage with his perceived reality. If I acted as if we were living in the same reality, with the same truths, we wouldn't get anywhere. That meant accepting that, in his mind, he had done nothing wrong.

Accepting did not mean condoning or embracing, but rather acknowledging. I had to allow his personal truth to shape how I would engage with him. Of course, I knew that Giuliano had made many mistakes, some of them incredibly harmful to me and others, but if I walked into a room with him and tried to convince him that he was wrong, I'd only succeed in generating conflict and defensiveness.

The other key insight from David was that I didn't need Giuliano to provide me anything—no answers, no apologies, no explanations. "If you go there hoping to get something from him, you are setting yourself up to fail," David warned me. "If you tell yourself a story that you need something from him, you are giving him power over you." Though I had been meditating for a few years at this point, and thinking about these issues obsessively, it didn't fully hit me until that moment. *He was right.* If Giuliano never apologized, never admitted any wrongdoing, was I going to live the rest of my life with an open wound, without closure? All because one man couldn't face the fact that he was wrong? My well-being only depended on that if I chose to let it. It was as simple as that.

This is a very Zen attitude, a bias for action and simplicity. *Stop overcomplicating things.* It's kind of annoying to hear, honestly, when you're so used to overthinking everything in your life.

"But how do I just stop caring?"

"How did you start caring?" David asked. "You just do."

I was reminded of Yoda: "Do or do not. There is no try." It wasn't a question of figuring out *how* to do something, it was a question of *doing* it. That was a mistake I'd made a million times: confusing a failure of willpower for uncertainty about how best to achieve something. You can sit there endlessly dwelling, coming up with strategies, debating which set of steps will fix your personal problems, or you can just fix them. You can just choose to let go.

Like my earlier epiphany in prison, this insight hit me suddenly, but it took me weeks to process it, to work out all its implications, and to feel it fully shape my actions. In the moment, it left me with a gaping question: If I didn't need Giuliano to say or do anything in order to feel at peace, then why on Earth was I putting myself through all this stress to travel back to Italy to meet with him? Why go at all if I had nothing to gain?

"Maybe you have something to give," David offered. At the end of our time, he left me with a provocative assignment. "This might be challenging to hear," he said, "but I want you to ask yourself if there are any ways that you are grateful for how Giuliano Mignini shaped your life."

A part of me instantly wanted to shout, "Fuck right off!" I already knew what my family thought of *that* idea:

"I can't believe you're willing to talk to that monster."

"Fuck that asshole."

"He's lying to you. It's a trap."

"He's just using you."

"He's the one who belongs in prison."

But I remembered what Mom had told me about kindness, and what I already knew was part of my mission in forming this relationship. I was returning to Perugia to be kind to him, to offer him the chance to feel seen. Not because he deserved it, but because I had it in me. My whole adult life, I'd felt like I had no agency as I was battered by a foreign justice system and by ruthless, unscrupulous media. Everyone associated my name either with a monstrous crime I hadn't committed or with a tragic thing that had happened *to* me. Neither of these said anything about who I really was. But this—this was something that wasn't about survival, that wasn't a reaction to someone else's action. This meeting didn't have to happen at all. I was making it happen. It was an act of radical empathy and compassion, something that truly spoke to who I am. It felt like the first moment of true agency I'd ever had in relation to this terrible saga. I would go to Perugia not to get anything from Giuliano, but to give something to him. What exactly? I still didn't know.

Homecoming

I'D LEARNED MY LESSON TRAVELING to Modena. This time, to avoid the media, Chris and I flew into Zurich and rented a car to drive across the border. We cruised through without even being stopped. Like the last trip to Italy, my mom came with us, both to help with Eureka and because she wanted to introduce me to the friends she'd made while I was trapped in a cell. Well, that, and her now permanent policy of never letting me travel to Italy without her ever again. On the way south, we stopped in Florence for lunch and so Eureka could get some stroller time. I wore big sunglasses and a large sun hat whenever I was out of the car. If I was recognized, the paparazzi would be on us like flies. If that were to happen, our plan was to just call off the meeting, hit the road, and drive back to Switzerland. So I was on edge walking through Florence, pushing my baby with Chris and Mom beside me.

Being surrounded by Italian speakers and immersed in Italian culture began to trigger me. But it was also summertime, and there was a flood of tourists strolling along the Arno, snapping photos of the Duomo. I started to feel rather anonymous, just a girl named Marie—as Chris called me when he had to get my attention in public—just another American tourist. Still, I wasn't about to take off those sunglasses.

I was also preoccupied, my mind continually drifting ahead in time to the upcoming conversation with Giuliano, or diving backward, remembering every single time I had tried to talk to him during my interrogation, during the investigation, and at trial, and *wasn't* heard. Chris and I developed a mantra for the trip: *Make good memories.* This whole country was a place I associated with trauma and injustice, but underneath all that, not quite snuffed, were pleasant memories of visiting Italy with my family as a teenager, touring Pompeii and excitedly telling Mom facts I'd learned from my Latin textbook, making dinner with my roommates in Perugia. Without proclaiming it as an official mission, I was becoming aware that one of my goals was to reclaim Italy for myself. A part of that was seeing the places and meeting the people who had impacted my mom.

That evening, we drove up a winding road into the small hilltop village of Piegaro, about thirty minutes from Perugia. Mom had arranged a safe house of sorts. Our plan was to stay there for a few days as I prepared for the meeting. Chris was even more paranoid about privacy than I was. He kept asking Mom, "You sure you can trust these people?"

Piegaro captured my heart immediately. The narrow, cobbled streets, built for pedestrians and wagons, barely wide enough for modern cars; the unexpected alcoves and stairwells where the village cats slept in the sun; the lone bakery, the lone butcher shop, the lone café at the center of town. It was a medieval village built over time without any plan, small stone houses and streets curving organically with the topography of the hillside. Nearly everywhere there were stunning views of the valley and rising hills of other small towns in the Umbrian countryside, the green heart of Italy.

We met Mom's friend Colleen, who guided us through the winding alleys to our sanctuary, a small flat that she and her husband, Tom, had converted from an old glass factory dating back to the 800s. Colleen and Tom were originally from Seattle, and after successful careers in law and architecture, they'd decided to move to this tiny town of three hundred people, buy an abandoned building, and renovate it into a vacation rental to live out their retirement.

Colleen had offered us the flat for free, and I soon learned that wasn't the first time she'd done so. While I was incarcerated, I was allowed six hours of visitation a month, and my family made sure that for four years, not a single visitation went by without someone from the family showing up to see me. The logistics of making that happen were difficult and expensive. Fortunately, my stepdad, who worked in computer security, was able to do his job remotely. Mom was only able to visit during breaks from her elementary school job. My stepdad spent months alone living in Italy, just to be there for those hour-long visits. At first, my family rented rooms in an agriturismo about an hour away from the prison.

Over a glass of wine that night, Colleen told me how she'd connected with my family. She'd been chatting with an Italian friend who owned a local winery, who asked her one day, "What do you know about that young woman over in Capanne prison?" Colleen said, "You mean Amanda Knox? She's obviously not guilty. This is crazy." Her friend concurred and offered to put Colleen in touch with a journalist named Sabina Castelfranco, who had grown familiar with my family over the years.

Through Sabina, she got ahold of my stepdad and said, "Listen, I have a place that's just twenty minutes from Capanne. You can live here for free. Just come."

My stepdad arrived that evening, and he spent the last year of my imprisonment living in Colleen and Tom's flat in Piegaro. Mom, too, had stayed there whenever she could get time off work. A total stranger had offered this kindness because she could. It was inspiring. But in the moment, I had to apologize to Colleen for seeming cold and robotic. I tend to dissociate in moments of crisis. I call it "going dead possum." This close to the meeting with Giuliano, I felt it happening despite myself.

These people had helped my family and become good friends. And it was important to Mom, especially, to share that with me, just as she wanted to sit down on the terrace overlooking the hills and toast the setting sun with an Aperol spritz. She got emotional as we did so. "I would sit here, day after day, staring out at this beautiful view, drinking wine and feeling guilty as hell," she said, "because I knew my baby was just twenty minutes away locked in a cage."

"To making good memories," I said, holding up my glass. Swallows swooped through the evening light, Eureka played with a flower at my feet, Mom and Chris at my side. It was a flash of paradise. In another life, I thought, I'd move here with my family and open up a little shop. We'd live out a quiet and meditative existence, eating ripe tomatoes and drinking wine. But, of course, over the next hill was that complex of cement and barbed wire, and it was calling to me.

My meeting with Giuliano was on Friday, so the next morning, Thursday, I hopped in the car with Mom and Chris and Eureka, and we drove out to Capanne. I couldn't say why I felt compelled to see it. I'd left it in such a rush, never thinking I'd return. Perhaps I wanted to feel what it was like for Mom to approach that fence. On the winding roads between Piegaro and the prison—roads that also ran to Perugia and cut through olive groves and vineyards, old stone walls and towers peeking above the umbrella pines and cypress trees—all I could think of was that I must have traveled these roads a hundred times on the way back and forth to the courthouse, but I had never seen them because I was inside that windowless prison van.

We pulled through the roundabout and came to a stop in the parking lot. I got out and took a moment to reckon with the place. Immediately, visions of the inside flooded my mind. The long, echoing hallway, the insane asylum doors, the barred windows, the cement-walled yard where I paced in endless circles. From the outside, it was not obviously a place of punishment. Nondescript gray buildings, a secured entrance, a barbed-wire fence. It could have been some government research facility, a military base, or a corporate defense contractor. But inside that barbed-wire fence, behind those cement walls, people I knew were still rotting away, not having left that place in the eleven years since I'd been rushed out of my cell in a whirlwind.

I stood there for maybe five minutes until I began to feel overwhelmed with anger. As we drove away, I just kept shaking my head in disbelief that I'd spent four whole years of my life in that place. I was angry that I'd had to wonder how to make a life worth living if confined for the next twenty-six years to that cement box. I was angry at the emotional and mental gymnastics I'd gone through to survive that disgusting wound in the Italian countryside.

Those years inside had been like living in an otherworldly limbo, some place divorced from time and space. But seeing it sitting there, drab and unassuming, off some random turnoff in the middle of nowhere, the facility took on a banal kind of reality. It was just some place, a place that had stolen years of my life. How small and petty and pointless. Seeing Capanne from the outside felt like the opposite of seeing a cathedral. Not awe but *ugh*.

I wasn't sure if this visit was helpful or not as I prepared to meet Giuliano. But it had called to me, and I wasn't here in Italy to ignore such calls. The loudest call was coming from Perugia itself. I had to return to that city I'd called home for five brief weeks, and I knew that now was the time.

Free

I'd been spooked that morning at the café in Piegaro. At six a.m., Chris and I went for a coffee, me in my sunglasses and hat. Mom was still getting dressed, but Eureka was with us, crawling on the cobblestones out front. It was a quiet morning in an already sleepy town, and there were only a handful of people up, so I figured it was fine to take off my sunglasses as I picked up my cappuccino—it was hard to see inside with them on—and immediately, an older woman in the café looked right at me and asked, "Are you Amanda?"

I felt like a mouse in the pantry that couldn't vanish fast enough. "I'm Marie," I muttered awkwardly, "from California," and I ran outside to a table on the terrace, where I turtled back into my sun hat and glasses.

We asked Colleen if she knew an older woman in town with a small dog, and it turned out the lady was a friend of hers. Collen hadn't told her I was coming. She had no reason to expect to run into Amanda Knox in Piegaro that day, but, like millions of people, especially in Italy, she knew my face almost as well as those of her own family. I felt terrible for lying to her, and I asked Colleen to pass on an apology and beg her to keep my presence in Italy a secret.

When we arrived in Perugia, Mom wanted to have a spritz at the Brufani hotel, and I was reminded how one of my lawyers, Carlo, had always fantasized about me returning to Italy and strutting down the streets of Perugia with my head held high. Even if a part of me wanted to say, "I'm allowed to be here as much as anyone! I'm not ashamed and I'm not afraid!" I knew exactly what would happen if I was spotted. It would be front-page news, and I'd be chased by a legion of press until I crossed the border back into Switzerland.

We settled on a driving tour of the city, and it was just as beautiful as I remembered. Situated atop a hill, and spilling out into the valley below, the medieval city is a maze of steep and winding streets that give onto piazzas and aqueducts and archways still standing from the Etruscan period. The sun-bleached buildings are crawling with ivy and painted like Easter eggs with muted pastel pride. The alleyways are so tall and narrow you wouldn't know the sky was there without looking directly up. The stone stairways were indented over centuries by the feet of popes and painters and peasants...and of course, students. So many students. The city is home to the University of Perugia, dating to 1308, and the University for Foreigners, where I took classes.

Passing through the old travertine wall, I was hit with waves of déjà vu. I had never driven these streets, only walked them, and so there was an unfamiliarity, compounded by time, layered over the shockingly familiar. The city I remembered jumped out at me in surprising turns. We rounded a corner, and suddenly there was the university, and there was the bookshop I frequented. "Look, the place I got coffee!" And before I knew it, we were driving down the narrow hairpin turn next to the basketball courts, that strip with no sidewalk where I had to dodge speeding mopeds on my way home from class. And there it was: Via della Pergola 7.

We could see the terrace where Meredith and I spent afternoons reading and playing guitar, looking out over the valley, eating stone fruits and chocolate. Someone's laundry was hanging there. Because, of course, someone else lived there now. How strange...someone probably took their afternoon siestas in the room where Meredith was murdered. They took their showers in the bathroom where Rudy Guede had left his bloody footprint.

The city was buzzing with the energy of tourists and students, but as we drove away, back to Piegaro, I felt a deep tranquility settle on me. It was inflected with sadness, with pity for my twenty-year-old self. I had been having the time of my life in Perugia. I was just a kid, and I was absolutely charmed by this city that beckoned me to explore and grow.

Life was beautiful, and I *felt* beautiful, and then I met Raffaele and everything was perfect. Until it wasn't. I tried to see those early, joyous days as clearly as I could in my memory, but I couldn't see them without thinking about what came after. But this quietness also came with a sense of peace. Seeing that laundry wavering in the subtle breeze, I realized that Perugia, and even Via della Pergola 7, was just a place. It was a place where a terrible thing happened, but it was also a place where young couples fell in love, where babies were born, and where poems were written.

Perugia was my place of joy before it became my place of horror and grief. Even then, it was someone else's place of hope or excitement. Every place was somebody's bad place and somebody's good place. Every picturesque winding road held a painful memory for the mother of a reckless driver. Every serene park had seen marriage proposals and tearful breakups. Perugia, and the house, transcended the events that occurred in them. It didn't have to be a place of pain or grief for me unless I held on to it that way. If I wanted it to be a place of healing, a place of beauty, it could be. The choice was mine to make.

Faccia a Faccia

MOM HAD BEEN SPILLING HER anxieties about the meeting with Giuliano the entire trip, little comments here and there tagged on at the end of conversations, and the night before, it all came to a head. "I don't trust this human being at all," she said.

She, along with my stepdad, was convinced that Giuliano was lying to me, that the two years of correspondence, which she had not read, was all a devious ploy to lure me back to Italy. In the worst-case scenario, he would try to have me arrested on new charges. In the best case, he would exploit me and use our meeting for his own ends. I had to remind myself that my mom had gone through her own life-shattering trauma, having her daughter wrongly imprisoned by this man. On top of that, she'd experienced firsthand how petty, vindictive, and absurd the Italian justice system could be. She could still vividly remember the day she had been arrested on Giuliano's orders, how she had been brought to an office, handcuffed, and charged with slander against the police, all because she had repeated to the press what I had told her about being slapped in the back of the head during my interrogation.

And my mom was in good company in worrying that Giuliano wasn't being honest with me. Retired FBI Special Agent Steve Moore, who'd helped coordinate my escape from Italy in 2011, told us just before our departure that he had discovered something truly troubling. In his research into the case, he'd learned that five days before Meredith was killed Rudy Guede was caught burglarizing a nursery school in Milan. He was found with a stolen laptop and cellphone, and an 11-inch knife. He was officially arrested. They took his fingerprints and mugshot. But a few hours later, Guede was mysteriously released without being charged, and the Milan police personally escorted him onto a Perugia-bound train, where he returned to face no consequences. Why on Earth would that have happened? Steve suspected, but couldn't prove, that Rudy Guede was actually a criminal informant for the Perugia police. Releasing Guede from that burglary had catastrophic consequences because he went on to murder Meredith just a few days later. Steve's theory was profoundly uncertain, but it was frightening nevertheless. Given all that, it wasn't crazy of her to worry about further absurd and unfounded charges.

Eureka was probably wondering what all the tense energy in the room was about, and why wasn't I just reading a book with her?

But even without knowing Steve's theory, my mom didn't trust the man who had prosecuted me when she knew I was innocent and she felt he must have known that too given the lack of evidence against me. "I always imagined him hearing a little voice in his head," Mom said, "and the voice is saying, 'This is bullshit. You've got the wrong person.' And him just ignoring that voice."

"But ignoring that voice doesn't mean he's evil," I said. "It could just mean he lacks moral courage."

"So he's a coward!" Mom said. She was understandably still very angry at Giuliano, and if I had, for a moment at least, convinced her not to judge him as evil, she was intent on judging him with another label.

"It also tells you something about the nature of the world," Chris offered. "If you learn that that level of life-crushing harm is capable from somebody who's not necessarily evil, it reshapes your perceptions about how harm happens. And how to mitigate harm and prevent harm in the future."

This was one of the many reasons I loved Chris. We shared a worldview that sometimes felt increasingly rare: giving everyone the maximum benefit of the doubt, realizing that compassion is not weakness, but strength.

Still, that night, as we went to bed, I was full of doubt. "No one thinks I'm doing the right thing here," I said. "Mom doesn't, my family doesn't, Steve doesn't, my lawyers don't. I mean, my stepdad calls him 'Pignini.' It's not helpful." I couldn't understand why things like that made people feel better. And it was so universal. That kind of name calling doesn't heal anything, and it certainly didn't make *me* feel better.

Such insults are designed to dehumanize their targets. It was my stepdad's way of saying that Giuliano wasn't human like the rest of us, that he hadn't behaved like a human being to begin with, and that he wasn't capable of growth or change. The irony here is that what Giuliano did to me was, I felt, a very human thing to do. Human beings mess up all the time. We are selfish and cowardly, and we self-delude and protect our egos at all costs, even when it means hurting innocent people. We fuck each other over. Pigs don't do that.

Despite my doubts, what I did feel sure of was that, whether Giuliano was cunning or cowardly, it didn't matter. That was a judgment about him. I couldn't control him. I could only control myself. And this felt like a test, a chance to prove to myself who I really was. If I didn't risk being hurt, I couldn't reap the reward of having had the courage to approach this situation.

Free

I woke before dawn and spent a few moments meditating at the window as the birds chased insects in the thermals over the valley. The sun, rising from somewhere unseen, touched the green crests of the hills to the west. I felt quietly determined, at peace, as free of anxiety as I had felt in a long, long time. I knew I was about to do something scary, but there was no way I was turning back.

Don Saulo had secured a private location for Giuliano and me to meet—a church-owned hotel just outside of Perugia called Villa Sacro Cuore. After winding through the hills for twenty minutes, we arrived at the road to the villa, which was unpaved and rocky, but slowly gave way to a manicured lawn, tall umbrella pines, and a large, elegant building, painted yellow—my favorite color—sitting on the edge of a hill overlooking the valley to the south of Perugia. We had arrived a good thirty minutes early, so I figured Giuliano and Don Saulo had yet to arrive. Mom did not want to go in, so we offered her the rental car in case she wanted to go on a drive. I didn't know how long this meeting would take. But she took her book and found a bench on the lawn a few dozen yards from the building. I picked up Eureka, and Chris and I entered the lobby.

I found a woman at the desk and told her, with a faltering hesitation, that I was here to see Don Saulo, and she said, "Sì, certo, ti stavamo aspettando. Saulo non è ancora arrivato. Vuoi un caffè?" *Yes, of course, we've been expecting you. Don Saulo has not arrived yet. Would you like a coffee?* She then led us upstairs to a small conference room and went to fix us two cappuccinos.

This was the first interaction I'd had with a Perugian local who knew exactly who I was, and she was so kind and warm toward me that it brought me to tears. After my acquittal, Perugians had launched an internet campaign where they posted photos of themselves holding up signs that read "Perugia vi odia." *Perugia hates you.* I realized that I hadn't been expecting this woman, or anyone in Perugia, to be kind. I'd been expecting the opposite. I was always expecting the opposite.

The conference room was lined with books on one wall, and on the others, photos of recent popes: John Paul II, Benedict, Francis. Adjoining the meeting room was a bedroom where Chris could hang out with Eureka as I sat down with Giuliano.

This was the room where it would happen. In mere moments, there would be nothing between him and me. The last time I'd been in a room to talk with him was the makeshift courtroom at Capanne, a few days into my imprisonment, where I'd desperately tried to explain that this was all a big misunderstanding, and he had used the opportunity to pounce on my every word, trying to entrap me in some incriminating admission.

I went over my notes about what I wanted to say and realized that I needed to look up a word. I'd forgotten how to say "grief" in Italian. As soon as I looked it up, it was obvious why. There isn't really a specific word for grief. Italians just say "dolore." *Pain*. Grief, of course, is a specific kind of pain, the pain for something that is lost. And if you want to say, "I grieve for somebody," you say "piangere," which means "to cry." It suddenly hit me how much even the structure of the language had set me up to be misperceived. Grief was synonymous with tears in Italian, and Italians are famously very expressive with their joy, their excitement, and their grief. Because I was not crying much in the days after Meredith's death, but was more numb in response to that sudden, shocking loss, it was perhaps inevitable that I was perceived as cold and unmoved, strange and suspicious. The divide I was trying to cross between me and Giuliano was deep, a lot deeper than the adversarial roles of prosecutor and defendant. It was as deep as language.

We heard a car pull up, and Chris peeked out the side window. There, talking by the terrace, we spotted Don Saulo and Giuliano. We

Free

couldn't hear them, but Don Saulo seemed to be coaching Giuliano in some way. They remained out there a good five minutes before entering the building.

Meanwhile, Mom was sitting on the bench under the shade of a tree, but she was not reading. She was hyperventilating. I didn't know this at the time, but she told me afterward that she spent the next few hours in a state of prolonged panic. She heard a siren in the distance, and she knew, she just *knew,* that Giuliano Mignini had set his trap, made the call, and they were coming to arrest me for some fabricated charge, to snatch her daughter away from her yet again.

As I heard the footsteps echoing up the stairwell, I was afraid of something else entirely: that my courage would fail me, that anger or despair or tears would overwhelm me, that I wouldn't be able to speak to Giuliano with kindness. I steeled myself, and then in walked Don Saulo, with Giuliano just behind him. And I fell to pieces.

Don Saulo was radiating warmth, his eyes were sparkling, and he looked as if he hadn't aged at all since the last time I'd seen him, playing music together in his office as I awaited the verdict that would set me free. I'd spent so much time mentally and emotionally preparing myself to face Giuliano that I hadn't even thought of what it would be like to see Don Saulo again. I hugged him and cried into his shoulder for at least a minute. He had been my closest friend in my darkest hour, an unfathomable source of kindness and generosity in a place whose very architecture was a manifestation of cruelty. And all those years in the prison, ministering to the trapped and traumatized, hadn't worn him down.

Giuliano stood patiently behind us until we released our embrace. So much for not breaking down in tears. Finally, I turned to him and took in the fact of his presence: he was as tall as I remembered, but less imposing, with a scraggly ring of gray hair around his bald pate, and a smile he might offer to a wounded animal. I was somewhat shocked to see him in casual clothes. I hadn't expected him to be wearing the black robes he'd worn in court, of course, but I also wasn't expecting a cargo vest, as if he'd just returned from a fishing trip. "It's okay," he told me in Italian. "Calm your butterflies."

I introduced him to Chris and Eureka, who matched the warmth Giuliano was beaming at her. She was oblivious to who this man was, and she became the buffer between us. I didn't quite know how to greet him. We didn't hug or shake hands, but he reached out a finger for Eureka to grab. He'd even brought a gift for her, a star-shaped music box with a pull string. She loved it.

We traded a few pleasantries about my travel from the United States and how beautiful Villa Sacro Cuore was, and then Chris and Eureka retreated to the adjoining bedroom while Don Saulo, Giuliano, and I sat down at one end of the long table.

I had prepared to begin this conversation by saying, "I'm here to listen to whatever it is that you have to say," but Don Saulo set the stage. "Amanda has some things she'd like to say to you, and I remind you to listen without interrupting." And suddenly, the onus was on me to begin this dialogue. Don Saulo had been sitting next to Giuliano, but he rose and came to the other side of the table and sat next to me. For the next fifteen minutes or so, my face streamed with tears, my breath came in heaves, and Don Saulo stroked my hair, petting me like a jittery rabbit. I looked Giuliano in the eyes and said, in Italian:

> I want you to know that I am innocent. I had nothing to do with Meredith's murder. You were wrong about me. I was treated as if I were guilty until and unless I could convince you and your

colleagues of my innocence. And I failed to do that. But I am not here to convince you of my innocence. I am here to let you know that whether you've realized your mistake or not, I do not think you are an evil person.

My breath escaped me, and I tried to regain control of myself. At that moment, Giuliano was tearing up as well. He reached out and took my hand and held it in both of his. My brain could not even process this, but I pushed through:

Your mistake, which caused great harm to me and my loved ones, and to Raffaele and his loved ones, is not the only thing that defines you. I want you to know that despite the fact that I am still hurt today, I am grateful for my experience, in which you played an important and influential role. I am grateful because I learned things about myself that I never would have known: both how weak and vulnerable I am, but also how strong. I am a very strong person. I know that in large part because of you. This experience crystallized for me my core values: curiosity, compassion, and courage. Curiosity for the truth, not just the version that most serves me. Compassion, especially for those who have made mistakes. And courage to overcome my own fears and pain in order to remain curious and compassionate toward others, especially those who have harmed me. We cannot change the past, but we can change the future. And the mistakes of our past are the opportunities of our future. It is never too late to live up to our values. And I believe *you* are a person of value. I do not wish you ill. I wish you peace.

Giuliano squeezed my hand, his eyes brimming. "I'm also here to grieve," I said. This was the word I'd looked up last minute. "I came to Perugia a naïve girl, and I returned home a traumatized woman. After these many years, I have been able to process what happened, and rise from the ashes, but part of me died here, and I'm here to grieve for her, and hopefully feel whole again."

Saying it out loud while staring into the eyes of my prosecutor, that metaphor took on a corporeal weight. I felt like I was at the funeral of my twenty-year-old self, that girl to whom nothing bad had ever happened. Returning to Seattle, I'd thought I would shed my prison clothes like snakeskin and emerge back into life as that bubbly girl. Of course, I couldn't. She was dead. It had taken me this long to realize it. I had returned to Perugia not just to meet with Giuliano, but to scatter her ashes and say goodbye.

Before Giuliano even responded, I felt triumphant. I'd said what I'd come to say and felt like I was finally enacting a truth about resilience, which is that after serious trauma, you don't get to go back to who you were, but you have to figure out how to have a say in who you become.

Then Giuliano, still holding my hand in his, responded. We talked for another ninety minutes, and he never let go. I cried much of that time, and there were moments of sharp disagreement. We bounced around a lot in the conversation, and rather than try to relay how it proceeded chronologically, I will tell you first what he didn't say.

He didn't say, "I'm sorry." He didn't say, "I was wrong." He didn't say, "What can I do to make amends?" He didn't say, "Please forgive me."

He maintained that he had done his duty, that he had followed the evidence. He said, "by the time I arrived, all I could do as a prosecutor was pursue the case against you, but I was not the one who first suspected you."

He told me that what had always bothered him about the case was that everyone held him accountable for his colleagues' actions, when in fact the police were making decisions before he became involved, and he wasn't even the only prosecutor. He pointed out that he was not the one who refused me a lawyer or who kept me up all night during my interrogation. And he was right about that. He said he felt a little trapped, by his duty and by the evidence, which he insisted he analyzed objectively. He had a job to do, but he was not the only one, and it was not pleasant.

Perhaps the best decision I made in making this face-to-face meeting happen was in asking Don Saulo to mediate. He had my back the entire time. He and Giuliano had known each other for decades, but Don Saulo understood the depth of what happened to me, and he wouldn't let Giuliano elide that. When we spoke of my interrogation, Giuliano acknowledged that what the police did to me wasn't "proper" because they did not advise me of my rights, but Don Saulo jumped in to say, "What happened to Amanda in that interrogation was torture. They tortured her." When Giuliano tried to find common ground with me, saying, "We both have been misrepresented as monsters. We both have suffered," Don Saulo swooped in to say, "Yes, but Amanda spent four years in prison."

Giuliano insisted that he couldn't imagine what he could have done differently. I pushed back with as much restraint as I could muster against the idea that he'd been perfectly objective and logical. In these tense moments, Don Saulo offered timely interjections: "Giuliano, I need you to listen to Amanda now."

"There's no going back in life," replied Giuliano. "I came to my conclusions on the basis of the facts. That's all." To which Don Saulo said, "I've been telling you for years, Giuliano, that you have all your facts and evidence, but there must be another explanation, because Amanda is not capable of causing such harm."

This was exactly what Giuliano had insisted upon in all his letters, so I wasn't surprised to hear him repeat himself. What I didn't expect is when he said, "That you would reach out to me after I asked for you to be condemned, it is a truly heroic act. Only people in books do such things." He said he was honored to meet with me and that I was by far his "favorite defendant." He said all this with total sincerity, all while still holding my hand in his. "Surreal" barely does it justice.

But it went beyond compliments. "I was suffering," he said, "when I asked that you be convicted."

"So you recognize that I am innocent . . ."

"We must respect the ruling of the Court of Cassation," he repeated.

I was gobsmacked. *Sbalordita.* Giuliano seemed to feel that even in retirement it was improper for him to contradict any of his actions as a public official or call into question any of the official verdicts. To his view, the Italian legal process had worked as intended. No ruling or sentence is considered definitive until it reaches the Court of Cassation, and along the way, the prosecution and defense balance each other out at the lower court levels. He was simply playing his part as the prosecutor, whose job, nay, duty, is to make the case for guilt. To him, the four years I spent in prison, the eight years on trial, it was all just part of the normal process of the larger court system arriving at the truth. "The final ruling acquitted you, and you are free, and I am happy that you are free." But still, he did not seem to see, or be able to acknowledge, that he had had a choice to prosecute or not, and that he chose to pursue a case against me with very weak evidence, without a sensible motive, all while the real killer was right in front of him.

And yet, he was so clearly moved by my presence and by this shared experience I had created for the two of us. He used the word "paradiso." *Paradise.* That's what this meeting was for him: one of the most treasured things to happen to him in his life. He knew that I had every reason to hate him, and he was deeply moved that I not only didn't hate him but that I would go to such lengths to connect with him. A part of me wondered if this feeling of his was amplified by the all-white outfit I was wearing, and even the presence of Eureka. Where he had seen a sly and murderous devil in the courtroom, did he now see a Madonna figure?

As much as he prided himself on being logical and objective, I don't think he reached his initial conclusions through logic, but through gut instinct, through a hunch that was terribly wrong. All those years of trial, my lawyers and I had tried to argue against his case with logic. Now, I had reached him not through logic, but through my presence, through emotion. If he thought of me differently now, it was not because he had found some new logical explanation, but because he saw the truth in my face. I could see the conflict in him. His "logical" convictions were at war with his emotional truth and pride and his sense of propriety. It was all tangled up, and he was in turmoil. But so was I.

Every time the discussion veered into our disagreements about the case, I found myself torn between my desire to hear him admit fault and the desire to have empathy for his inability to do so. I was falling into a trap. I didn't want to be permissive, to condone his behavior, so didn't I need to demand accountability? Was I just enabling his delusion that he didn't do anything wrong when I said things like, "I recognize your reasons for doing what you did"?

But not expecting anything from Giuliano was about more than having a stoic "admit what you can't control" mindset. It was about establishing a connection based on mercy and forgiveness in the absence of preconditions, in the absence of true accountability and justice.

I wanted to live in a merciful world, not the punitive one I'd grown up in. Punitive thinking pervades every aspect of our lives, from preschool to prison. Our very language conflates in the word "judgment" two very different ideas: the ability to form an objective, authoritative, and wise opinion on the one hand, and moral condemnation and castigation on the other. We're taught that it really matters who's right, who's wrong, who's to blame, who's to praise, whom we reward, and whom we punish. When something goes wrong, we are taught to believe that it is because there is something wrong with the wrongdoer, and that they deserve to face consequences.

Prison had reaffirmed an intuition I'd long felt that there was something wrong with that way of thinking, but at the same time, I felt that righteous pull toward what I did and didn't deserve. *I didn't fucking deserve to go to prison! I didn't deserve to be branded a killer!* But demanding that Giuliano admit fault was only thwarting my own purpose. I was only making him defensive, which I knew came from a place of fear. Of course he was afraid of being wrong! It's terrifying to be that wrong about something so consequential in a society that gleefully punishes wrongdoers.

After a long and winding conversation, at turns combative and pleading, the two of us talking past each other, I returned to my initial purpose: to simply be kind to him.

"The justice system established us as enemies," I told him. "I'm grateful that you are meeting me as a friend. I think that's uncommon, that it speaks to your character, and that together we can be an example. We can change this story. Right now, there are two stories people believe: the story of the monstrous girl who got away with a heinous crime, and the story of an innocent girl falsely accused of being a monster *by* a monster. Neither of those are true, but our story doesn't have to end there. Together, we can write a new story. As long as people view my innocence as an open question, they will speculate about me instead of honoring Meredith and holding Guede to account, and the Kercher family will never have closure."

I didn't know if this was something Giuliano would ever be capable of, but I hoped that if I offered him an image of himself that was worthy of esteem, an opportunity to be part of the process of affirming the truth and bringing healing to the Kerchers and everyone else harmed in this saga, he might step up and be his better self.

He told me that people had attacked me not knowing who I really am, but now that he truly knew me, he would tell them the truth. "I'm going to tell people that you're not a monster," he said, "and I hope you'll tell people that I'm not a monster."

"You made a terrible mistake," I said again. I had been firm on this the entire time, and I would not let him forget it. "But I don't think that makes you a bad person. And I wish you well." Then I gave him a hug.

And he said, "I wish you well, too. I want to make this better for you."

Chris and Eureka joined us, and we all walked outside into the gardens surrounding Villa Sacro Cuore. Giuliano saw my mom sitting on the bench and made eye contact with her. Mom took one look at him and bolted for the car. "Look," I said. "My mom has not forgiven you. To her, you are still the person who put her innocent daughter in prison for something she didn't do."

And I wondered, had *I* forgiven him?

A Dream Deferred

ON THE MORNING OF NOVEMBER 2, 2007, I awoke in Raffaele's bed. We'd spent the prior evening cooking, reading *Harry Potter* in German, smoking a joint, making love, and watching my favorite film, *Amélie*. I had known this sweet, nerdy boy for just a week, and we had given ourselves over to a mutual infatuation in a way that is only possible in the blissful unreality of a foreign fling, that fragile impermanent space where new love can blossom instantly, as if you'd found your soulmate, only because both of you know, though you hide it even from yourselves, that sooner rather than later, you will each return to your lives, alone again, and worlds apart.

In my broken Italian, and his broken English, we nuzzled and kissed and talked excitedly about our plans for the weekend. Raffaele wanted to take me on a trip to Gubbio, an ancient medieval town in the Umbrian countryside that was known for its truffles. We would spend a romantic weekend there, walking the cobbled streets, touring the cathedrals, and, of course, eating truffles! I had never tasted a truffle. I imagined them like delicious dirt. I pulled myself reluctantly away because I had to run back to my apartment to shower and get a change of clothes. It would only take half an hour, then we'd be off on our romantic getaway.

Free

But when I returned home that morning, I found that my apartment had been broken into, Meredith's door was locked, my two other roommates weren't home, and something was terribly, terribly wrong. Five days later I cried myself to sleep in a prison cell. That dream of truffles in Gubbio had shattered like a childhood fairy tale under the crushing weight of reality.

Both Raffaele and I were put through brutal interrogations, subjected to physical and psychological abuse. We were threatened with years in prison, denied bathroom breaks, sleep, and of course lawyers (we were only "witnesses," not "suspects," Giuliano would later claim, and were not entitled to legal counsel). The police thought I knew something I wasn't telling, and since Raffaele was my alibi for the night of the murder, they wore him down and coerced him into signing a statement saying that I was not at his apartment on the night of the murder and that I asked him to lie for me. Later, he recanted.

And so my paramour became my codefendant. And as our trials progressed, he faced the same fate I did: decades in prison. But while the prosecution and media and what felt like the whole world had become obsessed with Foxy Knoxy, he was Mr. Nobody. No one cared about who he actually was, a meek computer programming student with no history of violence, who was awkward and shy around girls (part of what endeared him to me). He was just along for the ride, and even his own family knew it. As we were convicted, and forced to appeal, they urged him to throw me under the bus. He could have cut a deal with the prosecution, extracted himself, and left me to rot. But that wasn't the truth. And he cared as much as I did about the truth.

Raffaele owed me nothing, but he was willing to face hell alongside me, even as I made it very clear to him in the letters we sent from our cells that our romance was over, and that I could not think of us in those terms anymore.

He took it in stride. Over those four years of prison, we saw each other only in the courtroom. Our relationship transformed into something more than friends, something not as intimate as lovers, but bonded. Our fates were tied together, and our sense of who we were, and what life was all about, was shaped by the same trauma.

In freedom, as rough as I had it, Raffaele had it worse. He was still in Italy. While I faced extradition, he was trapped in his own country. He couldn't get a job, couldn't date, and couldn't escape being the "boy accused of murder." And then, the "boy re-convicted." I wrote a memoir, as did he, and I saw him once when he came to Seattle to give a reading. It was a sad reunion. We still had that sword of Damocles hanging over our heads. When we were finally definitively acquitted by the Court of Cassation, we celebrated over the phone. "It's over! It's finally over! We're free!"

Since then, our lives had been moving in very different directions. He was still searching for a career and a family, while I had found my partner in Chris and had my beautiful daughter Eureka to brighten my days. We kept in touch through WhatsApp, trading messages every so often. But I wouldn't say we were close, even though the connection we have can't ever be severed. It's scar tissue, tough and sinewy.

Raffaele was living in Milan when I returned on this mission to meet with Giuliano. I told him what I was doing, that I would let him know how it went in the aftermath, and that if I was able to remain undetected in Italy, perhaps we could meet up. Being back in Perugia after fifteen years, driving past my apartment and down the street where Raffaele had been living, memories flooded back in vivid detail. We'd lost so much, and most of it we would never recover: our naïveté, our reputations, even our old digital cameras that had captured those moments of young romance. Among all the things we'd lost, that trip to Gubbio felt so small and inconsequential, something I'd barely remembered, a plan waylaid by tragedy. But Gubbio was less than an hour away from Perugia. Nothing was stopping us from finally taking that trip.

I called Raffaele and said, "Let's do it. Let's finally go to Gubbio and eat truffles." So he drove five hours from Milan to meet up with me, Mom, Chris, and Eureka.

As we strolled through the medieval town, Raffaele pushed Eureka in the stroller while Chris and Mom walked behind us, giving us a little space to catch up, and so I could tell him about the meeting with Giuliano. The Gubbio trip we had planned fifteen years ago was supposed to be a romantic getaway, and this was very different. I felt a lot of overlapping things: nostalgia for what could have been, sheer gratitude at how my life had turned out, sadness for Raffaele, who was still searching for many of the things I'd found. He was sweet to join me here, given the circumstances, and to jointly reimagine this intimate experience as a familial one. He didn't hold it against me, even as I saw that longing look in his eyes as he watched me and Chris and Eureka. I imagined that a part of him was thinking of that alternate universe, where Meredith was never killed and we were never arrested, and we went to Gubbio that day, and perhaps these many years later, happily married, we were returning with our baby to revisit a place from our early courtship. I was certainly imagining that myself.

We strolled into a small piazza where a clown on six-foot-high stilts was making faces at children and tying balloon animals. Raffaele pushed the stroller closer so Eureka could see. The clown bent down and said, "Che bella bambina. Questa è Sua figlia?" *What a beautiful little girl. Is this your daughter?*

"No," Raffaele replied.

I wished I could make it all better for him. Snap my fingers and grant him love, family, children, and peace. But I knew he was on his own journey, as I was, and that our lives would continue to move in separate directions. Coming together like this, in Gubbio, felt like we were honoring that love we'd felt fifteen years ago, honoring the gauntlet we'd survived together, and acknowledging who we'd become in the process.

Of course, we stopped at a café for some truffles and ordered a spread: crostini with fresh tartufo, tartufo hummus, tartufo with cheese. The truffles were exquisite: earthy, dark, pungent, and deeply savory—delicious dirt. I wondered if my twenty-year-old self would have enjoyed them as much as I did now. It occurred to me that all the drama of our trials, the imprisonment, the struggle to find meaning in it all—if it had to be a flavor, perhaps it would be tartufo. I wouldn't describe any of that experience as bright, acidic, or sweet. It was bitter and hard to swallow at first. But to the woman I'd become through all that, I could taste how nourishing it had been.

"How is it?" Chris asked Raffaele as he took a bite of truffle crostini.

"Buono," he said. *Good.*

There was one more thing Raffaele wanted to do. The town of Assisi was just a short drive from Gubbio, and Raffaele said we had to go. He wanted to visit the tomb of St. Francis. Raffaele is Catholic, and he wears a small cross around his neck. St. Francis of Assisi, I knew, was his favorite saint. He had actually taken me to Assisi fifteen years prior, back in 2007, just a few days before Meredith was murdered.

Raffaele wanted to make another pilgrimage to the tomb, which is situated in a large crypt below the Basilica of St. Francis, a white stone church lined with porticos that projects a grandeur that is at once clean and spare and humble. As we approached, he told us the story of St. Francis, the son of a prosperous silk merchant who lived the rich kid life until a strange vision led him to embrace a life of poverty, traveling the hills around Assisi, restoring old chapels.

St. Francis became the patron saint of animals, the environment, and of Italy. He is also the patron saint against dying alone, and against fire. I wondered if Raffaele had prayed to him while we were tied to the stake.

We descended with the line of religious pilgrims into the lower basilica, where ribbed vaults displayed elaborate frescoes of St. Francis and other saints. Then I left Eureka with Chris and Mom, and Raffaele and I descended the narrow stairs down to the burial chamber.

We paid our respects to the remains of the saint, and after a minute or so I made to return to the stairs, but Raffaele wasn't ready. He said he would join me shortly. He was down there another few minutes, and when he emerged, he told me what he'd been doing.

"The last time we were here," he said, "I made a prayer to St. Francis that we would always have happy memories together." Hearing that, my heart folded in on itself. Just a day or two before our arrest… "I think it was a curse," he said with a laugh.

"What did you say to St. Francis this time?" I asked.

"Forse non ci siamo capiti," he said. *Maybe we didn't quite understand each other.*

I'm not Catholic, and I don't believe there's anyone listening to such prayers, but I do believe that our lives are what we make of them, and that we can will ourselves into heaven or hell, if we have enough conviction. I think the Raffaele who asked St. Francis for happy memories for the two of us, a young man in puppy love, didn't even know how to believe such a thing. But the Raffaele I saw that day, I could see him choosing the light in the midst of darkness, just as I had. We would have happy memories from here on out. That was true if we wanted it to be.

The next day, Chris, Mom, and I drove toward Switzerland. On the way there I received an email from Giuliano.

Dear Amanda,

I have no words to describe what I felt at Villa Sacro Cuore. I hope it was a unique experience for you, too. Especially when we hugged. I will not forget it.

I was still processing the meeting with Giuliano, my reunion with Raffaele, and all the emotions I'd felt seeing Capanne prison and the house I shared with Meredith. I didn't have words then, either. As we crossed the border, I said aloud, "Ciao, Italia! Alla prossima!" *Goodbye, Italy. See you next time!* It was a casual phrase. The kind of thing one says absently when departing. But it felt true in the moment. There *would* be a next time.

Blessings

The Other Side of the Coin

AS I LEFT ITALY, I found myself thinking of Meredith, of the peaceful, everyday moments we shared in the weeks we lived side-by-side. How we trudged home from the grocery store together, taking turns lugging heavy four-packs of two-liter water bottles uphill, dodging cars speeding around the tight street corners, sunbathing on the terrace, her reading a mystery novel while I practiced "Hey Ya" on the guitar, sipping espresso together after class while Laura and Filomena, our Italian roommates, watched soap operas. Once, while out on a walk, I discovered a hole-in-the-wall vintage store and ran home to tell her about it. We went back together, and she bought a sparkly silver dress she said she would wear to a New Year's party back home. I remembered when she handed me her camera and asked me to take a picture of her by her bedroom window because she wanted to show her family the view of the valley below. She had such an effortless sophistication. I remembered how much I loved her accent, and that when she loaned me a pair of her tights, she felt like a big sister. And I remembered the last time I saw her, slinging her purse over her shoulder on her way out to meet up with her British friends, waving goodbye to me with a smile I will never forget.

Today, all these memories feel both very close and very distant.

Distant, because I have to dig through over a decade of trauma just to reach them. I have to look past the autopsy photos and crime scene footage I saw, the slurs I was called, the death threats I received, the accusations I fought, the imprisonment I endured, and the slanderous headlines that juxtaposed our names and faces, unfairly interlocking her death with my identity—all before I can think back on my fond memories of her.

But despite all this, these memories still feel very close, in part because when I first arrived in Italy, Meredith was an integral part of my life. But I think it's also because I've never really had the chance to mourn her. As I quickly learned in freedom, many people thought I had no right to mourn Meredith. They believed that I had something to do with her murder, or that Meredith had been forgotten in the wake of my trials, and that this was somehow my fault. Either way, Meredith and I were inextricably linked, and so it was somehow a further injustice that I lived while she perished. To those vocal critics, the only dignified path for me was to disappear and quietly count myself lucky to be alive.

When Meredith's family repeatedly went to the media and tried to resurrect interest in her as a person and in the justice she deserved, they were doing so because of a legitimate complaint. It wasn't Meredith's name in the headlines; it was mine. If I had been able to better articulate this early on, I would have said, "I agree with you! If this case had been handled correctly, I would have been a footnote in this tragic story, just like Meredith's other two roommates, whom no one remembers. Meredith deserves justice, and she deserves to be remembered."

But at the same time, I also couldn't accept that the tragedy of her murder, and of her erasure by the media, somehow meant that I should never talk about my own trauma or that my own fight for justice was somehow an offense to her memory. Slowly, I've found the words to articulate this dilemma.

I call it the *single victim fallacy*. When a crime occurs, there is an initial victim: in this case, Meredith. The authorities, by attempting to solve the crime and punish the perpetrator, are trying to address that victimization and offer some solace to the victim's family. But when they arrest and convict the wrong people, they create further victims. That's Patrick Lumumba, Raffaele, and me. In their zeal to arrest the perpetrator, the police detained Patrick for two weeks based on an incoherent statement they'd coerced me into signing, despite Patrick's rock-solid alibi; they then forced his business to remain shuttered for three months, which led to its collapse and derailed his life. And in their refusal to admit error, the authorities pursued an unsubstantiated case against Raffaele and me. All three of us are further victims.

Wrongful convictions often confuse our sympathies because they multiply victimhood and pit victims against one another. The single victim fallacy is the idea that there can only be one true victim in any situation, and that acknowledging the suffering of an innocent person in prison is somehow akin to denying the victimhood of the person who was murdered. *It is not.*

Unfortunately, this fallacy rears its ugly head all too often in wrongful conviction cases. The family of the initial victim is offered a villain by the prosecution, and they accept that story as a crucial part of the grieving process. But when the conviction is overturned, suddenly their sense of closure is ripped away from them. That's why it is extremely rare for victims' families to support innocence claims.

I've reached out to Meredith's family in a couple of ways over the years. I sent them a letter through their lawyer while I was still in prison. I wrote them another letter after I got home that I passed along through a journalist they were in touch with. I've been reluctant to push more than that because I understand how painful the very idea of me must be to them, especially if they still think I had something to do with Meredith's murder. But whether they realize it or not, we've always been on the same side.

Very few people ask me what it feels like to have lost a friend. Meredith and I were young women going through a similar stage in life in a brand-new place. We were both studying and meeting people and expanding our sense of the world. We only knew each other for five weeks, but friendship, like romance, blossoms quickly in such circumstances.

I often feel as if Meredith and I are two sides of the same coin. And when that coin was flipped, I got heads and she got tails. What happened to her could so easily have happened to me. If she'd been away that night, and I'd been home, would she have discovered the crime scene, would she have been wrongly convicted, and would she be reflecting all these years later, feeling like she was both incredibly lucky and tremendously sad?

I know what I would want for her if our roles were reversed: to live, to thrive, and to not let anyone take the preciousness of life away from her. I would want her to resist being cowed by the cruelty of those who would tell her to disappear and be ashamed of living her life while her friend was dead.

I barely had a sense of self-identity when I was arrested for murder. I was in that delicate space of exploring who I was, who I wanted to be, and how I wanted to think of myself. Then, the Italian courts and the global media swooped in and stamped me as a psycho slut killer. But however the world saw me, I still had to figure out how I saw myself. And I've wrestled with how to think about my own victimhood.

Many of the women I was imprisoned with were guilty of the crimes they were convicted of. Several were overcharged and over-punished, and I believed one of my cellmates when she insisted she hadn't known the lining of her luggage set, a gift from her new lover, hid cocaine. But most of the guilty owned up to their crimes. Some were even career criminals and defiantly proud of it: drug dealers, thieves, and prostitutes. I remember one of my cellmates, a pickpocket just a few years older than I was, fondly describing how she once stole three mopeds in one day, just for the pleasure of joyriding around the city. Another Roma woman told me she'd seen me wandering the streets of Perugia in the weeks before I was arrested and had considered stealing my backpack, but decided I probably wasn't carrying anything worth stealing. (She was right.)

These women had left a string of victims behind them. That's why they were in prison. But as I got to know them better, I realized that many of them were themselves victims long before they ever committed crimes. They had suffered poverty, neglect, and abuse. Having been exploited, they learned to exploit. Having been hurt, they stopped caring about how their actions hurt others. They were driven by a dual sense of entitlement and defeat, which left them cynical and adversarial. *Me vs. the World.*

By the time I returned home from prison, "victimhood" had become a cultural flashpoint. I saw people wearing various degrees of injustice and disadvantage like scout merit badges, just as the powerful were framing accusations against themselves as witch hunts. I found that these ways of thinking about victimhood didn't square at all with my experience.

I am certainly a victim of unjust imprisonment and of irreparable reputational damage. My youth and my innocence were stolen from me, and my life was forever altered. But even as I meditated on how badly I'd been fucked over, even as I saw my peers folding their disadvantages into their sense of self, the world was also telling me that I was not a victim at all. *Meredith was the true victim.*

This complicated cocktail of experiences—my time with the women in Capanne prison, the comparison to Meredith's victimhood, the thought that Meredith and I could have easily swapped places, being told to shut up and disappear—all that informs how I think about my own victimization. It's made me grateful that I grew up with so many joys and opportunities. It's made me grateful to be alive. It's made me realize that the injustice I endured made me stronger, that the hatred that came my way (and that has not stopped) could not break me. It's only made me more resilient.

There is a way of thinking about victimhood that is not about zero-sum point-scoring or comparison. I remember learning about the art of kintsugi when I was studying Japanese as a teenager. When a bowl or a vase is shattered, it is repaired with gold metalwork that both firmly bonds the cracks together and highlights them. Such bowls are stronger than they were before and are more beautiful. This is how I think of my victimhood today. The key thing is that kintsugi bowls don't repair themselves. They require patience and skill and a refined aesthetic sensibility. This is where agency comes in.

Defining myself as a victim was never satisfying because it didn't say anything about my character or my actions. It didn't say anything about *who I am*. It was merely about something that had happened *to* me. But the work I have done to fuse my own cracks with gold does reveal who I am and what I value. I am not angry or ashamed about the traumas I endured. At this point, I couldn't imagine myself without them. I wouldn't erase them from my past because they are my greatest source of strength.

Seneca, the Stoic philosopher, famously said, "I judge you unfortunate because you have never lived through misfortune. You have passed through life without an opponent—no one can ever know what you are capable of, not even you." His insight is that difficult periods in our lives are ultimately formative experiences; they make us who we are. Having experienced misfortune, having survived trial by fire, we have the opportunity to walk away with a better understanding of ourselves.

This doesn't mean that we shouldn't feel negative emotions when we encounter misfortune and adversity in our lives. It does mean that we shouldn't feel *only* negative emotions, though. That's an embrace of victimhood I can get behind. And it's one that allows me to carry the awkward burden of Meredith's legacy more easily.

However much I may wish it otherwise, the fact is that her identity has become so wrapped up in mine that most people can't think of me without thinking of her, or think of her without thinking of me. It's a burden I never wanted, and one that's especially awkward considering that I really didn't know Meredith all that well. But I feel privileged that I got to know her, as briefly as I did, for who she was, and not, like the many millions who know her name, merely in the context of her murder. Meredith remains a central figure in my trauma, but she played no role in the cause of my own victimization. As I carry her memory with me, I think of her as part of the gold filigree that holds my shattered pieces together.

The Art of Freedom

THE WEEKS AFTER I RETURNED home from Italy, I felt extraordinarily light. I had checked off a box that had been looming in my subconscious since 2007. The story I had been given had demanded this ending. I felt like finally—after a decade of surviving, of trying to prove I *didn't do* the thing I was accused of—I had finally *done* something. It felt good to have made something that didn't need to exist, something that was wholly original.

I'd be lying if I said, in the aftermath, I don't feel any desire for what I didn't get. I didn't get an apology. I didn't get an acknowledgment of wrongdoing. I didn't get a big public announcement of his belief in my innocence. But I've learned that while bad things can happen in an eyeblink, the good things take time. Change takes time. Growth takes time. I had given Giuliano a big opportunity for change, an opportunity he was not fully ready for. I gave him something to grapple with that he never expected in his wildest dreams.

And I'm still slowly and continually reaffirming to myself the slippery truth that it's not about what I deserve or what he deserves, because I turn my head and find that kind of thinking creeping back upon me. I remind myself that blame and punitive measures rarely resolve conflict or lead to situations where anyone can truly learn from their actions and the harm they cause. That mindset is exactly what led Giuliano to think that he was entitled to harm me in the first place. He felt justified in putting me through years of torture because, well, *someone* had to be punished, and he thought it was me. If the actual consequence of committing such a crime was rehabilitation, and release when deemed no longer a threat to society, I'd have been let out of prison the day after I was arrested.

Our letters have continued, and in them I often feel like I'm employing the open-ended encouragement I've learned from being a parent: kindly observing, gently guiding, dropping suggestions and nuggets of wisdom. For instance: true apologies are specific and without excuse; everything you say before "but" doesn't count; we are what we do and how we act; it is tragically easy to cause tremendous harm while believing we are doing the right thing; when we feel righteous, that's when we must be most humble and self-aware.

In his letters, I sometimes see Giuliano grumble and roll his eyes like a teenager. I listen as he makes excuses and tells me I just don't understand the Italian legal system. But I also see him desperate for my acceptance, eager for my reassurance and affection. And I give it to him over and over again.

I am trying my best to accept the apology I will never get. I've been thinking a lot about closure and how my deep wounds will figure into my life moving forward. I don't want to be returning over and over to the well of my pain. And yet I tear open my stitches whenever I give a talk to support the Innocence Project, or when I'm vulnerable on my podcast with another human who knows how it feels to be utterly lost. For better or worse, I know that there is something valuable in my painful experience, and I've been fortunate enough to be able to not only make meaning out of my misfortune but offer some insight to others in the process.

For a long time, I thought that getting closure about Italy was about moving past my trauma, finding a way to leave it behind. I know now that it's the source of my strength. Human beings are anti-fragile, physically and psychologically. When our bones break, they knit back together even stronger than before. When our psyches shatter, they reassemble themselves with more peace and perspective and power. There's a paradox there, because just as I wouldn't wish you to break your bones so they might grow stronger, I wouldn't wish my wrongful conviction on anyone. Yet I wouldn't trade it for the world. I also know that we don't choose the traumas we inevitably face. Yours will be different from mine, but we all face tremendous loss in our lives: the loss of loved ones, of our own innocence, of who we used to be.

It's a losing game to try not to lose *anything*, or for that matter, to try not to lose *everything*. Because you will, in the end. The only winning game is to accept loss as the other side of gain, as the negative space that allows us to appreciate the beauty of the joys and loves and people that life places before us. I am now a mother of two, since the birth of my son, Echo, in September of 2023. I look at him and at Eureka, both of them so warm and loving toward a world that has so far been warm and loving toward them, and I see my own youthful spirit there, even as I know that one day, inevitably, someone will be cruel to them. They will be hurt. And there is nothing I can do to stop it. I hope their trauma will not be as extreme as mine. I hope they will learn to be stronger and kinder through their misfortunes. I hope that makes them free.

Freedom, as I've learned, is a practice. For me, I practice freedom by embracing the grace of the God I don't believe in, grace that none of us deserve. That's the way Catholics talk about it. I prefer to think that we all deserve grace, kindness, and forgiveness, no matter who we are, or what we've done, or what we've failed to do.

It's often not easy to be kind, especially to those who've hurt us. But it's liberating. In my most Zen moments, all that pain dissolves in my gaze. It returns, inevitably. That's when I have to be kind to myself. Life is hard! Having compassion for your own failings is often harder than having it for those who've hurt you. I remind myself that it takes courage to be kind, and that bravery is not the absence of fear, but the decision to act in spite of it. Even as I do this, I continue to ask myself whether I'm getting anywhere. I don't have the answers to escape suffering, to find closure, to heal trauma. I don't know how to be truly free.

But I know how to try. I know that the greater your misfortune, the greater your opportunity to be free. The worst experience of my life blessed me with a sense of purpose, a humbling and encouraging perspective to always fall back on, and the ability to forgive myself and others. I've discovered a road out of the traps of arrogance, bitterness, and hatred—all sources of unnecessary suffering.

For the longest time, I felt trapped in a life not of my own making. I was trying desperately not to be seen as Foxy Knoxy, the psycho slut killer, then trying just as hard in freedom to not be "the girl accused of murder." I'm no longer trapped in a life I didn't choose. I don't feel defined by what I *didn't* do. Instead, I'm defining my life day by day.

What does that even mean? Most of us live with the assumption that being free means that we can make independent choices, that we are unconstrained by external coercion. Setting aside the thorny philosophical problem of free will, being free of coercion is certainly important, but it doesn't capture what matters to me most. I prefer to think of it like this:

To be free is to be aware of how we are immersed in our circumstances.

That's what *agency* really is: *clarity*. Without that clarity, we are not living our lives; we are living the story of our lives. We are born into our identities, and it feels as if we cannot be stripped of our histories and context, of our role within the grand human drama. When we're told, "You can be anything!" inevitably we start thinking, "Well then, why the hell am I *this*?" We suffer when the story of our lives isn't proceeding the way we want it to.

Because we feel like the protagonists of our own stories, I think we feel like we should have a say. Or that what becomes of us should at least make some sense. So, when something happens that seems to come out of nowhere, something that seems random, it induces awe—as in bug-eyed, mouth-gaping, heart-stopping, deer-in-headlights awe. We are paralyzed.

I feel blessed that I was struck by this so suddenly. This nightmare was my life. This was my story. But this feeling can also sneak up on you until you find one day that there's something off about your life, that surely this isn't the life you're *supposed to be living*. If agency is clarity, all you need to do to take back control of your life is to see more clearly. The feeling of freedom comes from realizing who we truly are, and how we truly exist. Things can't be otherwise. Yes, I am the "girl accused of murder," and yes, I am so much more than that.

Examining this has taken me down surprising paths—some joyous, some difficult—and I now feel more empowered in my helplessness than ever. If this all sounds paradoxical, that's because freedom is paradoxical. You can feel free in a prison and trapped in a penthouse. You can't choose your life, but you can choose how you feel about it, which will affect your life moving forward as you encounter an endless string of new challenges.

I don't know what problems I'm going to face tomorrow, but I do know that my perspective will continue to evolve, and that my story

Free

is only over if I want it to be. I promise you that if you feel impossibly stuck, *you're not*. Freedom isn't waiting for you tomorrow, or some distant day in the future when you finally close the door on everything that haunts you. Freedom is right here, right now, and it always has been.

A Benediction

May you never confuse kindness with weakness.
May you accept the apology you will never get.
May you choose to give when you don't yet know what you want or need.
May you reach for the stars so that in failure you walk on the moon.
May you choose, at the fork in the road, the path that will change you.
May you expect others to be worthy of respect,
    even as they act without honor,
        and may those around you expect your best
            even when you are at your worst,
                for expectation is a doorway.
May your courage be compassionate.
May your compassion be curious.
May your curiosity be courageous.
May your enemies become friends,
    or if not friends, then fools,
        for we are all fools at times,
            and may you find wisdom in the fool's mouth.
May you choose the company of those you want to succeed,
    and who will roll in the mud with you when you fall.
May you *yes, and* your life.

Free

May your pain clear the fog that has you walking in circles.
May you remember that you are not alone even when you are alone.
May you forgive yourself.
May you be free from suffering.
    May you be free to grow, to change, to love.
        May you be free.
            May you be free.
                May you be free.

Acknowledgments

It takes a village to save a life.

This book would not exist were it not for my husband, Christopher Robinson, who lovingly pushes me to be my best self, staunchly refuses to allow me to second-guess my worth, and whose own literary talents inspire me and have informed every stage of this manuscript.

I'm so grateful to my first readers: Phil Klay, Chris Ballew, Jeff and Cindy Hoyt, Thomas McCafferty, Mark Olshaker, Tom Wright, and Eric Frith, who encountered this manuscript in its ugly duckling stage, and kindly guided it toward puberty. I'm grateful to my agents, Jay Mandel, Laura Bonner, and Matilda Forbes Watson, and to my editor, Colin Dickerman, who recognized the potential of this manuscript and helped me elevate it to maturity.

Early versions of some of the material in this book appeared in *The Atlantic*, *The Free Press*, *The Independent*, *Medium*, *Oprah Daily*, *Broadly*, and *Westside Seattle*. I'm grateful to the editors of these publications, and to Sam Harris and the team at the Waking Up meditation app, where I honed many of the ideas in this book through a lecture series called "Resilience."

I will always be grateful to my Italian attorneys, Carlo Dalla Vedova and Luciano Ghirga, and more recently, Luca Luparia and Martina

Acknowledgments

Cagossi of the Italy Innocence Project, for believing in me and tirelessly fighting for justice. And I'm grateful to Bob Barnett and Ana Reyes, for being willing to represent me pro bono should I have had to fight an extradition battle.

I would not be the woman who could write this book without the help and influence of so many:

To Don Saulo Scarabattoli, for holding my hand when no one else could...

To my friend and codefendant, Raffaele Sollecito, for accompanying me on this journey of survival...

To my friend and adversary, Dr. Giuliano Mignini, for taking my outstretched hand, despite the backlash...

To my family—Edda and Chris Mellas, Curt and Cassandra Knox, Deanna and Vince Hanson, Ashley Knox and George Edwards, Delaney Knox and Ian Boudreau, Elizabeth Huff, Michael and Janet Huff, Christina and Kevin Hagge, Dolly and Monoj Nair, Rob and Dee Selk, Willow Hagge and Brit Streepy, Kyle and Jessica Hagge, Nicholas and Isaac Huff, Justin and Kerry Selk, Anil and Nilesh Nair, and Jackie Dawson—for going to the ends of the Earth to free me and support me as I readapted to freedom...

To those total strangers who became supporters—Giulia Alagna, Anne Robichaud and Pino Alagna, Doug and Anne Bremner, James Cook, Corrado Daclon, Bruce Fischer, Rocco Girlanda, Jim Lovering, Thomas Mininger, Steve and Michelle Moore, Karen Pruett, Nigel Scott, Tom and Colleen Simpson, Joe Starr (RIP), Tom Sykes, and Mark Waterbury—for supporting my family during my trials and imprisonment...

To my friends and new family—Sunny Bertollini and Mark Hinshaw, John and Renatta Emerson, Kate Endle, Laura Gordon, Mike Heavey, James Kaelan and Blessing Yen, Josh Karp and Steph Kesey,

Acknowledgments

Dean Kelly, Gavin and Molly Kovite, Taige Lauren, Brett Lither, Madison Paxton, Jake and Sarah Pederson, Brett Prim, Tim and Eileen Robinson, Kyle Robinson, Leila Aram-Panahi, and Jordin Mitchell, Maya Sears, Andrew Seliber, Colin Sutherland, James Terrano, Nicole Vandenberg, and Tom Wright—for being my community when I felt like a pariah...

To my innumerable friends within the Innocence Movement— including Justin and Heidi Brooks, Steve Drizin, John Eldan, Keith Findley, Jason Flom, Monty Free, Mark Godsey, Greg Hampikian, Mark Howard, Saul Kassin, Meredith Kennedy, Zieva Konvisser, Dan Krane, Richard Leo, Seth Miller, Peter Neufeld, Laura Nirider, Bill Oberly, Courtney Reed, Barry Scheck, Mike Semanchik, Jennifer Thompson, and Lara Zarowsky—for defending me and supporting me in telling my story...

To my freed and exonerated family—including Jarrett Adams, Donovan Allen, Marvin Anderson, Obie Anthony, Jason Baldwin, Brian Banks, Alan Beaman, Orlando Boquete, Ted Bradford, Kristine Bunch, Sabrina Butler, Mario Casciaro, Antione Day, Bill Dillon, Anthony DiPippo, Cornelius Dupree, Damien Echols, Ryan Ferguson, Heidi Goodwin, Sunny Jacobs and Peter Pringle (RIP), Josh Kezer, Ginny Lefever, Eddie Lowry, Denis Maher, Greg Mingo, Michelle Murphy, Alan Northrup, Juan Rivera, Khalil Rushdan, Marty Tankleff, Chris Tapp (RIP), Raymond Towler, Anna Vasquez, and so many more—for guiding me in my transformation...

To my teachers—Michael Danielson, Kris Johnson, Giuseppe Leporace, David Shields, and Mischa Willett—for helping me hone my mind and my writing before, during, and after prison. And to Mary Karr, who urged me over coffee one day to write the book that only I could write...

To Phil Bevis and Patrick Robinson, for taking a chance on hiring me when I was still a convicted killer, and to Dwayne Clark, for launching my speaking career when I'd never once told my story to a room full of strangers...

To my Sisterhood of Ill Repute—including Daisy Coleman (RIP), Lorena Gallo, and all the women out there who've been put through the public shaming ringer—for making it easier to bear the scarlet letter...

To my mentors and role models—Sam Harris, Jon Ronson, and David Zelman—for inspiring me to be more resilient, more kind, and to become a better thinker...

To the ethical and keen-eyed journalists and influencers—including J-Ax, Nikki Battiste, Jessica Bennett, Alexandra Berlin, Rob Blackhurst, Nina Burleigh, Sabina Castelfranco, Paul Ciolino, Maria D'Elia, Candace Dempsey, Brian McGinn, Stephen Robert Morse, Renee Muza, Luca Pallavidino, Alessandro Penna, Doug Preston and Mario Spezi, Frank Sfarzo, and Charlotte Theile—for studying the case carefully and daring to tell the true story when it was unpopular and unprofitable...

To the comedians I'm blessed to know—Whitney Cummings, Jena Friedman, Jenny Johnson, Bert Kreischer, Leah Lamarr, Annie Lederman, Zosia Mamet, Chris Porter, Joe Rogan, Nicole Schreiber, Hannah Stocking, Alanna Thompson, and Theo Von—for supporting me in finding and expressing the humor to be found within my tragedy and grief...

To Bo Burnham, Flight of the Conchords, The Lonely Island, and Weird Al Yankovic, for pulling me out of innumerable dark moods over the last ten years...

To all those who have contributed to the success of my podcast *Labyrinths*—including Canon Bryan, Levar Burton, Charlie Darnall, Henry Devries, Sophia Gates, Samantha Geimer, Malcolm Gladwell, Klaus Heinzelmann, Graham Johnson, Kristen and Ville Jokinen,

Acknowledgments

Alyssa Katherine, Kevin Kelly, Alison Levine, Chandler Mays, Mistress Cyan and Goddess Genesis, Dave Navarro, Emily Oster, Megan Phelps-Roper, Michael Pollan, Andre Sapp, Maya Shankar, Brent Spiner, Paul Stamets, Tim Urban, Kelly Walker, Jesse and Alex Weaver, and Andrew Yang—for thinking out loud with me for the last few years and helping me find my way to the insights in this book...

To my Hollywood family—including Olivia Fanaro, Lisa Harrison, David Jalenko, Ann Johnson, Monica Lewinsky, Warren Littlefield, and KJ Steinberg; Karey Burke, Carolyn Cassidy, Taylor Morgan (Robinson) at 20th; Craig Erwich, Jordan Helman, and Sasha Silver at Hulu; and Dana Walden at Disney—for lovingly and doggedly shepherding this story to the screen...

To my sangha at the Puget Sound Zen Center, and our abbot, Koshin Christopher Cain, for meditating with me on the impermanence of all suffering and for being there in my times of need...

To my children, Eureka and Echo, whose very existence is both a blessing and a deepening of my understanding and appreciation for everything that happens to us in this life...

To Meredith (RIP), whose legacy I will never stop honoring, and her family, because I still hope we can share our grief one day...

And again, to my mom, because I've been so lucky in my life, and nowhere more fortunate than in growing up with a mom like her...

...THANK YOU all for saving my life.

About the Author

Amanda Knox is an exoneree, journalist, public speaker, author of the *New York Times* bestselling memoir *Waiting to Be Heard*, and co-host, with her partner Christopher Robinson, of the podcast *Labyrinths*. Between 2007 and 2015, she spent nearly four years in an Italian prison and eight years on trial for a murder she didn't commit. She has since become an advocate for criminal justice reform and media ethics. Her writing has appeared in *The Atlantic, Time* magazine, the *Los Angeles Times*, and many other places. She sits on the board of the Innocence Center and serves as an Innocence Network ambassador.